Faith and A Fast Horse

Faith and A Fast Horse

A Novel by Charles Russell

ISBN 13: 9781973782520
ISBN: 1973782529

FOR JOHN CHARLES RUSSELL
My grandson, who was born on September 3, 2013

My wish is that he will read this book sometime in the future and remember how much his Coachie loved him.

Acknowledgments

WITHOUT THE SUPPORT AND ENCOURAGEMENTS of my wife, Patricia, this book would never have gone to press. She is my best friend and will always be the love of my life.

A special thanks to Glenda Watts for editing the book. She is a special person in our lives.

The cover was created by Pencraft Graphic Design. Mary and Denise do amazing work, and I appreciate the professionalism they bring to my books.

Author's Note

THIS IS THE FOURTH BOOK in the series following the life of a ranching family in New Mexico. I continue to see myself as a story teller rather than a writer. I have attempted to make the characters seem real by portraying their strengths as well as imperfections. To me, they took a life all of their own and in large part determined the path they would take throughout the book. Many times they would change the way I was portraying them and move in another direction, giving me no choice but to follow them. I know that must sound strange but it is true.

I told the stories for people to enjoy and hopefully be able to put aside problems they were experiencing for at least a few hours. However, throughout the four books, the tragedy of not accepting people who are different was included, whether because of color, social status, handicap, or religion. Also, in each story, people are portrayed as being able to change their behavior for the better.

Of course, the stories have a happy ending. Life is too short and too difficult to have it any other way.

If you can't fly then run, if you can't run then walk, if you can't walk then crawl, but whatever you do you have to keep moving forward.

Martin Luther King, Jr.

CHAPTER 1

Lacy

I STILL COULDN'T BELIEVE IT. I had just won the barrels at Cheyenne, moving me up to number 2 in the world. My dream had come true, and with little more than five months before the finals in Las Vegas, I was sitting pretty.

We were on our way home for ten days before our next rodeo. We had agreed that we would drive straight through and be in New Mexico at the ranch by tomorrow at noon. Ordinarily, we would have waited until morning, but both of us were anxious to get home. I was driving and Jack was asleep in the back seat. I had volunteered to drive first since I was too excited to sleep. We had a new 2000 Dodge, one ton dually, and a four-horse slant trailer with living quarters. It was a wonderful rig, and we had already put over 20,000 miles on it. I was having trouble staying within the speed limit. With the Dodge diesel, I couldn't tell I was even pulling a trailer.

I was hauling two barrel horses and Jack's roping horse. Thank goodness, both were sound and running good. I couldn't have asked for a better year. Maybe it was just my time, after six years, to win a world championship. I had been to the finals three times but never finished better than ninth. I didn't see how my life could be any better.

Traveling down the deserted highway at one o'clock in the morning gave me plenty of time to think. We had been married for five years, and Jack had been everything and more than I'd expected. He was instrumental in my success this year. We built our rodeo schedule around my barrel racing and didn't consider his roping. He had no chance of making the finals this year, but had been okay with that. In fact, he and his dad had become so close that I expected him to stop rodeoing soon and devote his time to ranching, which he loved. I had never seen a father and son who enjoyed one another's company the way he and Bo did. When we were home, they were inseparable. At first, I was a little jealous, but in time, I realized that was just the way it was going to be. His dad treated me like a daughter and was becoming like the father that I never had. I loved Jack's family and had never realized the support and security that a family provided.

Bo's mother treated me like a daughter, also. I had always thought my mother was the most beautiful woman I'd ever seen; however, being around Lexie and seeing how beautiful she was, both inside and outside, changed my mind. She kept hinting about grandchildren, and we had been trying without success.

Zack, Jack's twin brother, was in his sixth year of college, pursuing a medical degree. We only saw him during holidays. Everyone said they both loved me and that I had to choose which one to marry. That was not true. Jack was my one true love. Zack was so predictable and careful while Jack was spontaneous and exciting. We fit together perfectly, and I'd never considered marrying anyone else from the time I was six years old.

Tommie Rose, their sister, was a missionary in Africa and we hadn't seen her in over a year. I admit that she intimidated me, and I didn't enjoy being around her. She was tall, beautiful, and so confident in everything she did. Of course, she was religious, and I was always afraid of saying something wrong in her presence. She had always been nice, but it was fine with me for her to be in Africa.

Jack's grandmother, who I also referred to as Mia, was special to me. I wanted to be just like her when I became older. She was strong, confident, loving, and the most patient person I had ever known. I attempted to do everything I could to gain her respect.

We lived at the ranch when we weren't on the road. We had moved into Jack's great granddad's house when his wife, Helen, had moved to Roswell to be closer to her sons. We spent little time at my mother's (Alejandra's) ranch. She had married again and her husband was despicable. He was ten years older than she was, and I truly believe that the only reason she married him was that he had won several world championships. He was rude, abrasive, and only wanted to talk about his exploits in the arena. Besides that, he constantly wanted to hug me. Jack had warned me that the next time he put his hands on me, he was going to deck him.

It was no secret that my mother had loved Bo, Jack's dad, and wanted to marry him. After Bo married Lexie, it had destroyed my mother. She was never the same and had remained angry and vindictive ever since. I stayed away from her as much as I could.

My thoughts were interrupted when Roany reached over and gave me a kiss. Roany was our dog and was riding in the front seat with me. She had shown up at our house several years ago, pregnant. She was a mixed breed but several people had told us she looked and acted like a Catahoula. We took care of her and found homes for her puppies when they were weaned; in fact, Mia took the last puppy. Roany adored Jack, following him everywhere he went. She was sweet but protective of our belongings, including the horses, sleeping in front of the stalls when we were at a rodeo. She didn't allow anyone to come close to them.

I wasn't the least bit sleepy. We had left at 10:00 that evening, and after three hours, we were only a few miles out of Colorado Springs. We had agreed I would drive for four hours and then let Jack take over.

When we got home, I was going to take a few days off and relax. I might not even ride for several days and give the horses a much-needed rest. Jack would be with his dad, and I would just lounge around and be lazy. Jack resembled his dad in many ways; maybe that was the reason they got along so well. I'd never heard a cross word between them. I had asked Lexie about the relationship and she had replied, "Jack is much like Bo and Bo gets more like his late grands every day. I guess it's a family thing. You can expect Jack to get more stubborn the older he gets. Also, if he doesn't like to be told what to do now, it will get much worse later. I love Bo dearly, but he can be a challenge sometimes."

I could make out the lights of Colorado Springs now and the traffic had picked up. I heard Jack stirring, thinking I should stop and let him take over. That thought was immediately followed by an explosion, and I screamed as the pickup veered sharply toward the ditch. Loud, deafening sounds engulfed the cab and suddenly, I was upside down… and then blackness.

CHAPTER 2

Zack

I WOKE UP WITH AN excruciating headache. I gasped for breath, thinking, what is wrong with me? I had never hurt like this. I looked at the clock and it was 1:05. I hadn't been asleep but two hours, having been working in the emergency room till late.

I lay there quietly a few minutes and the pain began to subside. Within a short time, I felt fine and my entire body seemed to relax. I got up and went to the kitchen for a drink of water. No way could I go back to sleep, so I found my notes from the day's work and started going through them.

I was in my sixth year of medical school. I had begun to wonder if it was worth it, needing two more years before I could finish my medical degree. I had no social life, very few friends, and of course had not been in a relationship long enough to consider marriage. I missed my family, especially, my twin brother, Jack. I had not been home since Christmas. It was not easy to admit, but I was homesick.

I was feeling better and couldn't imagine what caused the pain. It might be that I could get some sleep now to prepare for another long day. I had just crawled into bed when the phone rang. Must be a call from the hospital needing me to come back to the ER, I thought. I picked up the phone before it could ring a second time.

"Zack, it's Mom. Don't panic but Jack and Lacy have been in a wreck. We know very little of the details at this time. A doctor from the hospital in Colorado Springs called a few minutes ago."

"Is that all the information the doctor gave you?" I asked.

"Yes. He did tell me that someone would get back with me shortly with additional information. I'll call you as soon as I find out something."

"Have you contacted Sissy?"

"No. It takes too long to place an overseas call, and I don't want to tie up the phone. I'll talk to her when I find out something."

"Let me know as soon as you hear anything. Could I speak to Dad?"

"Zack, your mom is calm, but we're actually frightened out of our minds. I can't believe they were on the road this late. They should've waited until morning to start home."

"Dad, I just wanted to hear your voice. We better hang up now so if a call comes through."

A chill went up my spine when I hung up the phone. The doctor should have had more information. It might indicate that he had chosen to let a human resource person call because the news was bad.

My hand was shaking as I made coffee. I sat down at the table and said a prayer, asking that Jack and Lacy be safe. Lacy was having a tremendous year and was a sure bet to make the finals, with a better than average chance to win it all. My mind refused to comprehend that something could happen to my brother. We had been so close growing up and had stayed that way into adulthood. We talked several times a week on the phone. He had become so much like our dad in recent years, not only in looks but his actions.

We had graduated from Artesia High School in 1994. Dad had bought a house there so we could attend a school with a good football program. Mom stayed with us during school and Dad had come down on weekends. Sissy had completed high school at Hondo.

We had both been starters beginning with our sophomore year. Jack was a running back and I was the quarterback. Jack had made all-state his junior and senior years; however, I didn't receive near the recognition that he did. Dad reminded me that I was much like him, just doing my job without the fanfare. Both of us did have scholarship offers, but Jack was not interested in college, and I realized that pursuing a medical degree would not allow me time to play football.

I kept looking at my watch every few minutes, anticipating the phone to ring. Only six minutes had passed and I began pacing between the kitchen and bedroom. Finally, the phone rang while I was in the kitchen. I made it to the bedroom and picked up before the first ring was completed.

"Zack, it's bad. A doctor told us we needed to get there as soon as possible. We have a friend in Ruidoso who has a plane, and we're meeting him at the airport. We should be in Colorado Springs in a few hours. Zack… are you still there?"

"Yes," I whispered, trying to control my emotions. "I'll get there as soon as I can. How's Dad?"

"Just being your dad. He hasn't said three words. He just draws into himself. We're leaving now. We love you and be careful."

I replaced the phone and sat down on the edge of the bed. I reached for the phone book, looked up the airport number and dialed it. Fortunately, I could get a flight to Denver with a layover in Albuquerque. The departure time was 4:00 A.M. I could rent a car in Denver and drive to Colorado Springs. It was only a little after two o'clock, but no way could I sit around here and wait. I dressed, put a few clothes in a travel bag and went to the airport.

With over two hours to wait before my flight, I walked from one end of the airport to the other, attempting to force myself to remain calm. The news was bad, no doubt. Working in the ER, I had witnessed phone calls telling the family they needed to come as quickly as possible. In most instances these calls resulted in the family being told the heart-wrenching news that their loved one had died.

I forced myself to think of the past and the relationship that Jack and I shared. He had never liked school and would have dropped out if not for football. It was a constant struggle to keep him passing and eligible. Right down to the last month of school, it was still a possibility that he wouldn't graduate. On several occasions, he had gotten into trouble, the last one involving a DUI in which he was arrested. They called me from the police station, telling me I needed to notify our parents. It took all my persuasion to convince them to release him to me. The police chief's son played football, and we were good friends.

Another instance involved a fight, which landed the opponent in the hospital. Jack was short-tempered and a boy had made a comment about Lacy. The incident occurred at school, and of course, he was expelled for three days. Mom had not stayed with us our senior year so it was my responsibility to look after him. I missed the three days of school, also, and we went home to explain the situation to Mom and Dad. Mom was furious, but Dad took up for Jack, saying that the boy got what he deserved.

Jack's problem was that he reacted without thinking of the consequences. It had always been this way, but to be truthful, I don't believe he cared about the outcome.

Jack received the recognition on the football field, but I held my own in the roping arena. In our final year of high school rodeo, I won the calf roping; however, Jack won the all-around. He'd finally talked Mom and Dad into riding bulls, with the solemn promise that he would not ever get on one after high school. Of course, he won the event, and that, coupled with our team roping title, earned him the all-around.

Dad detested team roping. He thought the only people who team roped were those that were too lazy to get off their horse. We finally convinced him to let us do the event, insisting that it would give Jack a chance at the all-around.

Every few minutes my anxiety would return, causing me to shake with fear. I kept repeating the same prayer. *Please, God, don't let Jack die. He has so much to offer his family and this world. Please God, don't let him die.* We needed Sissy here. Her faith was greater than anyone I knew. Jack and I did have some things in common. One of them being our respect and love for our sissy. She could do no wrong in our sight, and it had been that way since we were teenagers.

Jack and I had talked about the reason Sissy had not married. We agreed it was because she intimidated all her suitors. She was tall, beautiful, confident, and aggressive, when she needed to be. Men just couldn't deal with that.

Finally, an announcement came from a speaker that flight 109 was boarding for Denver.

CHAPTER 3

Lexie

We were only a few minutes from the airport, and Bo still hadn't said a word since we had left home half an hour ago. I was struggling to keep from breaking down. I was only a step away from totally losing it and going into a crying rage. My baby was hurt bad, maybe even worse, and Bo was dealing with pain the only way he knew. He had withdrawn into himself like a turtle in his shell. I attempted several times to make conversation and received only an inaudible murmur.

I had not attempted to get in touch with Tommie Rose. I knew it would mean being on the phone for at least twenty minutes. Maybe after we reached the hospital in Colorado Springs I could call her.

I kept thinking that we were on our way to a hospital due to an emergency call the same way we were twenty-eight years ago. The memory of going into the emergency room and finding that my brother had been killed still haunted me. Now, I was terrified as to what we would find in Colorado Springs.

I tried again to get something from Bo. "How long do you think it will take to get to Colorado Springs?" I asked.

"It shouldn't take over a couple of hours. He has a Learjet," he answered softly.

"How long do you think it will take Zack to get there?" This time, no answer, only a shrug of the shoulders. Before I could ask anything else, we arrived at the airport.

Within a matter of minutes, we had boarded the plane. We exchanged a few words with Stewart Enfield, the owner, and settled down for the trip. We had been friends with Stewart for years, in fact, he was on the board of the bank that Todd, my brother, ran. He knew Bo well enough not to attempt conversation with him, but he did express his regret to me.

"We appreciate your help, Stewart. It would've taken us hours to drive to Lubbock and get a flight to Colorado."

"No problem, Lexie. My pilot is on call and I'm glad to be of help. It shouldn't take over a couple of hours to get you there. I know both of you are out of your mind with worry. Did you contact your brother?"

"Yes, I called Todd before we left. He's coming later. I also notified my dad and Ms. Nancy. Dad isn't able to travel and Ms. Nancy won't leave him. I'll keep them updated by phone."

"How is your dad?"

"He does okay. He must be on oxygen at night and is careful what he does during the day. His heart is weak, but if he doesn't overdo it, he's fine." After that, quietness followed, and we settled down for the trip.

My mind kept going to Zack. He would be devastated. He and Jack were as close as brothers could get. Their differences had worked to bring them closer together. They still looked enough alike that people would get them confused. Zack had always looked after Jack and been there for him, especially when he was in trouble. Jack did the same for Zack; however, he seldom was in trouble, being a model student who used good judgment.

Nothing ever came between them, as proven by Lacy. It was obvious to all of us that Zack adored her but she chose Jack. Jack and Lacy were a beautiful couple and as far as I know, it had been a successful and happy marriage. Just the fact that Jack sacrificed his roping to help her get to the finals was proof of how much he loved her. Lacy was sweet, unlike her mother, and we had always gotten along well. She seldom mentioned her mother and never spent time at her ranch.

Every few minutes my thoughts would go back to the accident. I'd say another prayer asking that Jack and Lacy recover. We needed Tommie Rose here with us. Her faith was so strong, and she would be a comfort to all of us. I would get in touch with her as soon as possible. Bo interrupted my thoughts.

"How much longer, Stewart?"

"About half an hour, I guess. I'm going to wait on you in case you need the plane for anything else."

"I appreciate that, Stewart."

Bo reached over and put his hand on my arm. "We'll need to get a cab to go to the hospital. I'm scared, Lexie. I can't lose Jack. I just can't."

"I know."

We landed, caught a cab, and arrived at the hospital at a little after 5:00 A.M. We asked directions to the ER and were escorted there by a nurse. We identified ourselves, and within minutes a doctor came through some swinging doors, introducing himself as Dr. Emerson.

"I'm terribly sorry, but I have bad news. The young man has been placed on a respirator. He is in a coma and his condition is virtually hopeless. If he has a living will, we would need to see it."

I reached and grabbed Bo's arm to support myself. I heard Bo whimper and then he turned and walked through a door leading outside. A blood curdling scream came from outside and then silence.

"What about the girl?"

"She's in bad shape. Broken ribs with possible head injuries and a severely mangled leg. She has not regained consciousness. She's going to lose the leg if she survives."

"Can I see Jack?"

"Sure. Come with me."

We went down a hallway and through several doors, before coming to a cubicle surrounded by curtains. We stepped through the curtain and there lay my baby. All kinds of machines were connected to him, and he appeared to be in a peaceful sleep. I went to the bed and took his hand in mine. It was cool and limp. At that point, I broke down, laying myself across him and cried. I don't know how long I lay there before a nurse came and helped me back to the lobby.

I went outside to look for Bo, finding him sitting on a curb, staring off into the dark. I sat down beside him and put my arm through his.

"Bo, we have to deal with this. It's real and we can't run from it. We have to come together as a family and support one another."

"I prayed all the way up here. God didn't listen to me. He's going to take my son." At that point he started sobbing.

"No, God is suffering with us. We can't abandon Him now."

Still sobbing, he said, "Maybe you can't abandon Him, but I can. He deserted us and we're going to lose our son."

"Bo, we have to see about Lacy. She's hurt bad, also. I'm sure Alejandra is on her way, but we have to look after her, at least until her mother gets here."

"I don't care about her. Why was she spared?"

"Bo, please don't say that. Jack loves her."

"You heard the doctor. Jack is going to die when he's taken off life support."

"Anger is not going to help anyone, Bo. I'm going to check on Lacy. We also need to find out about the horses."

"You go ahead. I'm going to sit right here for a while."

Back inside, I was directed through a door that read Intensive Care and to a room. Lacy was hooked up to several tubes but appeared to be breathing normal. I was stunned at how bruised and swollen her face was. I asked the nurse how she was doing.

"It's too early to tell, but it is positive that her vital signs are good. We should be able to tell more tomorrow. Her left leg is badly mangled and surgery will be done as soon as the doctors believe it will be safe. In my twenty years, I've never seen a limb in that condition."

I thanked the nurse and went to find Bo. He was still outside sitting on the curb. "Bo, I have to get in touch with Tommie Rose. I'm going to ask if I can use one of the phones in the hospital. Do you want to come with me?" Instead of answering, he got up, which I assumed meant yes. He followed me back into the hospital. A receptionist escorted me to a small office with a phone. I was able to reach Tommie more quickly than I expected.

"Tommie, I have bad news. Jack and Lacy have been in a wreck."

"Just how bad is it, Mom?"

"Worse than bad. Jack is on a respirator with massive brain injuries and Lacy is in intensive care with severe injuries."

"I'll get there as soon as I can," she said.

"We need you, Tommie. How long do you think it will take?"

"At least 36 hours, maybe longer. Mother, please don't let them take him off the respirator before I get there."

I gave her the name of the hospital in Colorado Springs and told her she might have to fly into Denver and rent a car. We said goodbye and hung up. I immediately called Ms. Nancy and described the situation to her. She was amazingly calm. I thought again what a strong woman she was.

"Lexie, we can't come. I'm afraid Tom couldn't hold up to the travel or the stress."

"I understand, Ms. Nancy. I'll keep you informed. Would you get in touch with Jimmy and tell him what has happened? Also, please call Pastor Stevens."

"Certainly."

After we had hung up, I turned and addressed Bo. "We need to check on the horses and the dog. I imagine the best place to do that is with the Department of Public Safety. The troopers on the scene of the accident should have that information." I looked through a phone book that was lying on the desk, found a number and dialed it. When I explained who I was and what I needed, they put me through to another extension. A man answered and immediately gave me the information I needed about our animals.

"Bo, the horses and dog were taken to a vet clinic on the west side of the city," I explained. "The officer gave me the number of the clinic. I'm going to see what I can find out," I stated, as I was dialing the number. An answering machine came on and suddenly I realized it was too early for them to be open. I had completely lost track of time. I looked at my watch and it was only 6:30, thinking, *had it been only five hours since this had all begun?*

"There's a hotel across the street. We need to get a room for us as well as for Zack and Tommie," Bo said. "Zack should be here by noon."

"Yes, you're right," I answered, relieved that Bo had recovered some of his composure. "Would you like to see Jack now?"

"No. Maybe later. I couldn't handle it now."

Zack walked into the front entrance to the hospital where we were waiting for him just before noon. He hugged me and his dad and immediately asked about Jack.

"It's bad. He's on life support," I replied.

"No," he whispered, with tears welling up in his eyes.

He turned away from us and I heard him sob. Bo reached for him and hugged him from behind until he turned back around.

"Did the doctors give him any hope?"

"Virtually none," I murmured. "The doctor didn't give us any specifics about the type of life support. If you would like to see him, I'll go with you," I offered.

"Yes. I can tell the type of life support he's on."

"I'll wait here for you," said Bo.

Entering the room where Jack lay, Zack stopped and stared for at least a minute. I know he was attempting to get his emotions under control before he spoke.

"The tube in his mouth goes down his throat and into his trachea. His brain is damaged and does not give him instructions to breathe. The respirator pumps oxygen into his lungs and expels the air. I assume the doctors believe the damage to his brain to be severe and he will not ever be able to breathe on his own. I need to ask the doctors more questions."

"What do you suggest we do?"

"Request a meeting with the doctors to determine how much they actually know," he replied.

"I'll do that. Your dad is struggling to accept this. I've never seen him this way in the thirty years we've been married, not even when his dad and his gramps died."

"He and Jack have become so close since I've been gone," he observed.

"That's true. I'm hoping that when Tommie gets here she can bring him to join us in our grief. She should be here sometime tomorrow," I explained.

I continued, "The horses are at a vet's west of the city. I have the address. Since you have a rental car we should check on them and find out how badly they're injured."

"Right. If you'll see about a meeting with the doctors, I'll go back and talk to Dad and you can meet us in the lobby," he said.

I told Bo and Zack on the way to the vet's that the meeting was arranged for two o'clock. We had no problem finding the clinic, and the vet came out to visit with us immediately. He introduced himself as Albert Glaze.

"I'm terribly sorry about your son and daughter-in-law," he said. "I do have some good news for you about your animals. I picked them up at the scene of the accident. The safety chains on the trailer had not been latched. When the front tire blew out and the pickup rolled, the trailer came loose. The brakes were activated and the trailer came to a stop without turning over. The horses were bunged up and bruised but nothing serious."

"What about the dog?"

"She has a broken leg. I've put a splint on it and she can get around. Strange things happen in accidents. I don't know how she survived. It appeared that the pickup had rolled over several times. You're welcome to see the horses and the dog. There's no problem with leaving them here until you get ready to leave."

"We appreciate it, Dr. Glaze," Bo replied.

CHAPTER 4

Bo

I HAD TO GET MYSELF together. For the past twelve hours, my brain had ceased working. Lexie had all but taken over the decision making. It all happened too suddenly and without warning. Jack was everything to me, and I had always believed he would, in time, take over the ranch. We looked, thought, and acted alike. It was almost like it was me in that room on life support, and I was struggling to deal with that. At first, I pleaded with God that Jack would be okay, then I was angry when we discovered that Jack was not going to live. Now, I realized that it was doing no good to blame anyone, including God.

I was glad to find that the horses and the dog were going to survive. When the vet offered to keep them for us, I said, "We appreciate it, Dr. Glaze, but we're going to take the dog with us."

"Bo, we can't keep Roany at the hotel with us," Lexie responded.

"Why?" I asked.

"Pets are not allowed," she said.

"We'll find a way," I replied. "Besides, she's not a pet. She's family and our family is going to be together."

Reaching over and touching my arm, she said, "You're right, we'll make it work."

When they brought Roany out, she hobbled over to me on three legs. I knelt and she pressed herself up against me. She and Jack were inseparable and when he was home she was with us all the time; thus, she spent more time with me than anyone other than Jack and Lacy. I picked her up and carried her to the car, holding her in my lap on the way back to the hotel.

I approached the receptionist's desk with Roany hobbling by my side. The receptionist was a lady, probably in her sixties. "I have a dog with me," I announced.

"I see that. We don't allow pets in this hotel," she replied, with a frown.

"She belongs to our son. He's on life support. We need her with us."

"We do not make exceptions."

"Look, lady, I'm about to lose a son. You can't imagine how much I love him. I want his dog to be with us. I will say 'please', if that will help."

Before she could respond, a middle-aged man came through an open door, behind the desk.

"You can keep the dog with you. I'm sorry to hear about your son. I manage this hotel and we can make exceptions in circumstances like this. We do have rules, but they become insignificant when compared to your situation."

We were early for the meeting with the doctors and had to wait for their arrival. Two came in on time, but they informed us that a third would be there shortly. They told us that we needed to wait, since he was the neurosurgeon. Thirty minutes later he came into the room and without introductions started talking.

"Sorry I was late. I was in surgery and it didn't go well," he announced. "Now, to the issue we are facing with the young man on life support. I understand that he doesn't have a living will. That complicates a decision that should have been made easy. I would anticipate that you want to keep him on a respirator. That would be a mistake. Based on tests, he has extensive brain injuries. Removed from the respirator, he would die immediately. That is a fact. I'm sorry. That's just the way it is."

"What's your name?" I asked.

"Dr. Adders," he replied.

"My son's name is Jack Skinner. He's twenty-five years old. You're speaking of him like he doesn't exist."

"Your son is already dead," he replied.

"How can you be so callous?" I asked.

"Sir, I do this every day. Like I said, I'm sorry."

"We're not going to make a decision until our daughter gets here. That should be sometime tomorrow. She's a minister and has a strong faith."

Shaking his head, he replied. "I confront religious zealots daily. They make no difference. The fact is that your son is in a coma with a traumatic brain injury, and leaving him on a respirator is only prolonging your agony."

"We agree with Bo," said Lexie.

"Yes," replied Zack.

"Have it your way," he replied as he was walking out of the room.

One of the other doctors who had introduced himself as Matthew Jordon spoke. "I apologize for Dr. Adders. He's a brilliant surgeon and saves many lives. As you could see, he is young and very confident in his ability. His work is his life and as you have probably guessed, he is an atheist. As he becomes older, all of us are hoping that his manners improve."

"Thank you, Dr. Jordon. We're devastated by the prospect of losing our son," Lexie said.

"I understand. Those of us who have children can relate to your sorrow."

"Could we meet with you again tomorrow when our daughter is here?" Zack asked.

"Yes, although I can't guarantee you that Dr. Adders will be present," he answered. "Now, we need to be going. The young lady's mother is here, and we have a meeting with her."

"How's she doing?" Lexie asked.

"She is conscious. It's still too early to determine the extent of her injuries."

"Thank you, Dr. Jordon," I said. "Please keep in touch."

After Dr. Jordon and his companion left the room, Zack commented, "That Dr. Adders is a piece of work."

"Definitely," replied Lexie.

"How old do you think he is?" I asked.

"Thirty-five at the most, maybe younger," Lexie replied.

"No matter how brilliant he is, he still has a lot to learn," said Zack.

"Yeah. I'd like to take him outside for some lessons," I added.

"Alejandra and her husband are here. Maybe they can find out more information about Lacy," Lexie said.

The afternoon seemed to last forever. Lexie and Zack took turns sitting by Jack; however, I still hadn't seen him. I was paged over the speaker to come to the front desk. A receptionist gave me a message she had written down from Tommie Rose, saying she would be here tomorrow before noon.

We were back at the hotel by evening and had supper there. Zack and Lexie agreed that they would take turns sitting with Jack. I told Lexie that I wanted to accompany her on the first shift.

"Are you sure?" she asked.

"No. But I need to see him."

My heart was pounding from the time we left the hotel until we reached his room. My breath caught in my throat when I saw him lying there with a tube in his mouth. I turned around and choked back a sob. Get hold of yourself, I demanded.

"Bo, you can step outside a few minutes if you like," Lexie said.

"No," I said, turning back around.

I stood there looking at my son who I had adored since birth, remembering what Dr. Adders had said, "He's already dead." Surely this couldn't be happening, I thought.

"Bo, let's sit down," Lexie said, as she pulled the two chairs in the room up closer to the bed.

Sitting down, I asked Lexie, "Do you think he knows how much we love him?"

"No doubt."

"He was a pill when he was a little boy," I commented. "I had to spank him nearly every week until he was about ten."

"I know, but as he grew older, you were the one person he looked up to more than anyone."

"It's easier to be honest now, Lexie. I was partial to Jack. I didn't mean to be. It was just that he was so full of life and liked the same things I did. He loved the ranch like me and my grands and was happiest when he was there. I don't believe he would've continued to rodeo much longer. In fact, if it hadn't been for Lacy, he would've probably already quit."

"That might be true, Bo, however, he has always been devoted to her. They got along so well. Both had a wild streak in them, confronting life like a charging bull. I know people said the marriage wouldn't last, but they were wrong.

I never said anything to you, Bo, about how you treated the boys. You have no idea, but the fact is that Zack is more like you than Jack. It's obvious to me and to your mother. We've talked about it several times. Just consider the following: Zack is quiet, like you; he always supports the underdog; he performs well under pressure, as you did; he played quarterback and is a leader; he did not receive the recognition he deserved; he was more consistent in the roping arena. Remember, he won the calf roping their senior year in high school rodeo. I will admit he's not as stubborn as you and Jack, but that's the only quality that you and Zack don't have in common."

"What if Jack doesn't live? What will she do?" I asked.

"She'll never go back to her mother's ranch. She doesn't get along with her, and she despises Roy. She contends that her mother married Roy because he had several gold buckles. She told me once that Alejandra never got over you. I believe that's true."

"We'll soon be fifty years old and married nearly thirty years. Surely by now, we can stop talking about Ali. Whatever happens, Lacy will always have a home with us. I was so angry at first, but I know how much she loves Jack."

We sat in silence for the next hour, lost in our own thoughts. When Tommie Rose was missing twenty years ago, I couldn't remember telling her I loved her the last time I saw her. I became obsessed with this thought until we found her. Now, here I sat with Jack, thinking the same thing. One thing for sure. I'd known men who lost their sons, and it had destroyed them. I could not allow that to happen to me.

My mother was seventy-three and even though she was in good health, it was only a matter of time until she would need me. She could care for Tom, who was in poor health, now. That would change at some time in the future. My thoughts were interrupted by Zack.

"I couldn't just sit in the hotel room. You've been here two hours. Let me give you a break. I would rather sit here with Jack than alone in my room."

"Is Dr. Adders right?" I asked.

"If Jack's brain injuries are as severe as he says, the chances would be minimal that he would breathe on his own when the respirator was removed."

"Do we just need to give up?"

"I don't know, Dad. How do you give up on someone you love so much? Sissy will have more answers than I do. We need her here. Our family is not complete without her."

"Are there many doctors like Adders?" Lexie asked.

"No, Mom, thank goodness. Most are compassionate. I have a feeling that this is his way of dealing with life and death that he sees daily. He attempts to blank out emotions. I would imagine that he's a lonely person."

"He's a sorry little turd and I can't stand him!" I announced. "Zack, we're going back to the room and try to get some sleep. I love you."

"Love you too, Dad. We'll get through this."

Lexie hugged him, saying, "Love you, Baby."

CHAPTER 5

Zack

I STAYED WITH JACK AFTER Mom and Dad left. I sat down in one of the chairs for a few minutes and then decided I was going to talk to him. Standing by the bed, holding his hand, I began, "Please fight hard, brother. This family needs you. I need you. Remember all those hunting seasons? Well, there's more to come. You used to get mad when I killed a bigger deer. One year you didn't speak to me for a week. Remember that giant buck you killed when we were only fifteen? It took us five hours to get him back to the pickup. That was the first-year Mom and Dad let us camp out by ourselves. We stayed at Dad's and Uncle Jimmy's favorite place, and we nearly froze.

Remember the great times we had at the high school rodeos? The girls always liked you better than me. I don't understand…since many times they couldn't tell us apart. I guess you just had the magic touch. And then there was Lacy. I always knew she would choose you, but I didn't want to accept it. We never fought over her. I guess we loved one another too much.

You must admit it, I looked after you. For instance, when we were seniors and Mom and Dad drove up one Thursday night when we weren't expecting them. You and Lacy were in your room and before they could get in the house, Lacy and I were sitting at the kitchen table, with me helping her do a math lesson. That saved you a tongue-lashing from Mom for sure. Another time, when we were younger, maybe like sophomores, you asked a girl for a date to a dance. When Lacy found out she threw one of her famous tantrums. You talked me into taking your place and the girl, to this day, thinks she went with you.

Remember that math teacher that was determined to keep you from graduating? I was the only one in class that could make an A. She delighted in proving how much smarter she was than her students by failing at least one-third of her class. The night before the final, I stayed up with you all night, studying. I know you believe you passed because of my tutoring, but I'm not so sure. I went to her class early that morning and told her these exact words. 'Mrs. Everson, I just wanted to let you know that someday I hope that I know math as well as you do. You've prepared me for college and a medical degree. I do appreciate that, and it's important for you to understand how much your class meant to me. My brother doesn't understand how smart you are. He's not going to college and will live on the ranch the rest of his life. I would very much like for him to graduate with me.' I tell you, brother, she was standing by her desk when I told her this crock, and she had to grab hold of it to keep from fainting when all the blood rushed to her head. You may have passed the test, but my talking to her didn't hurt anything.

Furthermore, I never told a soul that you were the one that nearly bit that kid's ear off when we were in the first grade. Dad had to pay the doctor's bill." An attractive nurse came in the room, interrupting me.

"You look like your brother. Are you twins?"

"Yes."

"Both of you resemble your dad."

"Yes. That's what people tell us."

"Your dad is one of the handsomest men I've ever seen. Your mother is beautiful, also. They don't look old enough to have sons your age."

"Do you take care of these type of patients?" I asked.

"You mean those on life support?"

"Yes."

"Not all of them. We're required to rotate shifts."

"That's because it's too depressing," I stated.

"That's correct," she answered, softly.

"Dr. Adders says he has no chance to live when he's taken off life support," I commented.

"I try not to get involved. I will tell you this. Dr. Adders is the most disliked doctor in this hospital. He is young, nice looking, and despised by everyone."

"But he's a brilliant doctor," I added.

"Yes, and he's seldom wrong, which he's quick to point out."

She checked the IV, respirator, and feeding tubes. Turning to leave, she said, "I don't see a ring on your finger so I assume you're not married. If you want a home cooked meal during your stay, I can provide that for you."

"I appreciate the offer. I'm not in the mood for any social events. I'm sorry and thank you again. No way could I think of anything other than my brother now."

A few minutes after the nurse left, two maintenance workers came in carrying a recliner. One of the men explained, "Nurse Houser told us to bring this in here for you. We don't refuse any of her requests. Her smile is worth whatever it takes."

"Thank you. I appreciate it." It was late and I was tired. I stood by the bed, holding Jack's hand, and said, "Good night, brother, I love you. I'm going to be right here beside you."

I sat down in the recliner, leaned back and dozed, off and on, throughout the night. Frequently, I was awakened by a nurse coming in. On one of these occasions someone slipped a pillow under my head.

Early the next morning, Nurse Houser came in with a cup of coffee. "How did you sleep?" she asked.

"Off and on. Thanks for the pillow and coffee."

"Sure, no problem. I'll be off for the next couple of days. Do you think your family will make a decision about life support within the next week?"

"I have no idea. My sister is coming in this morning. We're asking for another meeting with the doctors this afternoon."

"Don't let Adders get under your skin. He has a knack for doing that."

"Thank you for everything," I responded, as she left. Looking at my watch, it was 6:20. I didn't want to leave Jack by himself so I stayed until my mom and dad arrived an hour later.

"Did you get any sleep?" Mom asked.

"Some. I did fine with the recliner."

"Why don't you go get something to eat and let me and your dad stay. Go back to the room and try to rest some. You might want to be around the lobby after 10:00. Tommie should be coming in by then."

"I'm going to check on Lacy before I do anything," I said.

"We saw Alejandra and her husband in the lobby of the hotel. We talked briefly, but they didn't have additional information from what we were given. She's conscious, but I don't know how alert she is. Maybe you can find out more information."

At the front desk, I was told that Lacy was in room 10 of the intensive care ward. The waiting room was crowded, and approaching the receptionist desk, I asked, "Would it be possible to see Lacy Skinner?"

"Are you family?"

"She's my sister-in-law."

"Her mother and dad are with her now," she replied. "After they finish, I'll check with a nurse and see if it's possible. Just have a seat if you can find one."

I waited twenty minutes until Alejandra and Roy came out into the lobby. Alejandra was crying, and Roy had his arm around her as they came over to where I was sitting. She hugged me, saying, "Oh, Zack, my little girl is going to lose her leg. The doctors said there was no choice. I'm so sorry about Jack. Is there any change in his condition?"

"No, he's still on a respirator. Could I see Lacy?"

"Certainly. She's conscious, but not lucid. I don't think she recognized us. She's drugged for the pain and will fall asleep and then wake up. She couldn't talk to us."

I thanked them, and without asking a nurse went into her room. She had her eyes closed. I reached for her hand and squeezed it. Opening her eyes, she said, "Jack". She closed them and was asleep immediately, but still held onto my hand. I stood there several minutes and then tried to remove it, but she held on firmly. Finally, I had to use my other hand to pry her fingers loose. She moaned as I placed her hand back on the bed.

As I left the room, I thought, when will she be alert enough to tell her about Jack? Do we even need to tell her before her surgery? Would the pain of losing Jack and her leg be too much for her to bear?

I returned to my hotel room, showered, changed clothes, and was back in the hospital lobby by mid-morning to wait for Tommie. I didn't have to wait long until I saw her walking across the parking lot toward the entrance. I could identify that walk from as far as I could see her. I knew for a fact that half a dozen modeling agencies had offered her a job. She was beautiful as well as stunning. Being tall, almost six feet, her long reddish brown hair pulled back in a loose ponytail and sprinkle of freckles on a flawless complexion, she turned heads wherever she went. A loose fitting white cotton blouse tucked into faded, well-worn jeans held up by some kind of African beaded belt did not hide her lean and fit body. Coming through the door, almost boyish looking, she saw me immediately. We met in the middle of the lobby and hugged. "Sissy, I'm so glad you're here."

"I came as quickly as I could. Is there any change?"

"No. He's still on life support."

"I've tried to call Mom's cell phone several times, but she didn't answer."

"She had to cut it off. She was getting a call from friends in New Mexico every few minutes. Of course, Dad doesn't have a cell phone."

"Are they with Jack now?"

"Yeah. We can go to the room. They're taking it hard, especially Dad."

On the way to the room, I told her about Lacy's condition. The greeting between them was emotional, with both Mom and Tommie crying. Dad just stood back and looked at the floor. She went over and hugged him, bringing the tears, which he tried to hide unsuccessfully.

"We're glad you're here," Mom said, wiping away tears.

"It was amazing how I was able to make connections. Ordinarily, it would have taken another day," she said, turning and going over to Jack. "Could I have a few minutes alone with him?"

We waited outside the room until Tommie joined us. "I imagine you're beat after that long flight," I said. "We have a room for you at the hotel across the street. We have another meeting with the doctors at 3:00 today. That would give you some time to rest."

"I have clothes in the rental car. Let me get them and you can take me to the room."

"Dad, I'll come back and stay with Jack while you and Mom go eat."

"Okay, Zack."

On the way to her room, I told Tommie about the first meeting and Dr. Adders' comments. I also filled her in on the condition of the horses and Roany.

"I've never seen Dad this way," she said.

"We're all devastated, but I don't even know a word to describe Dad's response. He and Jack have become so close since I left home. Of course, he was always Dad's favorite anyway."

"I'm going to shower and rest for an hour," she said, as we reached her door. "I'll meet you in the lobby after that and we can visit before the meeting."

I picked up a sandwich in the cafeteria and returned to the room to relieve Mom and Dad. After they left, I stood beside the bed and resumed my one-sided conversation with Jack. "Well, brother, our Sissy is here and things are going to get better. Remember how angry we would get when she would beat us in the roping arena. How could a girl rope better than us? Finally, we just gave up and viewed her with respect and admiration. As we became older that feeling increased. By the time we entered high school, she could do no wrong.

Remember when Bear died? We were in high school but of course, we didn't rope on him anymore. Sissy was in college and drove all night to be with us. We loved that little horse with the big head and feet. She helped us bury him in the apple orchard. We chose the location because he loved apples. It seemed that when she was around, the bad wasn't so bad and the good was even better.

Remember how the older boys would ask us about Sissy? They wanted to know what she liked and disliked, to get up enough courage to ask her out. It was kind of sad that a girl could intimidate boys the way she did."

At the allotted time, I left and met Sissy in the hospital lobby. She called Mom on her cell phone, and we all met in the cafeteria for coffee before the meeting with the doctors.

"Tommie, tell us what you think about Jack," Mom said.

"I honestly don't know. Hopefully, the doctors can provide information which will help us. I do believe we need to move with caution and not hurry our decision."

"Do you think there's any hope?" mumbled Dad.

"Yes, with faith. I have based my life on that," she responded. "I've come from an area where death is common. Children are starving, AIDS is ravaging the population, and a shot of penicillin could mean the difference in life and death. All we have is faith. I believe in miracles. I have witnessed them firsthand. That doesn't mean Jack will live."

"You're a minister, Tommie. Why would God let this happen?" asked Dad.

"It's not that simple. I truly believe that God suffers with us. Could he change it? Certainly. Why doesn't he? I have no idea. We must trust him and believe in him. I admit, I don't have the answers. I don't even have the questions, but I believe. That's what's important."

"So your suggestion is that we don't remove the life support until we're sure," I said.

"Yes," she replied.

We arrived at the meeting fifteen minutes early. The doctors were five minutes late but all three were present. This time, introductions were made before the meeting, which was led by Dr. Jordon.

"Have you made a decision?" asked Dr. Adders.

"No," I answered."

"Why the delay?" he asked.

"Our sister believes we should proceed with caution and take more time," I responded.

"That's ridiculous. I told you his brain injuries are severe. When the respirator is removed, he will not breathe on his own."

"We disagree," I said. "We're going to wait."

"That is stupid," he said, looking directly at Tommie Rose. "You are only prolonging the inevitable."

"What makes you so sure?" Tommie asked.

"Because I know what is best!" he replied.

"Dr. Adders, I have the verse that fits you, and please listen carefully," Tommie said, looking directly at him.

"But man, proud man,
Dressed in a little brief authority,
Most ignorant of what he's most assured,"

Interrupting her, he shouted with anger, "I'm not going to listen to you spout Bible verses to me!" He got up and left the room, slamming the door behind him.

Silence followed his exit. Finally, Dr. Jordon said, "It seems I spend a great deal of time apologizing for Dr. Adders. He is a brilliant physician, but he lacks manners, and I'm sorry. Also, I know that William Shakespeare would be pleased with his verse from 'Measure for Measure' being identified as Biblical Scripture."

"Dr. Jordon, if my family agrees, we would like to keep Jack on life support for another week. That will give us time to pray and talk about an upcoming decision," announced Sissy.

We agreed verbally with her and the issue was settled, at least for the next seven days.

CHAPTER 6

Lacy

I KEPT WAKING UP FOR a few seconds but couldn't keep my eyes open. My whole body felt numb. I remember Jack standing by me, holding my hand. People came in my room, but I couldn't talk. I tried to figure out where I was and remember what happened but couldn't. I dreamed that I was at the National Finals. One time I won, in another I hit a barrel in all ten go-rounds.

Finally, I woke up and everything was clear. A person was in the room in a white dress and she said, "Why, hello there. It looks like you are with us again, young lady."

"Who are you?" I asked.

"I'm Nurse Faraday. I've been taking care of you for the last week."

"Where am I?"

"Darling, you're in the hospital in Colorado Springs. You were in a bad wreck, and you haven't been fully conscious since you were brought here."

"All I remember is my husband, Jack, coming in and holding my hand."

"Let me get your mom and dad. They'll be anxious to talk with you," she said.

After she was gone, I tried to remember a wreck. Nothing came to my mind about what happened. I knew my name and my husband's name. I couldn't even remember my horses' names. Slowly, I began to remember why I was in Colorado Springs. We had been at the rodeo in Cheyenne. Suddenly, the pain was terrible in my lower body, and I cried out.

The nurse came back into the room. "Honey, we've taken you off most of the pain medicine so you'll be able to understand your situation. I'm so sorry, but you're going to hurt for at least a while. Your parents have been contacted, and they should be here anytime."

"How badly have I been hurt?"

"Your parents will be here shortly, and a doctor will also be present to visit with you. Now, hang in there, Baby. Things are going to get better."

"I know my husband's okay. He came to see me." Before the nurse could respond, my mother and Roy came into the room. Mom was crying and wringing her hands, and I didn't look at Roy."

"Oh, Lacy, you're awake," she said, coming to my bed and grabbing my hand. "I've been so worried about you."

"I want to see Jack," I said.

"That's not possible now."

"Why? He's been to see me and held my hand. I remember." My mother turned around to the nurse as if looking for help.

"A doctor is coming in shortly, and he'll explain everything," the nurse stated.

My mother had said a doctor would come in, but instead, three doctors were in my room when they explained mine and Jack's conditions. When they told me about my injuries and that they were going to remove my left leg, I started screaming. I gained enough control to argue with them, but all three were adamant that there was no choice. When they explained that Jack was in a coma with severe brain injuries and on a respirator that was keeping him alive, I told them to let me die.

A fourth person remained in the room after the doctors left and introduced himself as a social worker. Speaking to my mom, he said, "Could I have a few minutes alone with Lacy?"

Without answering, my mom and Roy left the room.

"My name is Jerry. Believe me, I understand your pain."

"That's impossible," I mumbled.

"No, Lacy. My wife and two-year old boy were killed in a car wreck. A drunk driver took them from me ten years ago, and I never got over it. I still grieve, especially at holidays. I wanted to die, also."

"Is that supposed to make me feel better?" I asked.

"No, of course not. You're faced with a tragedy. Somehow, I believe you are up to meeting this challenge. You're young and strong. Also, I did some research on you in preparation for this conference. You're a competitor. You don't like to lose, and you have dreams of being a world champion."

"That's impossible! How many world champions have one leg? I don't want to live without Jack either! He's my life," I sobbed.

"What about your mother and father? They're worried about you. You don't want to hurt them," he stated.

"That's how much you know. My mother cares little about anyone but herself. That man with her is not my father. I can't stand him. Jack's family is my only family."

"Would you like for me to have them come to see you?"

"Yes. I need them."

"I'll be back to talk to you later," he said.

After he left, the pain came back even worse than before. I pushed the button the nurse had shown me, if I needed anything. Within seconds, the nurse was in the room.

"I'm hurting!" I cried.

"I'll connect you to the IV, and you should receive relief in a manner of minutes."

"I just want to die," I whispered. Shortly, the pain was gone, and I was dreaming again. I would wake up and see images in the room talking and one of them appeared to be Jack. I could not make out what they were saying. Then I seemed to be in motion, with my bed moving and people walking beside me. After that, only darkness.

The next thing I remember is someone shaking me and telling me to wake up. I couldn't keep my eyes open, and every time I closed them the nurse would shake me again.

"Lacy, you need to wake up! You're in the recovery room and the surgery is over. Wake up! Come on now, open your eyes. That's better. How do you feel?"

"Tired and dizzy," I mumbled.

The nurse kept talking to me until I was fully awake and then said, "I'm taking you to the intensive care unit for at least a day. After that, they'll take you back to your room."

"My leg's gone, isn't it?"

"Yes, but you came through the surgery well," she replied.

"Big deal. Am I supposed to be happy about that?"

"A team of doctors will be in to talk with you after you're back in your room and rested."

I was in and out of it for the next 24 hours before I was taken back to my room where my mother and Roy were waiting. My mother was crying again, and Roy was consoling her.

"Oh, Lacy. The doctors said the surgery was successful, and you came through it with flying colors. I'm so thankful. My prayers were answered. My baby is going to be okay. I couldn't have made it without Roy."

"Yeah, sure, Mom. They took one of my legs off. Jack is in a coma and is probably going to die. Everything is great. You're ridiculous!"

"But Lacy, you're alive."

"Big deal. What do I have to live for?" I sobbed. "Please, just let me be alone."

"Okay, Baby. We'll come back in a few hours when you're feeling better," she replied.

My mother and Roy weren't gone but a few minutes when Bo and Lexie came in, with Lexie saying, "We wanted to check on you, Lacy. We won't stay but a few minutes."

Still sobbing, I said, "I'm glad to see you. Please tell me about Jack. I thought he came to see me, but now I realize it was Zack."

"Lacy, it's not good. He's still in a coma and is on a respirator. They call it life support because it is breathing for him. Dr. Adders believes that once he's removed from the respirator, he will not breathe on his own."

"How many days has it been since the accident?" I asked.

"This is the fifth day. We need to talk with you about a decision that we made. Since you are conscious and alert, you need to be included. We had told the doctors that we wanted to leave Jack on the respirator for seven days from the time we met with them. The meeting was two days after the accident. That would mean the respirator would not be removed for four more days. One of us has been with Jack night and day. In fact, Tommie Rose and Zack are with him now. We agreed that whoever was sitting with him would talk to him as much as possible. Of course, it is a one-way conversation, but we're hoping that will make a difference. Also, we have prayed about it every day."

"I can't live without him," I said.

"Don't say that, Lacy. We love you like a daughter," she responded.

"That's right," said Bo. "We need you, Lacy. You're family and we're going to take care of you. We need to know if you trust our decision about removing the respirator after seven days."

"I know you love Jack, like I do. I would never go against a decision you've made. Could I see Jack?"

"I don't know why not. We'll talk to the doctors," Lexie said.

Both of them bent over and kissed me on the forehead before they left, saying they loved me.

Alone again, I thought of Jack and how much I loved him. I couldn't imagine living without him. I kept wanting this to be a dream in which I would wake up and everything be okay. I began hurting again, and summoned the nurse who gave me a stronger pain reliever. The last thing I remember is wishing that I wouldn't wake up.

CHAPTER 7

Lexie

IT WAS OUR EIGHTH DAY in Colorado Springs, and all I could think about was that tomorrow the respirator would be removed. The accident had occurred Sunday night, July 30. We had met with the doctors on August 1 and asked that Jack remain on the respirator for a week. Tomorrow would be August 8, and there had been no change in his condition.

One of us had been with Jack day and night. We took shifts during the day, and Zack insisted on staying at night. He had a recliner and said that he could sleep, which we all doubted. We had agreed that whoever was with Jack would talk to him even though it would be a one-sided conversation. It was confusing that his heart was beating on its on, yet Dr. Adders kept insisting that he would stop breathing when he was taken off the respirator. Each morning and evening the four of us would gather around his bed. We would join hands, including Jack's, and Tommie Rose would lead us in prayer, asking for his recovery.

I would hate to even think of this ordeal we were going through without the presence of Tommie. She was our strength and the main reason for our hope. When we were together she would often tell us of her experiences in Africa; including the terrible toll that AIDS was taking;

the widespread famine and starvation of children; the miracles she had witnessed and the strong faith shared by those working with her.

On one of the occasions when we were doing our evening prayer, Dr. Adders came into the room. After we finished, he asked, "Do you think that will make a difference?"

"We certainly hope it does," I answered.

Shaking his head, he replied, "I've never seen it help anything. In fact, it only gives false hope to a hopeless situation."

"You still believe he's going to stop breathing when we take him off the respirator?" Zack asked.

"Most definitely," he said. "The brain has suffered extensive damage and that's the only reasonable outcome."

"Dr. Adders, this family believes. I know that you do not. That is your right even though I disagree with you. I will tell you this; there comes a time in everyone's life when all we have is faith in God and hope. For this family, that time has come. I would ask you to respect that." As she was speaking, Tommie, had moved closer to Dr. Adders. Because of her height, when she finished she was looking him directly in the eyes. He turned and left the room, mumbling during the exit.

We had been forced to go shopping for clothes, since we left home without packing. The hotel room had become our home. We took turns taking Roany for walks; thus far, she hadn't been a distraction for the guests. We had been eating most of our meals in the cafeteria. We seldom left the hospital except for several trips to the vet to have Roany's leg examined and check on the horses. Zack had kept the rental car for us to use. We did go to the wrecking yard to see the Dodge, and it was obvious why Jack and Lacy suffered serious injuries. From what we could gather by viewing the wreckage, both front doors had come open. Lacy's seat belt kept her in the cab but evidently, when it rolled over, her left leg was caught in the door and was crushed. The back doors remined closed and Jack's injuries probably came from being thrown against the cab when the pickup rolled over several times.

I was not only worried about Jack and Lacy, but Bo had become a concern as well. During the time we had been here, he had lost weight. Not just a small amount, but probably as much as fifteen pounds. I continually encouraged him to eat, but he would say he wasn't hungry. I was already stressed to the limit, and when he refused to eat breakfast on the day before Jack was to be taken off the respirator, I lost it.

"Bo, you've got to eat! You're going to starve, which is adding to our stress. Why can't you see that?"

"The last thing I need is for you to nag me. I told you. I'm not hungry."

"Would you please eat something? If nothing else, just to keep us from worrying about you. Bo, I know the pressure has been mounting with each passing day. Eat something and give us one less thing to worry about." He ordered and we ate in silence.

Tommie came in before we had finished, sat down, and said, "Dad, I'm glad you got your appetite back."

"I'm eating to keep your mother from nagging me," he replied.

"Would you like to go with me to visit Lacy?" she asked.

"No, I need to take Roany for her walk," Bo answered.

"Yes, I'll go with you," I said. "I haven't spent enough time with her."

Arriving at Lacy's room, there was a note on the door which read, "Do Not Enter." A nurse passing by said, "They're changing the dressing. It shouldn't take long."

A nurse came out a few minutes later and told us to go in.

"We wanted to check on you," I said.

"Thank you for coming. I'm still waiting to wake up from a nightmare. Has there been any change in Jack?"

"No," Tommie answered. "The respirator will be removed tomorrow. We've been praying that he'll breathe on his own. One of us has been staying with him night and day."

"I want to be there with him when it's done," Lacy said.

"Do you think you're able to be moved to his room?" I asked.

"Yes. They put me in a wheelchair this morning for an hour. They insist that I need to be up some and not remain in bed. Something about blood clots. Would one of you come get me?"

"I will," Tommie replied. "You don't want your mother to bring you?"

"No. I wish she'd go home and take that man with her. I can't stand him. I know she's worried about me, but I become even more depressed when they're around."

"We love you, Lacy, and we're going to be here for you now and in the future," I said.

"How are the horses?" she asked.

"They're fine. They were bruised up but nothing serious. The vet has agreed to keep them as long as we're here."

"I lost out on going to the National Finals, but that's nothing compared to losing Jack. I have no reason to live without him. I've thought about it constantly. We were so wonderful together and life was fun. Without him, it's just a black hole."

"Don't say that," Tommie said. "You have your entire life ahead of you. No matter what happens, you'll still be a beautiful young lady. Right now, it's vital for you to refrain from having a negative attitude. That will do nothing but make matters worse." She went over to the bed and took her hand. "Like Mom said, we love you and you're family."

"I still haven't been able to look at my leg or where it used to be. I know they removed it below the knee. The nurse keeps encouraging me to watch her change the dressing. She said that eventually I would be able to change it myself. It must be done every four hours. The social worker comes by every day. He's nice and I don't mind talking to him, but I don't know how much good it does."

"It'll take time, Lacy," Tommie said.

"I know. How is Mia and Tom doing?"

"Worried, of course. Ms. Nancy said to tell you she loved you. My dad is okay when he doesn't overdo it. They would like to come but can't afford to risk it." I said.

"How's Jack's dog?" she asked.

"Right this minute, she's lying up in the middle of our bed in the hotel," I answered. "I'd say she's doing fine."

For the first time, Lacy smiled, saying, "Jack loves that hound."

"She does have a broken leg but it's doing well," Tommie said.

"It's still hard to believe that we were on top of the world and then this happens. I keep asking myself why this happened to us."

"Lacy, we don't have those answers now and never will. We have to move forward with our lives and maintain a strong faith," Tommie stated. "I firmly believe there doesn't have to be a reason bad things happen, or for that matter, good things. We're not being punished or rewarded for what we've done. We must keep living our life and trusting in God."

"Will you promise to come get me when the respirator is removed?" she asked.

"You have my word, Lacy," Tommie responded.

We told her again that we loved her before we left. We met Alejandra and Roy in the hallway. We greeted one another but didn't stop and visit. My relationship with Alejandra had not improved nor had it become worse. You could say that we tolerated one another and were social when it was required at family gatherings. I knew that she had never gotten over Bo and despised me for marrying him. That was thirty years ago, but some things never change. Over the years, she had become angrier and that had taken something away from her beauty. Lacy, on the other hand, had not inherited her mother's attitude and was kind, considerate, and sweet. She resembled her mother when Alejandra was her age but that was as far as the similarities went.

Roy was far from mine and Bo's favorite character. He was one of those people who didn't hear much of what you said because he was preparing to tell you something about himself. There was something there with Lacy also that she had never told us. At least that's what I thought. He had been a World Champion steer wrestler, and we believe that was the main attraction for Alejandra. After he retired from rodeo, he adapted to an easy lifestyle on the ranch and gained considerable weight, which didn't help his looks. At family gatherings, Bo had always avoided him, but Jack had been courteous enough to listen to his stories.

After we passed them in the hall, Tommie asked, "Does she leave Daddy alone now? You know it was no secret when we were growing up. I know you thought we weren't aware of her feelings for him. It was so obvious, even to the boys. We used to talk about it and even Lacy acknowledged it by the time she was in her teens. I don't know how you did it. Of course, my friends in school thought Dad was a dream. They said he should have been a movie star."

"I really don't think Bo realized how serious Alejandra was until after we married. I honestly believe that Bo considered her more like a sister than anything. Certainly, that wasn't what she wanted. I keep thinking that women will stop noticing Bo as he gets older. So far that hasn't happened. He's almost fifty and women are still making fools of themselves around him. You know, Tommie, I don't think he even notices. Maybe I'm naïve, but that's what I believe."

"Mom, you're so beautiful, it's not surprising he doesn't pay attention to anyone else. How do you stay so fit and trim?"

"I help out on the ranch, which I enjoy. Also, I spend a lot of time working in the orchard. It's still one of my favorite projects, and our neighbors always have plenty of apples. Ms. Nancy still helps me, and even at 73, she can do a day's work."

Visiting about outside events took our minds off Jack for a few minutes. However, by the time we returned to the hotel lobby, Tommie commented, "I dread tomorrow, but in a way, it will be a relief to find out what's going to happen.

"I feel the same way, Tommie."

"Is Dad going to get through it?"

"I honestly don't know. I've never seen him this way. He hasn't slept over an hour or two each night we've been here. He gets up and leaves at least six times a night. I asked him where he goes and he said, 'Walking.' Your dad has always been calm and in control under pressure. Of course, the only time he has experienced anything close to this is when you were kidnapped. He's twenty years older now, and I credit that for at least part of his conduct. Also, we had reason to believe we would get you back. I know Bo, like the rest of us, realizes that Jack's chances are slim."

"I'm going to relieve Zack, whether he wants to or not," said Tommie. "He spends all night with Jack, and he needs to get out for some fresh air."

She left, and I went to look for Bo, hoping I could get him to eat some lunch.

CHAPTER 8

Zack

I LOOKED AT MY WATCH and it was 3:00 A.M. It had to be the longest night of my entire life. I couldn't get comfortable in the recliner and finally had sat upright. I tried to read a magazine, which was difficult with the dim lighting. Today was the day the respirator was to be removed. We had been informed in a meeting yesterday afternoon that the procedure would be done at 10:00 in the morning. I had requested that the feeding tube be kept in place, hoping for the best. Dr. Adders was present at the meeting, as negative and obnoxious as ever.

Nurse Houser came in talking. "What are you doing awake?"

"Can't sleep. Too much on my mind."

"That's not true. Only one thing is on your mind," she said, checking the IV's and respirator.

"You're right. Less than seven hours and we'll know."

"I know it's been tough. Don't go away, I'll be back in a second."

She came back carrying a straight back chair, placing it next to the bed. "Move over here in this chair. I'm going to take a few minutes and give you a massage. I'll just consider you a patient."

She worked on my neck and shoulders for fifteen minutes. She had magic in her fingers. By the time she finished, I had relaxed. I moved into the recliner, lay back, and was asleep in no time.

I woke up three hours later when she brought me a cup of coffee. "Thank you for the massage. It worked wonders. That was the best I've slept since I've been here."

"No problem. I like to see positive results of my work."

"Anyway, it was kind of you," I said.

"That offer for a home cooked meal is still open if you change your mind," she said, walking out the door.

Mom, Dad, and Tommie were there by 7:00 and insisted that I go eat breakfast. I put up a feeble argument but agreed. It felt good to be outside. Even though it was only the ninth of August, a light jacket would have felt good. I walked around the parking area for fifteen minutes before going to my room. The phone was ringing when I opened the door. Answering, it was Mia.

"Zack, I wanted to check in with you. I know the respirator will be removed today. Are you making it okay?"

"As good as can be expected, I guess. We're all kind of stressed out. How is Gramps?"

"He keeps apologizing for me not being able to be there. I couldn't do anything if I was with you. I can pray here at home. Pastor Stevens has been coming by every day. He's been with this family in every crisis we've faced."

"Someone will call you, Mia, when we know something."

"I know. I love you, Zack. Please tell Jack I love him, too."

"Okay. I'll do that. Love you, Mia." After hanging up, I thought what a remarkable lady my grandmother was. By the time, I showered, shaved, and had breakfast it was 9:00. I went by Lacy's room, and she was already in a wheelchair.

"Ready?" I asked.

"Yeah. Thank you for coming after me."

Mom, Dad, and Sissy were all in Jack's room when I returned. They greeted Lacy, with each giving her a hug.

"Who is that pretty nurse that keeps coming in here talking about you?" Tommie asked. "She brought us a cup of coffee."

"Nurse Houser," I stated. "She's been nice."

"We appreciated the coffee," Dad said. "If my grands were here he would prefer a shot of Jack Daniels. That might not be a bad idea."

"I still remember B-Boy. He taught me and Jack a lot. Of course, some of it got us into trouble."

"He was a special man. I remember what he did for me, and I'll always have a place in my heart for him," said Mom.

By 9:45, several personnel began arriving in the room. Dr. Adders was one of the last, in fact, he was a few minutes late. One of the doctors explained what would be done and asked if we had any questions.

"We requested that the feeding tube remain," I said.

"Yes. It will," he answered. "If you like, you can gather around the bed."

We formed a circle around the bed, with Lacy holding Jack's left hand and me holding his right hand. Mom, Dad, and Tommie filled in between us. The doctor removed the tube from Jack's mouth and throat, and the silence was deafening. We all had our eyes fixed on Jack, watching for a sign of life. We waited and waited.... nothing.

"See, I told you what would happen. You should have listened to me. I tried to tell you," Dr. Adders proclaimed.

I heard a strange sound come from my Dad. To this day, I can't describe it, but the next thing I knew he had a chokehold on Adders. He had one hand around his throat, and Adders was on his knees turning purple.

"Now, you son-of-a-bitch, you know how it feels not to be able to breathe," Dad said with a growl.

I moved as quickly as possible and grabbed my Dad around the shoulders to pull him off Adders. I was no match for his strength and if not for Tommie Rose he would have killed him right there. She moved quickly and pried Dad's hand from his throat, with Adders falling to the floor unconscious. Within seconds, a stretcher was carrying Adders out of the room.

Then I heard Mom cry, "He's breathing, he's breathing! Oh, my God, he's breathing!" Looking at Jack, I could see his chest rising and falling. Gathering around the bed, all of us had tears.

The doctor who had disconnected the respirator spoke, "We don't need to get our hopes up too much. It's not unusual for someone to breathe for a day or two when taken off the respirator, then stop breathing. It is encouraging that he is breathing on his own. I am aware of your staying with him continuously the past week and talking to him. I commend you for that. Now, we must wait and see what happens."

He was interrupted by two police officers coming through the door, accompanied by one of the staff that had taken Adders out on a stretcher. "That's the man," he said, pointing at Dad.

They went directly to Dad, with one of them saying, "Mr. Skinner, you are under arrest for assault." They put his hands behind his back and handcuffed him, reading him his rights during the process. Dad didn't say anything.

The rest of us were speechless until Sissy said, "Officers, that doctor was terrible, when we thought Jack had died. Dad was emotional and acted without thinking."

"Regardless of the circumstances, ma'am, your dad did attack a physician who's in critical condition. The hospital administrator assures us he's going to press charges. Now, we're going to take him to the station and book him. I'm sure you'll want to make bail."

"Tommie, you and Mom follow them and I'll stay with Jack," I said. We all gathered around the bed again, and Tommie gave thanks that our prayers had been answered. After that, Mom and Sissy followed the officers and Dad out the door, leaving me and Lacy with the one doctor who remained.

"Was that unusual conduct for your dad?" he asked.

"Very much so," I answered. "My dad's one of the calmest and most level-headed men I've ever known. He's not been the same since Jack's accident."

"That's true," Lacy said. "He's a wonderful man and seldom ever becomes angry. That doctor is awful."

"Yes. We all tolerate Dr. Adders because he's an outstanding surgeon. Maybe the best in the country. It was unfortunate that your dad was arrested, but Adders may think twice before he pops off about a patient again. Your dad was so quick to reach him; I didn't realize what was happening."

"My dad was an outstanding athlete. I could never have gotten him off Adders if it hadn't been for my sister. I hope that the hospital is understanding about my dad's reaction."

"The hospital administrator will support him no matter what. This hospital has gained much needed publicity because of Adders. People come from all over the world to have surgery here. Don't look for any help from him."

"Well, we appreciate the information," I said.

"About your brother. If he breathes on his own for three or four days, there is a good chance he will continue to breathe without a respirator. Of course, the question now is how long will he remain in a coma. We have no way of knowing. Also, without doubt, he has suffered severe brain damage. When, and if he does come out of the coma, there is no way of knowing what quality of life he will have. I'm sorry to keep giving you discouraging news, but you need to know what you're up against. Your brother has already proven Dr. Adders wrong, so at least you have hope. Now, I have patients needing my attention. It has been an interesting morning," he said, smiling.

A nurse remained in the room with Jack after everyone left, so I took Lacy back to her room. After two aids helped her back in bed, we visited a few minutes.

"Zack, I'm so thankful we still have hope. That gives me a reason to live. Jack is a fighter, and he may recover after all. I know it will be a long and difficult journey, but at least he's alive."

"You're right. Now we have to concentrate on getting you on the road to recovery."

"I'm going to try harder. The social worker keeps emphasizing that attitude is everything in recovery. I'm going to work on that."

"Good for you. Now, I need to see what I can find out about Dad," I said.

"Will you let me know?"

"Sure. Just as quick as I find out anything."

CHAPTER 9

Bo

I WAS TOLD AT THE police station that a standard bail would not be applied in my case. I had assaulted a physician at a medical facility and a judge would have to set bail. That meant I would be forced to spend the night in jail and attend a bond hearing in the morning.

"Isn't there something we can do?" Lexie asked.

"No, ma'am," replied the officer. "This is a special case and a judge must set bail. Charges are being filed against your husband as we speak."

"That's ridiculous!" Tommie exclaimed. "My dad's not a criminal."

"I'll be okay. I shouldn't have reacted the way I did," I said. "Lexie, you and Tommie need to get back to the hospital to be with Jack. Just let me know if there's any change. We need to be thankful he survived being taken off the respirator."

Before leaving, Lexie looked at the officer and said, "You better take care of him."

"Don't worry. I'll put him in a cell by himself."

After being photographed and fingerprinted, I was taken to a cell. A clock on the wall indicated it was a few minutes past 11:00. I thought, did all this really happen in an hour?

Sitting down on the hard bed, the first thing that came to mind was my grands spending the night in jail seventy years ago. My mom's prediction had come true. I was becoming more like Grands the older I became. A feeling of panic engulfed me as I realized that I could have killed Adders, if not for Zack and Tommie. To be truthful, I lost control of myself and barely remember the attack; however, it was vivid in my mind that Adders seemed pleased that he was right since we thought Jack had died. It was hard to believe any doctor would be pleased that a patient had died.

Only ten days ago, everything in my life was going great. My favorite time of year was coming up. It was the end of summer and we would start working the calves we had weaned. We were now running 900 momma cows on the two ranches. The calf crop had been good and we'd sell most of the calves in the fall. We had put up round bales to last the winter, and all we needed was several hundred square bales for the horses.

Jimmy Light, my lifelong friend, was still working for me. He and his wife, Felicia, had built a new home on the ranch fifteen years ago. Jimmy had trained Grands' and my father-in-law's race horses back in the '80s. They had been extremely successful, with his share of the purse money being substantial.

Jimmy and Felicia had two children. Jimmy, or Poco, was just out of high school and working for us on the ranch. He wasn't their child by birth but had been raised by them. His mother had suffered a stroke when he was born. His dad had been our jockey, Angel, at the time. Jolynda Kay, their daughter, was a freshman at Eastern New Mexico.

My mind kept returning to Jack. We now had hope, even though it was slim. Lexie had handled it better than me. She was right about my eating. I had lost weight due to not eating and so little sleep.

The first thing I was going to do when I got out of here was to contact the insurance company about the wrecked pickup. I know Jack had it insured because they were making payments. From the looks of it, the only option would be to have it totaled and get a new one. Also, I needed to check on getting the trailer repaired. Looking at it, we were amazed at how little damage it had sustained. For the first time, I began to feel some optimism and less helplessness, with some jobs to get done.

At mid-afternoon Lexie and Tommie returned with news that a bail hearing would be conducted in the morning. They also said they had hired a lawyer to represent me, and he would be here shortly.

"Any change in Jack?" I asked.

"No," replied Lexie.

"Dad, we did find out that Adders wasn't injured seriously. They thought he fainted from fright. He's already been released," Tommie informed me.

"I guess that's good news. He should thank you and your brother for that."

"Are you going to be okay, staying here tonight?" Lexie asked.

"Sure. Probably going to be good for me. It'll give me time to think about what a fool I've been. I keep thinking of the night Grands spent in jail for assault. Of course, he had a better excuse, since he had been drinking."

"Don't be too hard on yourself, Cowboy. We all still love you," Lexie said, smiling.

"Remember, Dad, even Jesus lost his temper a time or two. He drove the money changers out of the Temple."

"We'll be back early in the morning. We're going to get through this," Lexie said.

After they left, I went over and lay down. I dozed off briefly but was awakened by the jailor and a young man dressed in a suit and tie. He introduced himself as my lawyer, and we spent the next half hour going over what had occurred at the hospital that landed me in jail.

Breakfast the next morning was not going to make for any weight gain. We had dry toast and scrambled eggs that were well done. Rubbery would be an accurate description. Lexie and Tommie were there by the time I'd finished. We visited until it was time for the hearing. An officer escorted me across the street to the courthouse but at least didn't handcuff me.

We had to wait as several other criminals went before the judge. Finally, he called my name, and we approached the bench.

"Mr. Skinner, the charge is assault. How do you plead?" asked the judge.

"Guilty, Your Honor," I replied. The lawyer and I had agreed that the best approach would be to admit guilt since it was obvious.

"Your Honor, there are extenuating circumstances," my lawyer stated. He continued to explain, in detail, what happened. He did a good job of relating the story as I had told him. The judge listened intently until he had finished.

"Does the District Attorney have any comments?" the judge asked.

By the time he had finished with his accusations, I had begun to believe I should go to prison for life. He described me as a madman who was intent on murdering the doctor who was trying to save my son's life. He finished with an emotional plea to hold me without bail because I was a danger to the hospital and doctors.

"Mr. Skinner, I'm going to set bail at $20,000; however, I'm issuing a restraining order that forbids you from going within 100 feet of the hospital. If you violate this order, you will be arrested and remain in jail until your grand jury appearance. Is that understood?"

"Your Honor, that would prevent my client from visiting his son who is in critical condition," stated my lawyer.

"That's my decision. You'll have to live with it," he replied.

Leaving the courthouse, I told Lexie and Tommie, "I don't know if I can do this or not."

"Dad, you have no choice. It's either that or go to jail. The grand jury doesn't convene for another two weeks."

"I have a suggestion," said Lexie. "Take care of the insurance claim, buy another pickup, and get the trailer fixed. After that, find a place to stall the horses that has an arena. You can take care of them and maybe even ride some. That'll give you something to do plus get the horses away from the vet's."

"I had already decided to buy another pickup and get the trailer fixed. However, I know nothing about Colorado Springs. I wouldn't know where to find an arena that stalled horses."

"Well, that's simple. Ask the vet."

"Okay. I'll start on that tomorrow," I replied.

I still hadn't given in and bought a cell phone. I didn't want to be interrupted while I was working and besides, it interfered with my privacy. Lexie kept insisting that I was just stubborn.

While I was at the vet's the next morning, the receptionist summoned me for a phone call. Answering, it was Lexie.

"Bo, you need to come back to the hotel. We have a problem."

"Is Jack okay?" I asked.

"Just come back and I'll explain. It involves a decision we have to make." I left immediately and in a matter of minutes was talking to Lexie and Zack in the lobby of the hotel.

"What's going on?" I asked.

"Dad, Jack has swelling on his brain. Dr. Jordon notified us a few minutes before Mom called you. It came about suddenly. He said the only option was surgery and we shouldn't wait long. Now, for the other problem.... he has insisted that Dr. Adders would be the best one to do the operation."

"Hell, no!

"Bo, Dr. Jordon said that Adders would be the best we could get."

"Adders was glad when we thought Jack had died. I don't want him touching him."

"Bo, you haven't been yourself since this happened. I have opposed you very few times in the thirty years we've been married. I'm going to talk to Dr. Adders about doing the surgery. This is my little boy, and I want him to have every chance that is available."

"Dad, I'm sorry, but I agree with Mom," Zack stated.

I took a deep breath, exhaled, and said, "I will not let him touch Jack even if it means going back to jail. He's my little boy, too."

CHAPTER 10

Lexie

I WAS NOT SURPRISED AT Bo's reaction to Dr. Adders performing the surgery. I asked Zack his opinion on what we should do.

"Let me talk to Sissy and maybe we can come up with something. I'm not even sure that Dr. Adders will consent to do the surgery. Maybe we should talk to him before we proceed any further," he suggested.

"You're right, Zack, I'm getting ahead of myself. Let me see if I can schedule a meeting with Dr. Adders. We need to meet with him as soon as possible. Tommie is with Jack. You can talk to her while I see what can be done about a meeting with Adders."

I was able to schedule a meeting with Adders at 4:00 in the afternoon. When we arrived, Dr. Jordon was present, also. Dr. Adders had a cloth wrapped around his neck. I wondered if it was just for show or if it was necessary for his injury. We greeted one another briefly, and I got right to the point.

"Dr. Adders, I apologize for my husband's conduct. He hasn't been himself since the accident. He and Jack are extremely close. I know you've been informed that Jack needs surgery immediately due to swelling on his brain. We'd like for you to perform the operation. We understand that you are the best, and we want Jack to have every chance."

Smiling, he responded, "I accept your apology, but you are not the one who attacked me. Your husband tried to kill me and would have if not for your children. He was a madman. I have never been treated like that."

"All we can do is say we're sorry," I said.

"That's not enough. Maybe if he apologized, I would consider doing the surgery."

"You've taken an oath to help people, Dr. Adders. Surely, you wouldn't violate that promise," Tommie said.

"That man tried to kill me. He might succeed next time. What if the surgery was not successful and your brother died? No, I will not do the surgery unless I get an apology and assurance that he will not do harm to me."

With that statement, Dr. Adders left the room. Dr. Jordon asked us the question that we all were thinking. "Will Mr. Skinner apologize?"

"After thirty years of living with him, I doubt it," Mom answered.

"I do have one other option," Dr. Jordon replied. "Dr. Adders has few friends. No, that is an understatement...he has no friends here. However, there is a physician that teaches at the University of Colorado that might influence him. He was his mentor while attending school, and he has stayed in contact with him. The man's name is Dr. Wilson, and he is the only person I have ever heard Dr. Adders praise. I would suggest that we contact Dr. Wilson and see if he could help you. I have his phone number and can call him and explain your situation.

"Thank you, Dr. Jordon. That would be our best chance. My husband is stubborn and angry. Not a good combination."

"Let me see what I can do. I'll get back with you shortly," Dr. Jordon said.

At 6:00 that evening, while we were in Jack's room, I received a call from Dr. Jordon saying that Dr. Adders would perform the surgery early the next morning. Zack stayed with Jack while Tommie and I went back to the hotel to talk to Bo. We found him watching the news. As he became older, he had taken more interest in politics. The presidential election was only two months away; hence there was plenty of news.

"Anything new today?" I asked.

"Not much. Republicans continue to hammer Clinton on Lewinsky even though he's not running. Clinton damaged the party with his conduct. If the Republicans win it will be on his shoulders. The irony is... he was a good president."

"Bo, Dr. Adders is going to perform the surgery in the morning. Please be reasonable about this and think about Jack's welfare."

"I don't believe my opinion about Adders is unreasonable," he responded.

"Don't you accept that Jack has a better chance with Adders doing the surgery?"

"Maybe, maybe not. Depends on how hard he tries."

"Dad, Dr. Jordon assured us that once he was in the operating room, it wouldn't matter who the patient was. We must trust him. Think how we would feel if we didn't let Dr. Adders do the surgery and it was unsuccessful. We would always blame ourselves."

"Bo, Tommie is right. Would you consider apologizing to Adders."

"It would be a cold day in hell before I apologize to him. Besides, I'm not allowed within 100 feet of the hospital. I won't interfere with the surgery. I had said that no way would I allow it. That was wrong and I'll stay out of the way."

"That does make me feel better," I said. "Now, let's go eat supper. See, I'm now a country girl. Evening meal is not dinner. I'm going to get Zack and we can have a family meal together."

I had inquired about a good place to eat close to the hospital and it turned out to live up to its reputation. We kept the conversation away from the surgery. Tommie spent a large part of our time together telling us of her work in Africa. She went as a missionary but served in other areas, also. Medical treatment was scarce; therefore, she not only served the spiritual needs but the physical needs of the people. Doctors, when they were available, needed nurses. She assumed that position whenever she was needed.

Some of her stories were heart-wrenching while others were filled with joy. It was obvious that she loved her work, and it made me proud of her to know what a blessing she was to the people she served. Her dad and Zack were hanging on every word she spoke

"Sissy, how long are you going to stay in Africa?"

"Now is as good a time as any to share some news with you. I'm going to take a year off and go home. I've spent the last five years working in Africa. My family needs me now, and I'm going back to the ranch to help you. Hopefully, Jack will need me, and of course, Lacy is going to require a great amount of attention. Also, I'm terribly homesick for mountain air, the smell of pine trees, cold weather, horses, and my mom, dad, brothers, and Mia and Gramps.

Bo, looking surprised, said, "Tommie, that's wonderful news!"

"Oh my, Tommie, thank you. We do need you, especially now," I said. "I can't even imagine your gramps' reaction when he hears the news. It will be the best medicine that he could ever receive."

After Tommie's shocking announcement, the mood around the table changed drastically, with even Bo perking up. I was pleased beyond words and totally surprised.

"With that good news, I need to get back to Jack. Is everyone ready to go?" Zack asked.

When we were back in our room, Bo and I talked several hours. He was more like his old self than he had been since the accident. Now, if tomorrow would just go well, we might get some normalcy back in our lives.

I was up early the next morning. I went to the hotel restaurant to get coffee and when I returned Bo was getting dressed. "Brought you coffee," I said.

"Thanks. When are you going over to the hospital?"

"The surgery is scheduled for 7:00 this morning. That's still an hour from now, but I can't just sit here and wait. I expect Zack and Tommie will already be in Jack's room."

"Keep me informed about the progress of the surgery," he instructed.

"That would be easier if you had a cell phone," I replied.

"I don't like cell phones. You know that. They're a nuisance. Zack or Tommie can come to the hotel. I'll stay in the lobby."

"Okay. We're not finished with this conversation about a cell phone, though."

"You're beautiful being assertive," he said, smiling.

"You're full of it, too," I said, kissing him, and leaving.

On the walk to the hospital, my steps were lighter and brisker. Bo was getting back to being Bo. Zack was in the room but Tommie had not arrived.

"Morning, Mom. You're early."

"I know. I would rather wait here than in the hotel. What did you think about Tommie coming home for a year?"

"I'm pleased beyond words," he said.

"Your dad is a different person since the news," I replied.

"I noticed the change immediately last night," he said.

Tommie came in before we could continue. I was startled by her appearance. She had put on makeup and was wearing a white pant suit that made her look stunning; not like any minister that I had ever seen. She had on high heeled boots which made her taller than me or Zack. Simple; but elegant, the cream colored, long-sleeved bolero jacket fit her slender figure like a glove. It was fastened by two pairs of large-pearl like buttons. The short jacket overlapped a broad waist band. No belt was needed for her tiny waist. There was nothing remarkable about the slightly flared pants. A fashion made remarkable not by its structure, but the structure it was covering. Of course, she brought something from her new homeland...a rectangle, serape-like stole with some kind of black and white African pattern was flapping across her shoulders, almost like wings.

"Sissy, you look beautiful."

"Thank you, Zack. I woke up this morning thinking I needed to dress up today. I bought some makeup in the little shop at the hotel. It's the first time in over two years I've put anything on my face. Where I've been, there's no reason to fix up."

Immediately after her explanation, two male nurses came in to move Jack to the operating room. Dr. Jordon arrived as they were leaving.

"The operation will take at least three hours. We have a family waiting room and will report progress of the operation from time to time."

"We appreciate it, Dr. Jordon. Thank you for everything you've done. I would like to have the name and address of the doctor in Denver who convinced Dr. Adders to perform the surgery."

"Certainly. His name is Keith Wilson. I will get his address for you later."

After three hours of stressful waiting, with several updates that appeared positive, Dr. Jordon came in, accompanied by Dr. Adders. "The operation went well. No problems whatsoever. Dr. Adders did his usual great work. Jack will be in recovery for several hours and be put in ICU for a day."

"Thank you, Dr. Adders," I said, shaking his hand. "You also, Dr. Jordon."

"We appreciate it, Dr. Adders," Zack said, shaking his hand. He acknowledged it with a nod and a smile. Zack also thanked Dr. Jordon again.

"What happened next demonstrated how unpredictable Tommie can be. She moved over to Dr. Adders, held out her hand, and when he took it, she reached and kissed him on the cheek. Adders, with his light complexion, turned red as a ripe tomato. He mumbled something, which nobody understood, turned and left the room.

Smiling, Dr. Jordon said, "Well, now, that's the first time I've ever seen him speechless."

CHAPTER 11

Zack

THE DAY AFTER JACK'S SURGERY, my dad's lawyer came to the hotel and informed him that the hospital had dropped the charges. Not only that, but the restraining order had been lifted. My dad thought it was a joke at first and then realized it had happened. When he informed me, he was dismayed at the action of the hospital.

"It doesn't make any sense, Zack. One day they want to send me to prison and the next they drop the charges."

"Strange things happen, Dad. Who knows? They may have had a change of heart. It doesn't matter. What was it that B-Boy always said? 'Don't look a gift horse in the mouth'?"

"You're right."

"It's hard to keep track of time, Dad. Tomorrow will be August 12, making it almost two weeks since the accident."

"I haven't been away from the ranch this long since college. I'm sure Jimmy is taking care of everything. We talk on the phone every other day, and he keeps me up to date. I've asked him to put off working the calves till I get home. It's not necessary that I be there, but it's one of my favorite times of the year."

"I'm surprised Todd hasn't come to be with us," I said.

"Your mom insisted that he stay in Ruidoso. There's nothing he can do here, and she feels like he's needed more there. You know, her dad's not in good health."

"That makes sense," I stated.

It was Monday, the fifth evening since the surgery, and I assumed my night shift, allowing Mom, Dad, and Sissy to go eat. Nurse Houser came into the room, making her nightly rounds.

"You have a neat family. They're all nice. What's Jack like?"

"Friendly, spontaneous, aggressive…a little on the wild side. He's more fun than I am," I explained.

"What makes you say that?"

"It's true. The girls like him better. We're twins and many people can't tell us apart, yet the opposite sex always was attracted to him."

"Does that include his wife? You would have married her, I bet," she said.

"Do you have a crystal ball or just noisy?" I asked.

"I know people. Sort of a hobby…reading them."

"Lacy chose Jack, which was the right choice. They fit one another," I said.

"Well, I believe you would be fun," she replied. "Are you involved with anyone?'

"No. I haven't had time for a relationship."

"That's not healthy" she said.

"I get along fine, thank you. Now you're getting personal," I stated.

"Okay. Why do you want to be a doctor?"

"I like to help people. Also, there was a doctor in my hometown who was a family friend. Growing up, I saw how much good he did for people. His name was Dr. Sadler."

"Will you return to your hometown to practice?" she asked.

"I have no idea," I answered. "Hadn't you better see about your other patients?"

"One more question. Are you a real cowboy?"

"Yes, I have been since I was old enough to walk."

"I love cowboys, especially bull riders. Do you ride bulls?"

"No. I only rope," I replied.

"Oh. Well, I guess that's okay."

"See. I told you so. Jack was a bull rider. Maybe that's why the girls liked him better. Don't you have other patients to look after?"

"Trying to get rid of me, huh?"

We were standing on opposite sides of the bed and before I could answer, we saw Jack move. Not only did he move, but both his eyes were open.

"He's conscious," I said.

"Yes. Take his hand and tell him to squeeze it," she instructed.

I did as she said but received no response. She left the room, saying she was going after a doctor. I called Mom on her cell phone but she didn't pick up. The signals were iffy here. I called the room and Dad answered.

"Dad, Jack's awake!"

"We'll be there in a minute." I heard him tell Mom before he hung up.

The doctor and nurse arrived just a few minutes before Mom and Dad. The doctor was examining Jack's eyes with a light when they entered. I hadn't seen the doctor before.

"He's conscious but not responding. That is not unusual for someone who comes out of a coma," he said.

"What's next?" Mom asked.

"He will alternate between sleep and being awake. Hopefully, on one of the occasions in which he's awake, he will respond to stimuli," the doctor answered. "I'll notify Dr. Adders and when he is available he can give you additional information."

After he left, Tommie asked that we join hands for a prayer of thanks.

The next morning, we met with a team of doctors, with Dr. Adders being present. Introductions were made before we began. Dr. Jordon led the discussion.

"We are hopeful for a recovery for your son, now that he has come out of a coma. However, it will be a long road. Dr. Adders, will you begin by explaining about the damage and what can be expected?"

Dr. Adders, in a pleasant voice, began, "Your son, Jack, has suffered damage to both sides of his brain. However, the right side was damaged the worst. That means the left side of the body will experience movement problems or weakness. The left side has some damage but not as much. That side of the brain is responsible for verbal and logical functions, including speaking, listening, reading, and writing. This is an oversimplification but may prove somewhat accurate. However, with the brain damaged, nothing is certain. I will say it is remarkable that your son survived, and I believe it is positive that the left side has less damage. In my experience, being able to talk and understand is important to the patient during the recovery period. I will answer any questions that I can."

"How long will it be before he can walk?" Sissy asked.

"Let me refer that question to Dr. Ellis, who oversees our rehab wing."

"Just a guess but I would predict three to four months. Ordinarily, I would say six months, but he's young and strong. It would be safe to say that at first he'll have a balance and coordination problem," he explained.

"Will he have mental problems as well?" Mom asked.

"Yes, more than likely, he will have problems with cognitive or thinking skills. Examples would be paying attention, concentrating, and remembering new information. He will become confused easily. Most times they're not able to be independent, but in some instances, they can. There is so much that we don't know, and it's only a prediction. Sometimes we're right. Other times we're not."

"Is there a chance he could have a full recovery and lead a normal life?" I asked.

"It would be a very slim chance, with the amount of damage. Not impossible but very unlikely. He has age on his side and a supportive family, which is important."

"What can we expect to happen next?" Sissy asked.

"Brain trauma patients go through several steps of recovery: the first step is a coma; in the second step, the person is awake but does not respond to stimuli, which Jack is experiencing; the next step would be reacting to stimuli but not in a consistent manner. There are six more steps but I would recommend that we take one at a time," Dr. Ellis explained.

"Thank you for the information. We understand how fortunate we are to have this hospital caring for Jack," Mom stated.

"Please understand, Mrs. Skinner, it wasn't a coincidence that Jack awoke from his coma. Dr. Adders' surgery was amazing, relieving the pressure on his brain. I am impressed every time I see him work," Dr. Jordon said.

"Thank you, Dr. Adders," Mom said, looking first at him and then Dad.

Dad cleared his throat and said, "We appreciate it, Dr. Adders."

Sissy and I followed in expressing our appreciation. Dr. Adders acknowledged us with a nod of his head and a smile.

The next two days yielded no change in Jack, but on Wednesday, August 16, with Lacy by his side and holding his hand, she started crying.

"He squeezed my hand," she said, through the sobs. "He squeezed my hand! Squeeze my hand again, Jack. Oh! He did it again! Blink your eyes, Jack. Blink, Jack. He did it! Did you see that?"

Lacy wasn't the only one in the room with tears. Tommie and I had seen the blink.

Each day after that, Jack's responses were unpredictable. Sometimes he'd react, other times he would not. He would seem confused and agitated when we gave him a command. The doctors keep assuring us that his responses were normal and to have patience.

Dr. Adders came back every day, and maybe it was only a coincidence, but it appeared to be when Sissy was present. He was friendly and totally different from the first several meetings with him. I mentioned this to Sissy and she scoffed it off.

"Don't be ridiculous, Little Brother. Remember, our dad tried to kill him."

"But we saved him, Sissy. Besides, I see the way he looks at you. He's got those hungry eyes."

Giving me a shove, she said, "You're terrible, Zack. Remember, the last time we had a real fight. I had you down sitting on you, and Mom had to pull me off. I think you were in junior high."

"I admit you were pretty tough, Sissy. Jack and I couldn't beat you roping until we were in high school. We would do the tie-down jackpots with Mom timing and Dad would win. You would be second and Jack and I would fight it out for third. No wonder you intimidated the boys."

"Changing the subject, Zack, but I have a suggestion. Why don't you go back to Houston in time to start the semester? I know they begin earlier now than they used to. I'll stay with Jack and Lacy to help them. I'm also going to suggest that Mom and Dad go back to the ranch, at least for a while. I know Mom worries about her dad. Also, Dad would like to go back, I'm sure. It's going to take several months before Jack and Lacy can return, but I'll be here to help, however I can."

"I've considered not returning to school this year," I said.

"No, that shouldn't happen. You must get on with your life. This situation we're in will be a long-term affair, maybe years. You don't need to change your plans, thinking that will make a difference for Jack and Lacy."

"I'd feel guilty leaving them before they improve more," I said.

"Guilt is not good, especially when it isn't justified. We have no idea how long it will take for them to improve, especially Jack. Also, I know that Lacy has never been comfortable in my presence. I believe that can be changed, by spending more time with her. I've done nothing for my family for the past five years. I've been serving others, which is good, but now it's time for me to be with my family."

"I'll think about it," I said.

The next week, Jack began to respond better to commands, and three weeks from the date of the accident he spoke Lacy's name. It was a reason to celebrate and we went out to eat that evening. Lacy was now on crutches and went with us. During the meal, Tommie brought up the idea that she had presented to me. At first, Mom objected, but after a lengthy explanation, she began to warm up to the proposal. The turning point was when Tommie insisted that they could come back anytime they chose, and she would call them with daily updates. Dad admitted that he was anxious to get back to the ranch.

I also agreed to attend the fall semester, which was starting in a week. I did inform them if Jack or Lacy experienced any major problem, I was coming back.

After leaving the restaurant, we went back to Jack's room. I stayed to spend the night after everyone left. Standing by Jack's bed, I told him, "We're so thrilled that you're recovering. I wish you could have seen Lacy tonight. She was beautiful. She's being a real trooper, getting around on her crutches. I expect you to continue to improve and one of these days be back in the roping arena. Sissy has kinda taken over the leadership role in the family without anyone realizing it. That shouldn't surprise you or me, knowing the kind of person she is. Good night, Jack. We all love you."

Nurse Houser brought my coffee early the next morning. I told her I would be leaving in a few days and appreciated her help.

"The offer is still open for a home cooked dinner."

"No, thanks, but I would like to take you out to eat. You choose any restaurant in Colorado Springs. Are you working tonight or tomorrow night?"

"I have off tomorrow night and that would be nice. I know just the place. It's expensive, but I have an idea that you can afford it," she said.

"It's a date then. Can we take your car?" I asked.

"Sure thing. You haven't even asked me my name. I'm not always Nurse Houser, you know."

"Okay. Let's have it."

"Courtney," she announced.

Mom, Dad, and I had agreed that we would leave on Tuesday, August 22. Dad had been able to buy another pickup to replace the wrecked one. He also had the trailer repaired and had moved the horses to an arena that rented stalls. Tommie had asked to keep the pickup, trailer and horses, saying that she wanted to ride during her stay. Also, she thought the horses would be good therapy for Lacy.

Dad had contacted his friend to pick him and Mom up in his plane, and I had made reservations to fly back to Houston.

We spent the day together on the 21st of August, visiting about everything from rodeo to horse racing to family events. My date with Nurse Houser was that evening, and Tommie was giving me a hard time.

"A doctor and a nurse. That's nice, Zack. Just think, when you open your practice you won't have to hire anyone. I saw this coming from a mile away."

"You're so smart, Sissy. You can't even see what a bumbling fool that doctor is making of himself. When he left Jack's room the other day, this famous brain surgeon ran slap dab into the door...he forgot to push it open."

"All right, Zack, let's call a truce. Neither one of us are interested in our admirers. We'll not talk about it anymore."

"Fine with me. Now, I need to meet Nurse Houser in the lobby for a strictly dinner date," I said.

The evening went fine, even though I wasn't used to dating. The meal was great, and we visited for an hour after finishing. As she stopped the car to let me out at the hospital, she invited me to stay for breakfast at her place. I politely declined, saying I wasn't ready for that kind of relationship.

If Jack ever found out I turned down a very attractive lady he'd never let me forget it.

CHAPTER 12

Lexie

ONE OF THE HARDEST THINGS I've ever done was leaving Colorado Springs to go back to the ranch. I finally came to grips with our decision by knowing that Tommie would be there to look after Jack and Lacy. I was anxious to get back to check on my dad, and Bo didn't put up any argument. The older we became the more reluctant we were to be away from home.

Tommie drove us to the airport in the new pickup that had replaced the wrecked one. We had also located an RV park where we parked the trailer. She was going to stay in the living quarters in order to get out of the hotel. Tommie was still a mystery after twenty-nine years. On the drive to the airport, I attempted to get some information from her.

"Tommie, do you realize that Dr. Adders is fascinated with you? Nurse Houser told me yesterday that the staff was thinking about raising a collection for you. She said that Dr. Adders was a different person. He was positive and even courteous to them. They attribute the change to you. What do you think about that?"

Laughing, she replied, "I could care less what Dr. Adders thinks. If a peck on the cheek changed him... that's great. I have no interest in him whatsoever, except the care he has provided Jack."

"That peck on the cheek got your daddy out of jail, also. We found out later that Dr. Adders was behind the charges being dropped and the restraining order lifted."

"Mom, Dr. Adders is not the only admirer I've had. While I was serving as a nurse in one of the African villages, a young man caught me alone in the medical tent. He spoke enough English to tell me he had a problem down there and pointed. Smiling, showing those big white teeth, he asked if I could fix it, and I told him I think I have just the cure. Turning around and opening a drawer, I took out a huge syringe with a five-inch needle. I don't know why we even had such an instrument. I turned and facing him said we will need to give you an injection in your problem area and you will be fine. He ran out of the tent, completely cured."

Bo burst out laughing. "Maybe that's what Adders needs."

"Tommie, you're never going to get a husband like that," I said.

"That's fine. Maybe I'll just be an old maid," she replied.

When we reached the airport, Stewart was waiting on us. Before we left, I had Tommie promise that she would call me every day for at least the first week. If she couldn't get me on her cell phone, she could call collect from Jack's room.

After we boarded and took our seats, Bo asked, "Can you believe our daughter? She has the number one brain surgeon in the country falling all over himself for her and she shrugs it off."

"She's always been her own person, Bo. Even when she was ten years old. Remember Mia finally telling us she had kissed Abel when he was dying of AIDS. She had been told not to get within three feet of him."

"She was some kind of cowboy. She could have rode-oed professionally. Flame was still young enough when she graduated from high school to compete on. She was practically unbeatable riding him," Bo commented.

The trip was short, with Bo and I visiting. We landed before noon in Ruidoso and were at my dad's by one o'clock. I had called Ms. Nancy, and she was expecting us. Both she and Dad met us outside, immediately after getting out of our car.

"Lexie, Bo, we're glad to have you home," she said, hugging us both.

"It's been a long three weeks," Dad said, hugging me and shaking Bo's hand.

We went inside and proceeded to tell them about the progress that Jack and Lacy were making and all the other news, including Bo getting arrested. We had withheld that information in order not to give them something else to worry about. They brought us up to date about the happenings on the ranch. One of the troublesome events was Jimmy getting bucked off a colt.

"I shouldn't have asked him to ride her. Jimmy does such a good job with young horses, and this filly has a world of potential," said my dad.

"Dad, Jimmy is going to have to learn to say no. He's too nice. Remember, Jimmy is nearly fifty years old. How badly was he hurt?"

"Bruised ribs and sore all over," Ms. Nancy said. "He's not able to do much. It's increased Poco's work load, but now that Bo's home, he can take up the slack."

"We need to work the calves right away. We may have to hire extra help," Bo stated.

We visited until mid-afternoon before starting home. Bo surprised me with his first question.

"What would you think about moving, Lexie?"

"Moving! Where?"

Smiling, he said, "The home place. There are several nice spots between Mom's house and Grands' old house where Jack and Lacy live. We could build."

"Why?"

"It's more like home. Plus, we're going to have to help Jack and Lacy. We'd be much closer to them."

"I never dreamed you'd think of moving from the Hondo Ranch."

We rode in silence for several miles, and thinking about the suggestion, I realized it made sense. Suddenly, I was excited about the possibilities involved in building my own home.

"What would we do with our house?" I asked.

"I've thought for awhile about hiring someone else. Jesse is not able to do much anymore and he needs to retire. He's been loyal to this family for over fifty years. I could help his sons on the North Ranch, and the new hire could help Jimmy on the Hondo Ranch. We could still all work together at times."

"When would we start this project?"

"Just as soon as you pick a location and come up with a plan. We may not be able to complete it before spring. Depends on what kind of winter we have."

"I'm surprised. When did you come up with this idea?"

Laughing he said, "Would you believe it was the night I spent in jail? I couldn't sleep, so I lay there and thought."

The next several weeks our life resumed a routine that was somewhat close to normal. The calves were marked, with me being chief cook for the cowboys. I would have breakfast ready at 6:00 each morning, which was before daylight. It consisted of bacon, eggs, fried potatoes, and biscuits. With eight hungry men, I cooked a tremendous amount of food. Ms. Nancy and my dad would come early, and she would help me. My dad couldn't do anything, but he enjoyed watching the activities. Lunch would be something fried, either steak or chicken, with potatoes and gravy. We usually had vegetables and a dessert which included cobbler or pie.

It was hard work but enjoyable. At the end of the day I was exhausted, but I wouldn't trade those days for anything. Also, it allowed me to get my mind off Colorado Springs, for at least a while.

Ms. Nancy helped me in the apple orchard, also. We made a good crop and had enough apples for everyone in the valley. We finally gave up and left the remainder to the deer. Jimmy was still an avid hunter, but he wouldn't shoot a deer in the orchard, saying, "They love apples and it's not fair. Besides, it's too close to the road and house."

Felicia, Jimmy's wife and my friend since college, continued to oversee the dinner theater in Ruidoso. She worked at her job but was more than a little allergic to ranch chores. She had gained weight and was heavier than ever. I felt sorry for Jimmy, who was thin and had to listen to her gripe at him for not gaining weight.

I stayed active and was able to maintain my weight at close to what it was after Tommie was born. I had a few gray hairs but with the auburn color, they didn't show as much. I considered myself fortunate to have a wonderful family. The exception was my mother, who I had not seen in years. We had met on several occasions at funerals of family members, but we had never had a conversation. I had tried, one time, to talk with her, but she turned and walked away. She had remarried twice, with the first husband dying, and the second one leaving her. She had to be one of the unhappiest people that could be found anywhere. Hate ruled her world and always would, unless something changed.

Tommie honored my request and called me with a daily update. Sometimes, there was nothing to report, and we just visited about happenings at the ranch. Other days, she would have news about progress Jack and Lacy were making. Jack able to stand on his own or Jack was speaking in broken sentences and was aware of what was happening around him. Both were going to therapy daily.

Tommie was concerned about Jack's frustration when he attempted something new and failed. Some days were worse than others. Lacy spent time each day encouraging Jack in his efforts.

"Mom, there's much more to Lacy than I thought," she had told me. "She's small in stature but has a world of determination. You know what a gorgeous figure she had, well, it's still there but she has lost some weight. She's going everywhere on that one leg, either with crutches or an invention that the rehab unit has agreed to use on a trial basis. It is called an iWalk 2, which allows one to place their knee on a brace and walk without crutches. It can only be used by below-the-knee amputees. My biggest concern is that Lacy won't even talk about riding again. She's convinced that it would be impossible for her to get on a horse."

My conversations with Tommie either lifted me up for the day or started me worrying about the future for Jack and Lacy, depending on the kind of report I received. Bo and I talked continuously about what we could do for them when Tommie brought them home.

I was concerned about my dad. Not seeing him for three weeks probably had something to do with it. I now realized how poorly he looked. It seemed that he had become old overnight, with the slightest exertion resulting in loss of breath. I knew that soon he would require oxygen full time rather than just at night. It made me sad to see him in this condition; however, he was 80 years old and had suffered two heart attacks. I loved him so much, and if not for him, I would've never had this wonderful life and family. He supported me when I made a terrible mistake at nineteen, and my mother disowned me.

I had, along with Ms. Nancy, determined a site for our new home. The location we eventually chose was only a mile down the road from Jack and Lacy's house. It was between two rises but was not low enough to obstruct the view. The area where the house would sit was flat with only a few cedars and would be about one-quarter of a mile off the road. Hopefully, that would eliminate some of the dust from road travel. It would only be two miles from the highway and three miles down the road to Dad and Ms. Nancy's.

We were facing a major challenge in selecting a plan. We had looked at dozens but were not satisfied with any. I didn't want a large house since it was only the two of us; however, it would require enough room for guests and hopefully, one day, grandkids.

CHAPTER 13

Tommie Rose

"CAN'T… SISSY," JACK SAID, AS he attempted to squeeze my hand.

"It's okay, that will come later," I said. We were doing exercises that the therapist had recommended we perform several times a day. His left side was weak, and he still couldn't use his left arm.

"Lacy… coming… today?" he asked.

"Sure. She'll be here any time." Lacy came every day to visit and give Jack support. She was doing great and getting around on her iWalk without any assistance.

"How's… Roany?" he asked.

"She's at the trailer. Probably watching TV." I had kept Jack's dog, thinking she might help with his rehab. I had asked to bring her into his room but my request was refused, with the nurse saying dogs were not allowed.

"How's… horses?"

"Good. Too fat, they need riding. You work hard and you'll be back in the saddle in no time."

"Thank you… Sissy… for everything."

Dr. Adders came into the room, before I could respond to Jack. He smiled and asked, "How is everybody today?"

"Good," I said.

"Is the patient making progress?"

"Yes," I answered.

"I would like to ask him some questions, if it's okay?" he said.

"Sure, you're the doctor," I answered.

"Jack, do you ever get dizzy?" he asked.

"Sometimes... when... I... first... stand up."

"Does it last long?"

"No... just a... few... seconds," Jack answered.

"Is your vision ever blurred?"

"No."

"Is there anything you need?" Dr. Adders asked.

"I'd like... to see... Roany," he replied.

"Roany?"

"That's his dog," I explained. They won't let me bring her into his room."

"Why?" he asked.

"The nurse said she had germs. It's a rule of the hospital," I said.

"The dizzy spells are probably a result of a drop in blood pressure when you stand up. Nothing to worry about," Dr. Adders explained. "It's a positive sign that your vision is good."

"Thank you...Doc..., for everything," Jack said.

"No problem. I need to be going now. If you need anything, let me know," he said, as he left.

"He's nice," Jack commented. "He... likes... me."

About three minutes later, a frowning nurse came in and said, "You can bring the dog to visit any time you wish."

"Doctor... likes me," he repeated.

I went back to the trailer immediately to get Roany. When I brought her to his room, it was a sight to see. When she saw Jack, she jumped up on the bed. Jack cried for the first time since the accident, and she licked his tears off. When it was time for us to leave, she wouldn't get off the bed. She ignored my command until finally I picked her up and put her on the floor. Jack was smiling when I left the room, dragging his dog.

I was glad to get out of the hotel room and move into the living quarters of the horse trailer. It was small but more private, and the limited space didn't bother me. The five years I spent in Africa, my living quarters were no larger than the trailer's. It was only a ten-minute drive to where the horses were stalled. I would get up early, read my Bible for half an hour, go feed, and be at the hospital by 8:00.

Within a few days after Mom and Dad left, Jack was receiving therapy. It was slow at first but after a few days, he began making progress. Occasionally, there would be a setback, and he would become frustrated, which was usually followed by anger. Seven weeks after the accident, which was late September, he could stand, and walk with a slow shuffle. He could use his right arm; however, the left side was still weak, and he had to carry that arm in a sling. His balance was not good, and someone had to be close by to keep him from falling. The physical therapist allowed me to be with them and assist when I could. Jack and Lacy were both moved to the adjoining wing of the hospital that specialized in therapy by this time. This wing had two floors with about twenty patients on each.

After we had been there a week and I had gotten to know some of the patients, I asked the administrator if I could have a Sunday service for the ones who could attend. He seemed pleased and agreed, telling me I could set up in the lobby on the first floor.

The first Sunday, I was surprised at having an attendance of sixteen. The administrator had a piano moved in, and one of the nurses volunteered to play for us. We sang several familiar hymns and I preached, what I hoped, was an uplifting message. I was pleased that both Jack and Lacy attended. I had to hold back the tears when they came in with Lacy on her one leg moving along on her iWalk, helping Jack shuffle along. They sat on the back row, with Lacy holding the hymnal when we sang.

Dr. Adders continued to come by the room daily. I would have preferred that he spend his time with patients who needed him. He had asked me out to dinner twice but I refused. I had no personal interest in him whatsoever. He was a nice-looking man, but his arrogance turned me off big time. I had accepted the fact, long ago, that I was too particular and didn't consider that to be a good quality. It was more of a weakness that I prayed would change over time. So far, the results had been disappointing.

I had dated some in college and even attended what social events were available in Africa with someone. Nobody, thus far, had lived up to my expectations.

I always went out in the afternoon to get the horses out of their stalls. I would put them on an electric walker, which was available, for half an hour, and during that time, I would clean their stalls. If I finished early, I'd get one of Jack's ropes and rope his dummy. I enjoyed roping and had missed it, finding it relaxing and a welcome relief from the hospital.

Lacy had gone with me on more than one occasion, and I kept after her to ride with me. There was an arena located within a short distance from the stalls. She kept putting me off until a Saturday the first week of October, when she finally agreed. I understood her apprehension, but it would be good therapy for her, both mental and physical.

We left the hospital earlier than usual to give us plenty of time. Lacy was back to her usual weight, and you would never know, looking at her from the waist up, that she had a handicap. She had to use the crutches around the stalls since the uneven ground would not allow the use of the iWalk. She had worn jeans with the empty left leg pinned up.

"Lacy, would it be okay if you rode Jack's roping horse? I know your barrel horses are going to be really fresh and full of themselves," I suggested.

"Sure," she responded.

"I've rode your horses a few times, and I have to admit it wasn't much fun. They kept looking for a barrel, hoping to get to run," I said. "They're great barrel horses, but I was used to Flame. I had roped on him and he was much calmer."

"I always wanted to rope, but Mom wouldn't buy calves or put in the effort that was required. What I did learn, your dad taught me. I was okay on the ground but never took it further than that. Jack kept promising me that he would help me. I believe he would have eventually, but of course, I don't know now."

"I wish Dad would have competed professionally, at least for a few years. He was amazing. The boys could never beat him, even when they were in high school."

"He has always been nice to me, even when my mother was so angry," Lacy said.

"Roping takes a lot of time and patience. For us, it was a family event, with everyone helping, even Mother. I would hate to guess how much time we spent in the arena," I said.

"Tommie, Jack and I could never repay you for what you've done for us. I don't even know how to thank you adequately. I always thought you were too good for me."

Laughing, I said, "You're sweet, Lacy. You don't need to thank me or repay me. You're family and we love you. We will always take care of you and Jack until you can take care of yourselves. Now, I'm going to saddle our horses and we're going for a ride."

CHAPTER 14

Lacy

I KEPT THINKING THAT AGREEING to ride was a mistake; however, Tommie had been so good to me and Jack, it was impossible to continue to decline. While she was saddling our horses, I kept repeating to myself, *you can do this, you can do this, be brave, you can do this, be brave.*

Tommie was something else. She was so sure of herself, which made her even more beautiful. Today, she was wearing jeans and a flannel shirt tucked in. She wore a cap which covered most of her hair and if not for her figure could've easily been taken for a man. She saddled the horse exactly like Jack, which made sense, due to the fact they both had been taught by their dad. She tightened the front cinch first, then the back cinch, then the breast collar. She didn't tighten them to riding level until she had walked the horses a few steps. She stretched their front legs to ensure that the cinch didn't pinch them due to a wrinkle in the skin.

It was easy now for me to see why her brother idolized her. Jack and I had been to the last two Sunday services at the hospital. Her message was positive, and I came away feeling good, wanting to hear more. I could understand why Dr. Adders was so enamored with her.

Both horses were tied while she was saddling them. She untied Cotton, which was Jack's horse, and finished cinching him.

"Okay, Cowboy, time to mount," she said.

I didn't know what to do. She led him over to me saying, "Lay down your crutches. I'll help you up on the right side. Just relax now and I'll give you a boost."

By now, I was shaking. She took my right leg and with little effort lifted me up into the saddle in one swift motion.

"There now. You're ready to go," she said, smiling.

I found the right stirrup and sat still until she had mounted my barrel horse. Cotton was short and wide in the front and backend. He was sweet and Jack was almost as attached to him as his dog.

We started riding toward the arena, which was only a few hundred yards, and I could see immediately that balance was going to be a problem. Since my left leg dangled with no support, I wasn't secure in the saddle. Anyone who doubted the importance of legs while riding, would understand if they were in my situation. I knew that only walking the horse would be possible without falling off.

Tommie was having problems with my horse and had to take it in tight circles several times before we reached the arena. No one was present, which was good.

We rode around the arena several times, and I began to feel more confident. Tommy continued to struggle with my horse and finally loped her around the arena five or six times to take the edge off her.

We had been there an hour or so when several pickups with trailers pulled up to the arena. Men began getting out and unloading their horses. I asked Tommie if maybe we should leave.

"No. Let's ride some more. You're beginning to get more comfortable. I can tell by watching you," she answered.

The next pickup that drove up was pulling a stock trailer and unloaded calves into a holding pen. By this time, some of the men were saddled and rode into the arena. One of them rode over to us.

"You'll need to get out of the arena. We have a jackpot every Saturday. You can ride outside the arena and watch the roping if you wish," he said.

The guy was overweight. No, fat is a better description. He was holding a Coors Light in one hand and the reins in the other. He had a gap in his shirt and his belly was showing. He had not shaved in several days. He would have been a perfect bad guy in a John Wayne movie.

"When you get ready to start, we'll be out of your way," Tommie replied.

"See that you do," he said, as he was riding off.

One of the younger men, hollered across the arena, "That little one can ride with me. Looks like she's about to fall off."

We pretended that we didn't hear the comment and continued to ride. Then one of the men started running his horse at full speed, coming within a few feet of us. Of course, Tommie's horse spooked and it took several minutes to calm him down.

"We better leave," I suggested.

"You're probably right," she replied.

As we started toward the gate, the beer drinker, called out, "You might want to hang around and see some real cowboys work."

At the gate leading outside the arena, Tommie dismounted, and gave the reins of her horse to me. She walked the short distance to the men, which was within hearing distance.

"Is your jackpot open to anyone?" she asked.

"There's six of us that rope. Do you have someone in mind? Maybe your husband or a friend?"

"Me," she answered.

Laughter followed from several of the men. "You're a woman, you gotta be kidding," stated the one still holding onto his Coors."

"No, I'm not kidding," Tommie said.

Laughter again. "Sure, we'll take your money. The entry fee is $25 for each go and we usually have six. It's winner takes all. We have an older man that flags for us and a friend is the timer. Do you have a rope and string?"

"At the barn. I'll be back shortly."

On the way to the stalls, we met the man who was going to flag. He introduced himself as Jeff, and we told him our names. Tommie didn't tell him she was going to enter.

After helping me off and unsaddling her horse, she said, "Lacy, I don't see why you can't drive the pickup. All you need is your right foot since it's an automatic. You can drive over to the arena, and I'll ride Cotton."

"Okay. Are you sure this is a good idea, Tommie? It's been a long time since you've roped."

"It has been a long time. It might be interesting, though. I've got a feeling these guys aren't much except talk."

I didn't have a problem driving to the arena. I decided to stay in the pickup, but with the window rolled down I could hear the conversation.

"We draw to see what order we rope in," said one of the older men, who was about thirty. The second go, we reverse the order. You need to pay the money up front."

Tommie drew a number out of a hat and then paid her entry fee. She mounted and rode over to where I had parked.

"I drew number six," she said. "These are the smallest calves I've ever seen. They should still be on their mommas. I'm glad I've been roping some on the ground, at least. That should help."

One of the men hollered at us, "Bring your little friend over here and I can help her with her riding." Tommie left before any more insults were directed at me.

Out of the five men who roped before Tommie, two missed, and the best time of the other three was a 13.5. Tommie was impressive as she built her loop and rode into the box with the pigging string in her mouth. The men should have gotten a hint that she knew what she was doing.

"Don't fall off now and hurt yourself," said the beer drinker. "We don't want a lawsuit on our hands. I might be willing to give you some lessons if you were nice to me." That brought a round of laughter.

Tommie nodded for her calf, roped him right out of the box, got off on the right side, was down the rope, and her hands were quick and sure as she tied him. The man had been calling out the times after each roper. This time he hesitated longer than usual before calling out, "11.2". The only sound that followed was me honking the pickup horn.

Tommie roped first in the next go, and this run was even better. Once again, the timer hesitated, even longer this time, before calling out "16.1". Tommie moved to the roping box and asked the timer, "Are you sure?"

Smirking, he replied, "I've never been more sure of anything."

Jeff, the flagman, rode his horse up beside Tommie and said, "You're a liar, young man. I'm not going to allow you to cheat this lady. You pay me fifty dollars to flag for you, and I sure can use the money, but I'll not be a part of this."

He continued, "This lady's name is Tommie Skinner and she's from New Mexico. That name probably means nothing to you. I'm old enough to have been around in

1970 and again in 1981 when her daddy beat Lowe in both match ropings. Bo Skinner was the best I've ever seen. The only thing that kept him from being a world champion was that he chose not to rodeo professionally. It's obvious that he taught his daughter well.

Now, that young girl in the pickup won the barrel racing at Cheyenne this year and then lost her leg in a wreck. She was sitting number 2 in the World at the time. You men should be ashamed of yourselves. Now, you give this lady her money for the first go round, and I'm certain she has had enough of your company. Is that correct, Tommie?"

"Yes. We need to be going. Thank you, Jeff."

"No problem. My church has been praying for your brother's recovery, also. Our minister visits the hospital and I'm aware of his struggle."

"I appreciate that," Tommie replied.

We stopped at a Mexican food restaurant on the way back to the hospital. Looking at the menu, Tommie said, "I appreciate food more after spending five years overseas."

We ordered, with Tommie asking for a margarita. When she noticed my surprised expression, she said, "I love margaritas. I reward myself once a week with a meal here. I guess it's unusual for a minister; however, I believe it's okay to have one a week. I think of myself as a normal person. I confess that I miss rodeo and cowboys in those jeans. Now, isn't that an awful thing for a minister to say?"

Laughing, I said, "No, it shows that you don't consider yourself perfect. Would you like Dr. Adders more if he was a cowboy and wore jeans?"

"No. It's his attitude that I dislike. It wouldn't matter what he did or wore. He doesn't consider himself to have any weaknesses."

The meal was wonderful after the hospital food, and visiting with Tommie about her work increased my admiration for her. She was modest yet confident, aggressive yet caring, and dedicated yet fun-loving. She made me feel good about myself. I knew that I was fortunate to have her here for me and Jack. Her riding and roping ability was more than amazing. She roped like a man and rode like the barrel racer that she had been.

The first thing I did when I was back at the hospital was go see Jack. He was just finishing his evening meal. I always tried to be with him when he ate. The left side of his face had no feeling and at times particles of food dropped from his mouth and I would be there to clean him up. As he became more alert, he realized what I was doing. It embarrassed him and he apologized, but I assured him over and over that it was fine. I was just glad to have him here with me.

I balanced on my right leg, jumped up on the side of his bed and kissed him, "Guess where I've been?"

"With Tommie."

"Right. We've been riding," I said.

"Really?"

"Yeah. I did good for my first time with one leg. It was fun. What was great is that I got to see Tommie rope."

"She's... good," he said. "She... beat me...and Zack... a lot... of times.

I then told him about her winning the Jackpot and how ugly the men were to her.

"She's... something... else," he said with a smile.

CHAPTER 15

Bo

LEXIE TALKED WITH TOMMIE EVERY day the first two weeks we were home and then every other day after that. Tommie was able to call Lexie on her cell phone, so I seldom spoke to her. Lexie would relay the information to me. All in all, everything seemed to be going well, with most of the reports positive.

It was the second week in October, and we already had experienced several frosts. Hay was put up and range cubes had been delivered. We were ready for winter, and like every year, we didn't know what to expect. I had noticed that the horses had put on winter hair earlier this year. Ordinarily that would mean a cold winter but you never knew.

I felt good about the decision to build on the home place. Lexie had chosen a location and plans for the house. My mother and Tom were pleased with our decision also. We had not told Tommie about our plans.

On Tuesday, October 10, when I came in for lunch, Lexie met me at the door saying, "Bo, Jake called about an hour ago, and asked that you get back to him."

Jake Yarborough had played center on our national championship team in 1971. He had gone on to play for the Houston Oilers, being selected to the All-Pro team eight times. He now lived in Houston and was a regional manager for an investment company. We had stayed in touch, talking at least once a month on the phone.

"Did he say what he wanted?" I asked.

"No, but I didn't like the sound of his voice. It contained a sense of urgency. I thought about coming to find you, but it was so close to lunch I decided against it."

I used the phone in the den and Jake picked up on the first ring. "Jake, what's going on?"

"Thanks for getting back to me, Bo. I have a problem, and I'm hoping you might be able to help."

"Sure, Jake. I'll do whatever I can."

"You better hear what it is before you agree. It concerns Carl Richburg and his wife, Diane. You remember, Carl, from our college days?"

"Crazy Carl. Of course I remember him. He put Idaho State's All American out of the game on the opening kick-off with the most vicious hit I've ever seen. That was thirty years ago, and I remember it like it was yesterday."

"Well, Carl works for me now. He runs one of my branch offices. He's a great employee. I wish I had more like him. You remember his girlfriend with the thick glasses, I'm sure. He married her and she became a doctor."

"I remember her well, Jake. I'm not surprised she became a doctor."

"Okay, here's the problem. She was working in the ER last night, and they brought in a ten-year-old boy who had a ruptured appendix. She operated on him and he didn't make it. Of course, it wasn't her fault and everyone in the ER said she did everything she could."

There was a pause and I thought maybe we had lost the connection. "Jake…you still there?"

"Yeah. The problem is that the boy was the son and grandson of one of the most prominent crime families in the United States. A Houston detective came to see me this morning and said they were concerned about retaliation from this family. I tried to downplay it, saying surely the family would be understanding. His response was, 'Don't count on it.'"

"Where is Carl and his wife now?" I asked.

"They're at my house. Bo, they're terrified. Maybe they should be. I don't know. This is all new to me."

"You want to bring them out here?" I asked.

"I don't know what else to do. If you could just keep them until we see there's not going to be a problem. You were the first person I thought of because I trust you. Also, your location was a factor."

"Of course, I'll help anyway I can," I stated.

"That's great, Bo. I'll drive them out there immediately. They only have the clothes they're wearing. They're afraid to go back to their house. We'll leave immediately and should arrive around midnight. Since I've been to your place several times, I won't have any problem finding it."

Lexie had listened to the conversation. At least to my part of it. "You better sit down to hear this," I said. I commenced to fill her in on the part she couldn't hear. She remained silent until I finished.

"This can't be real! It sounds like a movie plot. What are we getting ourselves into?" she asked.

"I couldn't say no. Jake was the reason Jeremiah and I were able to stay in college. He's a friend. Carl is a friend, also."

"But, Bo, we'll be putting our entire family in danger!" she exclaimed.

"What would you have had me do?" I asked.

Silence followed my question. "They would never look for them here," I stated.

"How do you know that? This is a crime family! They kill people! They steal. They're evil. I don't know, Bo. I just don't know. How can we get ourselves in such a situation? We have Jack and Lacy to look after. We have your mother and my father to take care of. Now, we have to protect people from a crime family." By now, she was crying.

"I'm sorry, Lexie. I didn't know what else to do. If you want to go back to Colorado Springs and stay that will be okay with me. You should be safe there."

"Robert Skinner, you can't be that stupid! I wouldn't leave you, my daddy, and Ms. Nancy here. I'm not worried about myself. It's our family that I'm concerned about."

"Well, like I said, I did the only thing I could. If Jake had someone else he trusted as much as us, he would have taken them there."

"Are they going to stay here?" she asked.

"No, I think the best place would be at Jack and Lacy's. I'm sure this will blow over in a few weeks, and they can return to Houston before Jack and Lacy are able to come home."

"I can't believe this. I received a good report from Tommie this morning and was feeling good about everything. Just when life was beginning to seem normal again, this comes up."

Trying to move on to something else, I asked, "What do I need to do to help you get ready for them?"

"You really want to know? Go into town and get you a cell phone. There's an AT&T store next to Walmart. Don't argue with me. Just do it. If we're going to do this, at least I want to be able to stay in touch with you."

I knew better than to argue so in the meekest voice I could muster, I said, "Okay, I'll do that."

"Now, I've got to get over to the house where they'll stay and get it cleaned up. It's been vacant for two months and it'll need airing out. I'll send a grocery list with you and items you will need to get at Walmart. When you return, come over to the house, and we'll go tell Dad and Ms. Nancy what we're doing."

"Are you sure we need to tell them?" I asked.

"Positive. I'm not about to endanger this family without informing them. I don't see any need to tell Jimmy and Felicia though. The same goes for Jesse and Lisa."

"What kind of phone do I need to get?" I asked.

"One just like mine. I'll write it down for you. Have them program it and phone me before you leave the store," she instructed.

"You're even more beautiful when you're assertive," I said, giving her my best smile.

"And you're so predictable. Every time I'm upset you give me that sweet talk. Now, I'll expect a call from you before I see you again."

An hour later, after getting my written instructions, I left for Ruidoso, knowing it was going to be a rough afternoon.

On the drive into town, I started talking to myself, which was becoming more common the older I became. *I don't need a damn cell phone. I should have just refused. I'm still the head of this household and what I say should be the law. I wonder if they'll give me one of those little holsters they carry them around in? I'm not wearing one of those! They look ridiculous. There's no way I can keep up with a phone. I lose my pocket knife at least once a week, I can never find the remote control, either. She gets more assertive with each passing year. Telling me what to do...what to wear and what to eat. But she is the most beautiful woman I've ever seen, I muttered, smiling. I wouldn't trade her for anything.*

I was in town before I knew it. I found the store, gave them the kind of phone I needed and waited...and waited.

Finally, they came back, telling me it was formatted and ready to use. I signed several documents and called Lexie's number.

"Hello," she said.

"It's me," I stated.

"Why, hello, Cowboy. Welcome to the 21st Century. Are you on your way home?"

"No. I haven't even been to the grocery store or Walmart yet."

"I'm proud of you. Now I can keep up with you," she said. "I'm getting things done, but I'll still be working when you get here."

"See you in an hour or two. Love you," I said.

"Love you, too."

It was late afternoon before I was back at Jack and Lacy's house, where I found Lexie still working.

"The house was dirty, Bo. I don't understand how dirt can get in as well as this house is constructed. It smelled musty, so I opened all the windows to air it out. Let me see your phone."

She inspected it, and gave it back with a nod. "It's the right kind. Now, do you know how to use it?" she asked.

"I have no idea."

"Don't worry, I'll give you lessons," she said. "Now, bring in the groceries and put the perishables in the fridge. By the time you do that, we can go talk to Dad and Ms. Nancy."

On the drive to their house, I asked Lexie, "How do you think they'll react?"

"Calm. Much better than me," she answered.

She was correct about her assessment. I told them the entire situation, and they sat quietly until I finished.

"You did the only thing you could. We'll be fine," said Tom.

"I agree. You couldn't refuse to help your friends even if it is a difficult situation. Anything we can do to help, just let us know."

"Aren't you the least bit frightened?"

"Not really," replied Tom.

"It's difficult to be frightened after going through that terrible ordeal with Jack and Lacy," explained Ms. Nancy. Everything else seems minor compared to that."

We thanked them for their understanding, leaving for home to wait on our new family to arrive.

CHAPTER 16

Lexie

THE FIRST THING I DID when we were back home was to get on the internet and look up the family of the boy who died. Lambenio was the name, and of course there was a wealth of information about them...all bad. The more I read the worse it became. Finally, I just turned off the computer.

I had to remind myself of something positive that happened. Bo has a cell phone, finally. Now, if he would just learn how to turn the computer on. I had accepted the fact that he was born 50 years too late. He would be totally satisfied with the technology that was available in 1940. Those traits did not stop him from being my love and my hero. He was being vintage Bo when he agreed to help his friends even under these circumstances. It was a testament to his leadership and trust that caused Jake to look to him for help. Someone who made All-Pro eight years must have a lot of friends.

I cooked a Mexican casserole that evening so we would have something for our guests to eat when they arrived. I would insist they stay the night with us and we could take them to their residence in the morning.

We stayed up and watched an old movie while waiting for them. Jake had accurately predicated their arrival time, as they drove up a few minutes after midnight. Bo met them at the door, giving Jake a hug and shaking hands with our guests. "Welcome to our home, Carl and Diane. This is my wife, Lexie. I don't imagine you remember her." After introductions, we moved to the den.

"We apologize for the imposition," Carl said. "Jake explained, on the way here, what you had gone through with your son and daughter-in-law. We didn't know what to do. Thank goodness for Jake."

"I'm sorry," said Diane, beginning to cry. "I have never had anything happen like this. I have done at least a hundred appendicitis but this one was difficult. The appendix had ruptured, which should have not been that big of a problem; however, they failed to bring him to the hospital for a lengthy time. Why, I have no idea. He died on the operating table. I didn't see the family afterwards. One of the other doctors informed them. I was told that they had asked who did the surgery and I wondered about that. Then the detective came to see me later that afternoon, telling me about the family and his concern for my safety."

"Have you had anything to eat? There's a casserole in the oven," I said, trying to move on to something that wasn't so upsetting for them.

"Thank you, but we got something to eat on the way," Carl answered. "We're totally exhausted from the stress. It's been a long and difficult day."

"We'd planned for you to stay here tonight. Tomorrow, we'll take you to the house where you'll stay," I said.

"Jake, we have a room for you, also," Bo said.

"I'd planned on going back to Roswell and getting a room," he replied.

"No way. You must be tired after that twelve-hour drive," Bo said. "We'll get you up early, feed you, and have you on your way back to Houston."

"That'll be great. My wife doesn't even know where I am. I told her I would explain when I returned."

"Let me show you to your room. It has a shower and please make yourself at home," I said.

"We want to pay you for doing this for us," Carl said.

"That's the last thing on our minds, Carl. Just forget about it. I'm looking forward to visiting with you about our football days," Bo said.

After getting them settled in their room and finding some night clothes for Diane, I returned to the den. Bo and Jake were in a deep conversation, which stopped abruptly when they saw me.

"What's the deal, boys. Are you afraid of what I'm going to hear?"

"We were discussing what action we might take in our current situation. We don't know whether to inform the local authorities or stay quiet. The real dilemma is how to determine if there is a danger to Diane, the impression that she received from the detective," Bo explained.

"I did find out a little information about the family," Jake said. "They live in Phoenix but are originally from Chicago. They're from a well-known crime family that originated in Sicily. A split occurred within the family, and they had to leave Chicago."

"Could we contact the law enforcement authorities in Phoenix and see what kind of information they can provide?" Bo asked.

"That's an idea. When I get back to Houston, I'll ask the detective to see what he can find out about the family. I'll get back with you as soon as I have any information."

I excused myself and asked Bo to show Jake to his room when they finished visiting.

By the time I was up the next morning, Bo had cooked breakfast. Maybe this wasn't going to be such a bad idea after all. First a cell phone and now cooking breakfast. Of course, the bacon was limp and the eggs were burned but he tried. The toast looked eatable.

"Good morning. Did you sleep okay, Jake?" I asked.

"Yes, thank you. I can make it back to Houston now," he replied.

"Have you and Bo been replaying your football days?"

"Yes, and visiting about our families," he answered.

"Maybe you can come back to visit and stay longer under more pleasant circumstances," I suggested.

"That would be wonderful. I love New Mexico. It's beautiful here and peaceful, after the hustle and bustle of Houston."

"It's home now. I wouldn't want to live anywhere else," I said.

"Lexie, I've never told you, but I had a wonderful professional career. I was fortunate enough to play on some good teams with great players. I was a teammate of the first great Black professional quarterback, and we're still friends today.

I received recognition, which some great players are denied. What I'm trying to say is, I owe it, in large part, to Bo. He came to Texas State when we were terrible. Looking back now, it's obvious that he was the reason for our success. Without that success, I would never have received the opportunity to play professional football. I am convinced of that. I can truthfully say that he was the best leader on the football field that I have played with. I just needed to tell you this. Maybe it will help you understand why I know that I can depend on him."

"Thank you, Jake. He's special even though he can be a challenge at times."

"Jake, me and Jeremiah would have never stayed in school without your support our first year. If I did play a part in your success, it pleases me greatly," Bo said.

"I need to give you some information about Carl and Diane. Carl has worked for me over twenty years. They're not like most couples. As you know, Bo, Carl was raised by his mother. She lived with them until her death two years ago. When I say they're different, I don't mean it in a negative way. Diane is brilliant, but she and Carl have no social life. They have each other and that's all. I've tried to invite them to parties, but they stand in a corner looking frightened. They have no close friends, except me.

I have been blessed, and I help them all I can. It's one of my ways of giving back. Diane reads and Carl watches sports on television. That's the extent of their entertainment besides work. Diane doesn't cook. They eat fast food for most of their meals.

They have no children. Carl told me it was not possible and didn't give any details. I suggested adoption but evidently that wasn't an option. If they have additional family members, I'm not aware of it. Don't get the wrong idea. They're good people and would never hurt anyone. Carl doesn't have a mean bone in him. It has always amazed me that he was such a vicious hitter on the football field.

An oversimplified description of them would be 'shy'. When they have nothing to say, don't think they're upset or angry with you. That's just the way they are. Maybe this information will help you."

After Jake's lengthy description of our guests, he thanked me again, said goodbye, and Bo walked him to his car.

Before I even cleaned off the table, I called Tommie on her cell phone. We had been fortunate to be able to get a signal, most days. She had another good report. Jack was walking and talking better. The therapy was doing wonders for him. Lacy would receive her artificial leg within a short period of time. She had more good news, saying that it looked like they would be home for Thanksgiving.

When Bo came back in, I gave him the news.

"That's wonderful. Thanksgiving is only a little more than a month away. Did you want to go visit them?"

"I don't see how we can leave, Bo. Not with the responsibility of looking after Carl and Diane."

"I guess you're right," he said. "Maybe they'll be gone in a week or so."

Before I could respond, Carl came into the room followed by Diane. "Good morning. Would you like coffee?"

"Yes, that would good," said Diane.

We sat down and drank our coffee in silence, until I announced that I would cook breakfast. After that, I would take them to their residence. Diane didn't offer to help me, which made me thankful for Jake's insight on their behavior.

We drove them over to the north ranch in my Suburban, with Bo trying to make conversation but receiving a limited response. Finally, he had success by bringing up football. Carl responded with comments and questions, but Diane stayed silent.

We gave them a tour of the house, left them our phone numbers, and started home.

"Bo, they may starve. They have to cook. Maybe I better go back and fix their lunch."

"They're not too old to learn, Lexie. We agreed to provide a place to stay, not board, also."

"It's sad, Bo. Imagine not having friends or family. When we have tough times, we always have family for support. Like now, with Jack and Lacy. You know what I'm going to do?"

"I have no idea, Little Girl."

"I'm going to have Pastor Stevens visit them and ask them to come to church."

CHAPTER 17

Tommie Rose

THE NEXT DAY AFTER LACY rode for the first time was Sunday, and we had a morning service for the ones in rehab. The number in attendance had grown to well over twenty. In fact, about the only ones who didn't come weren't able.

Jack and Lacy had not missed a Sunday and were in their usual seats.

I had a new member today who stood at the back by the entrance. I started to go back and ask him to take a seat but decided that Dr. Adders could stand if he wanted. He could make a quick exit if he decided. He had asked me out to dinner several times, but I had not accepted. He still came by, with the pretense of checking on Jack, almost every day.

My sermon that day was taken from Romans 14:1 and dealt with tolerance. It was one of my favorite messages, and the main thrust was not to judge others by their differences but to accept them as God has done.

Dr. Adders stayed for the sermon but left immediately after I finished.

Jack and Lacy were the last to leave, and we sat down and visited for a few minutes.

"Tommie, your sermon was great," said Lacy.

"Thank you. It's one of my favorites. Nelson Mandela is one of my heroes. While in Africa, I witnessed his efforts to bring the country together. Apartheid was ended in 1991 under his leadership, but it continued to be a struggle to enforce while I was there."

"Sissy... when are... we going home?" Jack asked.

"I've talked with your therapist about a release date. He's pleased with your progress and amazed. He believes that Thanksgiving would be possible, but he's reluctant to give us a firm date. Lacy is another matter entirely. They're pleased with her progress; however, her leg has not healed well enough for fitting a prosthetic."

"I don't care about that. I can get around on my iWalk. I can be fitted later for an artificial leg. I won't delay us getting home," she said.

I had noticed a man standing in the doorway as if wanting to say something to us. Before I answered Lacy, I asked him what he needed. He walked over with his hat in his hand.

"Ma'am, you don't recognize me, do you?"

Suddenly, I did know who he was. Minus the beard, the open shirt, and the Coors can, he was the man who had given us a hard time yesterday. "Yes, now I recognize you," I said.

"I came to apologize to you and the other lady. I'm sorry for making such a rear end of myself yesterday. Several beers bring out the worst in me, but that's no excuse. I keep my horse at the stable and I'd like to give you my cell number. If you ever need someone to feed for you, I'd be glad to do that."

"Why, thank you. I accept your apology. I appreciate your offer to feed. There're days it's difficult for me to take care of the horses."

"I've never seen a girl rope like you," he said.

"Don't... feel... bad. She used... to... beat... me, too," Jack said.

"Your dad must have been something else," he said. "Jeff told us more about the match ropings after you left yesterday."

"Dad...was...amazing," Jack replied.

"Well, I'll be going. Here's my number," he said, handing me a piece of paper.

"Thank you. I see your name is Bubba. Is that your real name?"

"No, just a nickname. My real name is Frank," he answered.

"I'm going to call you Frank. This is Lacy, who you know, and this is my brother, Jack." He shook Jack and Lacy's hand.

"I'm sorry for the interruption, but I've felt terrible since yesterday. Call me or text me if you need me to feed," he repeated, before he left.

"That was nice," Lacy said.

"Yes, it was. Now, back to our talk of going home. Lacy, you don't want to stay long enough to be fitted with a prosthetic? You do realize that it would make it possible for you to ride again with balance."

"I don't care about that. How many one-legged barrel racers have you seen? I can ride around the ranch without falling off," she said.

"It's settled then. Hopefully, we'll spend Thanksgiving at the ranch.

The next week, I gave in and accepted a dinner invitation from Adders. It was against my better judgement but a conversation we had influenced my decision. He had come by Jack's room and asked if he could visit with me privately for a few minutes. We stepped outside the door and he began.

"I know the point you made last Sunday in your sermon was directed at me."

"Which one?" I asked, smiling and feeling satisfaction.

"When you said that intelligent people should accept those with less ability and treat them with respect," he explained.

"That's true. We should never feel superior to another," I said. "If the shoe fits, wear it, is what I say."

"What about people who label others as arrogant, rude, and selfish? Doesn't your God love them also? Isn't that passing judgement and feeling like you're better than they are? Yet, you may know nothing about the person because you will not even give them a chance."

Suddenly, I was caught totally off guard. I hadn't thought of it that way. Knowing I was right in my analysis of him, I was comfortable passing judgement on his conduct. Somewhat meeker, I said, "You got me where it hurts. You're right."

"Is tomorrow night okay? I know this great place to dine that has wonderful steaks. I imagine you're a meat eater," he said.

"Okay," I said. "You win. You're correct. I grew up on steak and potatoes."

After he left, I said to myself, *you deserved that*. Now, you have a date with a guy you despise. Another problem was what to wear. I had no doubt but what it would be a nice restaurant, probably requiring a reservation. I probably should just wear jeans, that would be good enough for him. Immediately, I rejected that notion. I wanted to show him I wasn't a country hick. That meant going shopping tomorrow. I had ignored Jack when I returned to the room, and he interrupted my thoughts.

"What'd...he want... Sissy?"

"He asked me out," I said.

"Turn him... down again?" he asked.

"No, we're going out to eat tomorrow," I mumbled.

"Why?" he asked.

"Let's just say I received a dose of my own sermon that didn't go down well."

"Better...not tell... Dad," he said.

"Don't worry. I know better than that."

The next afternoon, I bought a dress at a nice shop downtown. It was eggplant purple with a boat neckline and slightly flared skirt. The long sleeve followed the flair of the above knee skirt. I also purchased a simple topaz necklace with matching earrings. My black leather pumps would work well enough with the outfit.

I had told Adders that I would met him in the lobby of the hospital that evening at 8:00. When I arrived, he was already waiting. I was surprised since he was always late to meetings. He was wearing dress slacks and a long sleeve sport shirt but no coat. He was not overdressed, which provided me some relief. I had no idea what we were going to talk about.

"You look nice," he said.

"Thank you." We walked to his car which, to my surprise, was a Toyota Camry that was several years old.

On the drive to the restaurant there was an uneasy silence. After several minutes, I asked, "What type of place are we eating at?"

"Actually, it doesn't specialize in any type of food. It has a variety of offerings, and I usually order the seafood.

It will be crowded so we may have to wait. They don't take reservations. It's not a fancy place, but it has good food.'

Another surprise. Surely, I'm going to be right about something. We arrived, and true to his predication, we had to wait. There was an outside waiting area that offered drinks. We were able to get a table, and he asked me what I would like from the bar. No way was I going to order anything but a Coke. He came back carrying my coke and a Bud Light.

"Who's first?"

"What do you mean?" I asked.

"I would like to know more about you. Do you want to go first or should I?"

"You start," I said. He commenced to tell me about himself, beginning with his childhood. From the time he could remember, he despised the name Theodore that they bestowed upon him. He had quickly insisted on Ted. His parents had been wealthy… from inheritances. They had not wanted him to interfere with their travel and adventures, so he was placed in a boarding school at the age of eight. He only saw his parents on holidays. He was not athletic and didn't fit in with the other students. He excelled in academics and graduated from high school when he was sixteen. His parents were in Europe and didn't attend his graduation.

He enrolled in Harvard, completed his undergraduate studies in three years, then went on to complete his medical requirements in another three years and was working as a physician by the age of twenty-three. He was hired at his current job two years later and had spent the last ten years in Colorado Springs.

"I'll take questions now." he said.

"Why are you so distant and uncaring about your patients?" I asked.

"I wasn't always like that. The first two years I was friendly with the families and my patients. It hurt too bad when one of them died. I suffered and it affected my work on the next patient. I dealt with it by removing my personal feelings from my work. It's that simple."

"Do you like being that way?" I asked.

"No. I have no choice if I'm going to be effective."

"Do you have friends?"

"Believe it or not, I do have a few friends. Not people I work with, however."

"Have you ever attended a church?"

"Only in boarding school, where it was required. I would prefer to stay away from religion. That is your area of expertise. Me asking you about your beliefs about medicine would be comparable to you asking me about religion."

"You did attend my service Sunday," I stated.

"Yes, and I did find it interesting. People have never accepted me because I'm not like most. Your sermon hit close to home."

"Now, you," he said.

"I told him about growing up in New Mexico, describing my family, and going to a tiny school. I described my horses and competing in rodeo. I divulged more about myself than I intended, going into detail about looking after my brothers and the special relationship I had with Gramps. He listened intently without interrupting until I finished.

"Tell me about your dad," he said.

"I've already told you about him," I replied.

"No, your real dad. Your biological dad. Did you know him?"

Stunned, I sat there several seconds without answering. "How did you know? Is it that obvious?"

"Probably not to most. But I've studied you more than most. You have many of your mom's features, but none of your dad's. You and Jack do have some similar features so he would be your half-brother."

"It's a long story. Not that interesting." I noticed there was no wait line now. Without realizing it, we had talked for over an hour. "I'm hungry. I thought you were taking me out to eat."

"Head fake, huh. Okay, let's eat," he said.

The meal was delicious and we visited another hour at the table. He told me more about his work, and I talked about my time in Africa. When he dropped me off at the hospital it was 10:30. It had turned out to be a pleasant evening, after dreading it. It was the strangest date I've ever experienced. He never touched me, not one time. Ordinarily, your escort would take you by the elbow when you entered or exited the car. He might hold your hand walking in or out of the restaurant, and of course there was the goodbye. Nothing. On the drive to the trailer, I thought, he must not have found me attractive.

CHAPTER 18

Bo

JACK, LACY, AND TOMMIE WOULD be home Thanksgiving. That was great news. Tommie insisted that we would be amazed at the progress that they had made, especially Jack. It had only been seven weeks since we had left Colorado Springs but it seemed like months. I would've liked to go back for a visit, but our current situation was not going to allow that.

The next two weeks went better than expected. I started going by and picking up Carl to help me with my projects, and Lacy did the same with Diane. I had water gaps to repair due to heavy rains this year, and Lexie still had apples in the orchard that she hadn't gathered. Carl wasn't much help at first, but he was a willing learner, and within a few days he was doing better. He seemed to be enjoying the ranch work even though he confessed to being exhausted at the end of the day.

After the first few days, Lexie was positive about Diane, saying she wasn't afraid anymore. She had begun teaching her how to cook some basic dishes. One of her proudest accomplishments was an apple pie that she baked. Lexie was like an old mother hen who had taken Diane under her wing. She said that Diane was willing to learn, which surprised her.

After two weeks, Lexie had expressed amazement at the change in Diane. "Bo, it's unbelievable. She talks to me now. It's evident that she's enjoying herself. She learns quickly, which is not surprising. What's strange is that she knows so little about basic responsibilities of a wife such as cooking and cleaning. Also, when we went into Ruidoso the other day, she was like a kid in a candy store. We went up and down main street going into every shop. She was amazed at all the offerings. When I asked her if she ever went shopping, she replied, "Not really. Not like this."

"Did Diane have her own medical practice?" I asked.

"No. She worked full time in the ER. That makes sense since it didn't require her to have any type of personal relationship with her patients. I'm sure she's an excellent doctor."

"Carl opened up to me the last several days. He said they wanted children but it didn't happen. They had considered adoption, but kept putting it off, and now he felt they were too old. He still has relatives in the Hill Country, around Fredericksburg, but they seldom visit them.

I've talked to Jake several times. He still doesn't have any information on the Lambenio family in Phoenix. He has a wealth of information on the family that still lives in Chicago. Like you told me earlier, it's not good; however, it looks like this scare might all be a false alarm. Hopefully, that's the case."

"It does look promising for Carl and Diane to return home before the kids get here Thanksgiving," she said.

Time passed quickly and by the first week in November, we were getting excited about Thanksgiving. The reports from Colorado Springs continued to be positive. Lexie, also admitted that she had enjoyed having Carl and Diane, despite her earlier apprehension.

It was Saturday morning, November 4, and Lexie was about to leave to pick up Diane and go into Ruidoso. We had a strong norther, with the temperature in the twenties. I was in the process of telling Lexie to be careful since we had snow in the forecast for that evening. Just as she was going out the door, Pastor Stevens drove up. He had been visiting Carl and Diane at least once a week, and they had gone to church with us the last two Sundays.

"Pastor Stevens, good to see you this fine morning," I said as he approached the house. Immediately, I noticed his sombere expression.

"Could we go inside?" he asked.

"Sure, that wind is biting this morning." Inside, the three of us sat down at the kitchen table, and I knew something was wrong.

"I have terrible news. Tommie Rose called me an hour ago and told me that Jack had a stroke, probably caused by an aneurysm. He didn't make it. I'm so sorry."

"There must be some mistake! I talked with Tommie this morning, and he was dong great," Lexie said.

I couldn't talk. Fear went through me, and I couldn't breathe. This can't be true.

"Tommie called me first. She didn't want to tell you over the phone. She asked me to do it. I don't know what else to say. I'm so sorry."

By this time, Lexie was sobbing and trying to talk.

I got up and went into the bathroom. I was still having trouble breathing. I looked into the mirror, seeing the tears. I started talking to the image. *You were no help to your family when the accident occurred. Truth is, you were a hindrance to their dealing with it. You acted like a weak fool. This time you're going to be strong for them and grieve with them. You're not going to run away and withdraw into a shell.*

I went back into the kitchen and took Lexie in my arms. She was still sobbing but could speak. "Bo, w-what are we g-going to do? We've lost our b-baby."

I didn't trust myself to speak. I just held her tight. Pastor Stevens asked if we wanted him to go tell our parents.

"If you'll give us a few minutes, we'll go. I would appreciate it if you went with us," I said.

"Certainly, I'll wait outside for you. Take your time," he responded.

After he left, I held Lexie out in front of me. "We're going to make it. I'm going to be here for you this time. I promise." She nodded, and I held her again until she could talk.

"We better go," she said.

We took our Suburban and Pastor Stevens followed in his car. On the way, we both expressed our concern about telling my mom and her dad. We were especially worried about Tom because of his heart condition. We also talked about what we should do next. Had Zack been notified? We needed to inform Lexie's brother, Todd. We should call Tommie and see about Lacy.

By the time we arrived, both of us had better control of our emotions. That changed when my mom came to the door and greeted us. Lexie broke down again going into her arms.

"Mom, we have bad news. Pastor Stevens is with us," I said.

Gathered in the living room, Pastor Stevens told them the message he had delivered to us. Mom put her head in her hands and Tom, Lexie's dad, put his arms around her.

For the next half hour, between episodes of grieving, we made plans for the remainder of the day. We would stay together. I noticed Tom's color was bad, and I asked him if he was okay.

"I have a tightening in my chest," he said. "I keep thinking it will get better."

"Lexie, I'm going to get Diane to come look at him. I'll be back in a few minutes," I said. Within five minutes, I was telling Carl and Diane our news and asking her if she could examine Tom.

"Yes. I was able to take my medical bag when we left Houston. I'll get it."

A few minutes later, she was taking Tom's blood pressure and asking, "Do you have some nitroglycerin tablets?"

"Yes."

"You need to take one now and we'll see if that helps," she said.

"Your blood pressure is not that elevated. Do you take oxygen?"

"Only at night," he replied.

"Let's get you on it now."

Diane was a totally different person as she treated Tom. This is where she was comfortable, and it was evident that she was confident in herself.

After another fifteen minutes and another blood pressure check, she announced that Tom was going to be okay.

"Keep the oxygen on the remainder of the day and tonight. I doubt if any of you get much sleep. I will stay here tonight with you, if it will make you feel better."

"We would appreciate that," my mom said. "Carl is welcome to stay, also."

Lexie called Tommie and Zack, as well as her brother, Todd.

Tommie was doing okay, but Lacy had become hysterical and had to be given sedatives. When she called Zack, he was already on his way to New Mexico. Todd came out as soon as Lexie called him."

With everyone there, I told Lexie I had somewhere to go and would be back shortly. She gave me a knowing look and nodded.

It was noon and snow had begun to fall when I parked at the cemetery. I hardly noticed the cold as I walked over to my grands' grave. I spoke to him as if he was standing in front of me. *Grands, it's been twenty years and I still miss you every day. I need you more than ever. We've lost Jack. I don't know how I'll make it without him. I loved him more than anyone can imagine. I have promised Lexie that I will be there for her. I wish I could understand why something like this could happen. Pastor Stevens says that God grieves with us. I'm not going to be angry with God this time. I will ask him for strength to get through this. I know that I can't do it by myself.*

I moved over to my dad's grave. *You were so strong and brave when you were ill. I hope some of that courage will be with me now.*

I moved back to Meme's grave. I spoke aloud this time. *You were the foundation of this family. I truly believe that after all these years. I'm going to pray to be like you as I face this tragedy in the life of our family.*

When I returned to the house, Diane was in the kitchen making sandwiches for lunch. I could hear her giving Carl orders. He had been the keeper of the fire since we had arrived, bringing wood in whenever needed. Our decision to keep them had turned out to be an advantage. If not for Diane, we would have had to take Tom to the emergency room in Ruidoso.

Lexie and I took our sandwiches into the den so we could talk.

"Bo, are we going to Colorado Springs to be with Tommie and Lacy?"

"Yes. I'll ask Stewart to fly us. We'll leave in the morning. Maybe we can be of some comfort to Lacy. Zack will be here tonight and he can go with us. We'll follow the hearse home with our family, including Roany, the horses, and of course Lacy. It will be crowded but that's okay," I said, choking up again.

We spent the remainder of the afternoon sitting by the fire, reminiscing about Jack. We would do fine for a while then one of us would break down. The longer we visited the easier it became. Carl and Diane remained in the kitchen, with her baking cookies, and Carl coming in only when he needed to add wood to the fire.

Zack arrived in the early evening, setting off an emotional response. When I saw him, it hit me how much he and Jack resembled one another. I think everyone had the same feeling, with that adding to the suffering. Things eventually settled down again, and we told Zack of our plans to leave the next morning for Colorado Springs.

"I had a lot of time to think on the drive here. Jack was doing great, per Tommie's reports. I know it's hard to understand how this could happen; however, it's not that unusual, with the type of injury that he suffered. I've seen it several times. Blood clots occur in cases like this with no explanation. It remains a puzzle to the medical community. It's not the fault of the doctors or the treatment he received in the hospital. It would be wrong to blame them."

Zack continued, "I also thought about the suffering it would cause on this family, especially with Lacy and you, Dad. We will be there for one another, which is a blessing. Many families are not so fortunate. What is strange, every time I thought of Roany, I choked up. I had to pull off the side of the road and stop several times between Brownfield and Roswell. She's going to be devastated and won't understand."

“This is a difficult time for you to miss school,” Lexie said.

“No, Mom. That’s something else that occupied my thoughts on the way here. I’m not going back to school. No use arguing with me. Eventually, I may complete my study but not in the near future. My place is here with family. I can’t take Jack’s place, but I can lend whatever support is possible to assist us continuing our lives without him.”

“Are you sure?” I asked.

“Positive.”

We stayed until 10:00 before going home. Zack left also, to stay at our place. Carl and Diane stayed with Mom and Lexie’s dad. This would be the saddest day our family had ever experienced.

CHAPTER 19

Tommie Rose

THE RIDE BACK TO THE ranch was crowded and maybe that was good. We had picked up our three horses at the stable that Frank (Bubba) had been taking care of the last several days. Dad was driving with Zack and Roany in the front. I was in the back seat with Mom and Lacy. We hadn't gone but a few miles before Roany was in Zack's lap. When I had suggested that she could ride in the trailer since we were crowded, Zack's answer was a short and firm, no.

It was an approximate eight-hour drive, but we had asked the driver of the hearse to stop about every two hours for a break. It was late in the afternoon, on Monday, November 6, when we arrived in Ruidoso at LaGrone Funeral Home. It had been a long, sad drive with little conversation.

The owner was expecting us since we had called before leaving. I went in and told him we would be back the next morning to make arrangements for the service.

On the drive to the ranch, I asked Lacy if she wanted to stay with Mom and Dad tonight.

"No. I want to go home," she said.

"Would it be all right if I stayed with you?" I asked.

"Yes. Thank you," she replied.

The first place we went was to Mia and Gramps' house. We had already called ahead and told them what time we should be there. Mia had supper on the table when we arrived, and after hugs all around, we sat down to a silent meal.

The next four days were beyond description for our family. Making funeral arrangements, notifying friends, selecting pallbearers, and having to greet guests as they came into our home were almost more than my family could bear.

Mom and Dad's guests, Carl and Diane, proved to be a blessing. They stayed with Mia and Gramps. With Diane being a physician, it was comforting to know that she was available. She also wrote me a prescription for Lacy who continued to have emotional outbursts. I kept thinking, hoping, we could just get through the service, which had been set for Thursday morning at 10:00. Of course, Pastor Stevens would deliver it. He asked me if I would like to assist and I declined, saying, "Thank you, but I don't believe I could."

On Wednesday, while we were alone, I tried to talk with Lacy about coping with her grief. "Lacy, I'm here with you. Please lean on me and the rest of the family. We're all going to be here for you now and always."

"I'm not interested in living anymore. I thought Jack was going to get well, and we could come home together. Now this! Why should I want to live? Without him it's not worth it."

"I loved him, too, Lacy; however, I know he wouldn't want us to grieve our lives away. Think about what he would say to you if he were sitting here now."

"Why? After he was recovering and doing well. Why would God do that? Why not just let him die in the wreck? If there is a God, it makes no sense."

"Lacy, these are questions that have been asked since the beginning of time. Some people try to answer them. I do not. Why? Because I do not know."

"Tell me something that you do know, Tommie. You're a preacher, surely you have some answers."

"I know that our family, which includes you, will come out of this stronger. We prayed for Jack to recover; now, we should pray that our faith grows stronger to cope with this tragedy. I truly believe that God is grieving with us. I know that Jack's passing is not God punishing us for our sins any more than God rewarding you for doing good when you won Cheyenne. I know that others are grieving like you and are asking the same questions that you do."

I continued. "I miss Jack already and will the remainder of my life; however, I will always love him and cherish the memories, and a time will come when we will be together again. I know that you have your whole life ahead of you. You can and will know joy again, even though now it seems impossible. I know that we must get on with living this life that has been given to us and not live in sorrow and pity. We can't change what has happened, but we do have some control of our future. I know that, even though it is difficult, you need to think of others and the grief they are suffering. Imagine for a minute what my dad is going through. Just think what it's like for my mom to lose a son. I know that you need to consider them and find ways to comfort them even in your grief." I paused to allow her time to respond.

"I'll try to do better. I-I never thought of anyone else but myself," she said. "I loved him so much, I didn't think of the sorrow others were feeling. How can you be so strong?"

"Lacy, the morning Jack died, I went to the trailer and cried three hours. I'm not nearly as strong as you think. Dr. Adders took off work and came to the trailer. He took me to a local funeral home and we made arrangements for them to pick up Jack's remains at the hospital. We spent the remainder of the day driving around the countryside and talking. I don't know what I would have done without him. Of course, you were under so much sedation it would not have done any good to stay with you."

"I'm going to do better," she repeated.

The service was held at the Methodist Church in Capitan. A huge crowd attended, with cowboys from all over the country in attendance, plus the locals who had watched Jack grow up. Several of Dad's friends from college were also present. Pastor Stevens, who was now 60, and had been a friend of the family for thirty years, conducted a wonderful service. Several of his stories about Jack's early conduct in church brought laughter from the crowd. He recounted the day that he baptized Jack and Zack and what our family had meant to him personally through the years.

The funeral procession to our family cemetery had to be at least two miles long. It was a beautiful, clear, fall day with frost covering the ground. Most people parked at the bottom of the hill.

Pastor Stevens said a few words and then announced that Zack would like to speak. I was surprised that he was going to be able to deliver the eulogy. He hesitated and I thought, he's not going to be able to do it. Then he cleared his throat and began speaking.

"My brother and I were close from the time we were born. We always had each other's back. It didn't matter if we were in the right or not. I knew him better than anyone and could almost

predict his behavior. He was kind, impetuous, hot-tempered, and loyal to his family and friends. He was a cowboy; not just an ordinary cowboy. He could rope livestock in the pasture and doctor them or compete in the arena. I remember one instance where he roped a cow we needed to doctor in a pasture with telephone poles. She went on one side of the pole and he and his horse on the other side. To this day, I have no idea how he got out of that mess."

He hesitated again. This time I was sure he couldn't go on. But after thirty seconds he continued. *"Jack was like his dad and his B-Boy. He loved this land and will be a part of it forever. Jack is no longer with us, but his memory will survive in the minds of those who knew and loved him. I-I loved him. I-I'm sorry, that's a-all I can s-say."*

CHAPTER 20

Bo

I FELT SORRY FOR ZACK and yet proud of him. I went over and hugged him when he had finished.

"Dad, I had to do that. I'm sorry I couldn't finish," he said.

"You did great, Zack, I'm proud of you."

Me, Zack, Lexie, Tommie, Lacy, and Mom stood in a tight group as people lined up to express their condolences. Standing together I'm sure gave us strength. Mom had insisted that Tom didn't come to the cemetery. He had stayed at the house with Carl and Diane. I didn't know some of the younger men and women who came by. Of course, many of the locals were present. People were well-meaning but became emotional when trying to express themselves. This made it hard on all of us. Finally, after forty-five minutes, Tommie whispered, "Dad, that's enough. We need to leave and go to Mia's. We've been through enough."

"You're right," I said. At that moment, the crowd opened enough for me to see Grands' grave. I thought of the time, twenty years ago, when we stood here. Jack and Zack were six and served as pallbearers. They broke down when Dr. Sadler was giving the eulogy, and Tommie Rose, who was ten, went over and put her arms around them for comfort. Now, here we were again, burying a beloved family member. Tommie Rose was still the one looking after the family, and maybe that was a sign of what was to come.

Jake had come to the funeral, and before leaving, I told him to come to the house for lunch.

Carl and Diane had the food set out when we arrived at Mom's. There was enough to feed the entire county. People had been bringing dishes for three days. Much of it would ruin before we could eat it. We had invited Pastor Stevens to eat with us.

With only family and the few friends, the atmosphere was more relaxed and conversation was easier. After we were seated and Tommie had said the blessing, Pastor Stevens asked, "Nancy, do you remember the time I came to dinner thirty years ago?"

"Do I remember? Oh, my goodness, that day aged me ten years. You were new, and I wanted to make a good impression. Helen, my dad's second wife, and I had threatened him to be on his best behavior. I'd warned him not get into the liquor cabinet and watch his language. Right off the bat, he gives this colorful description of how fast Jeremiah could run. I could have crawled under the table."

"What did he say?" Lacy asked, speaking for the first time since the service.

"I can't repeat it," Mom said.

"I was at school, Lacy, and wasn't here, but I heard what he said. Jeremiah was my roommate and was a tremendous athlete. My grands said he could run like a scalded ass ape," I explained. That brought laughter from around the table, which was much needed after what we had just gone through.

"That didn't bother me," said Pastor Stevens. "I spent a couple of hours with Bob Matthews that day and gained a whole new perspective of this country. That had a profound influence on my decision to remain here for thirty years. He offered me a cigar, which I accepted. It made me sick, but I was able to get up the road a piece after leaving before I pulled over and threw up."

More laughter followed. "I'm sure you knew about the session meeting where they were going to terminate you?" I said.

"Yes, I heard about that," said Pastor Stevens. "I had left immediately after the sermon so I was not present."

"What happened?" Jake asked.

"I was there, this time," I said. "Pastor Stevens was seeing a young lady from Hondo, who was Hispanic and a Catholic. After the service, while outside the church, my grands was told a session meeting was called and the reason for it. He went back inside. My mom told me to go with him to keep him calm. The president of the session said he was getting a lot of complaints about Pastor Stevens and he made a motion to release him immediately. When he asked for a second, my grands stood up and said, 'Hell no, you're not going to get a second, and you never will as long as I'm breathing.' I don't remember the rest of it; however, Mom can probably tell you, since she heard it all from the parking lot. Anyway, it got real quiet for at least a minute before a session member whispered, 'I move to adjourn.' Everyone except the president voted for the motion." Laughter, again followed my story.

"Your grands must have been something else," Jake said.

"Yes, he was. He was very colorful. Jack and I got into a lot of trouble repeating some of his quotes," Zack said.

"A day doesn't go by that I don't miss him. However, Bo is rapidly filling his shoes," my mom said.

After we had finished, Jake asked if he could talk with me a few minutes alone. We went upstairs to the balcony and sat outside.

"Bo, I was informed before leaving Houston that the issue with Diane and Carl has been resolved. It was all a misunderstanding from the beginning. The grandfather who was asking about Diane, come to find out, was not angry with her. He had only wanted to tell her it wasn't her fault. The boy's stepfather failed to bring him to the emergency room, telling his mother he was faking. She begged him but he flat out refused; hence, the mystery of why he wasn't brought earlier is solved. No doubt the boy could've been saved if not for the stepdad. The mother of the boy left the stepdad because of this. However, that's not all the story. The stepdad was found dead two weeks later. The ruling was suicide by hanging. Actually, the ruling was correct. He did commit suicide when he failed to take his stepson to the emergency room."

"So now, Carl and Diane can go back to Houston with you," I said.

Smiling, Jake replied, "Not quite. They want to stay here."

Confused, I asked, "What do you mean? Don't they want to go home?"

"They want to move here. With all that has been going on in your life, you may not have noticed, but they're not the same couple who I brought out here. Now, I'm going to let them tell you the remainder of their plans."

Later that evening, I had a chance to talk with Carl and Diane. I told them about my conversation with Jake and his explaining about the misunderstanding with the boy's family.

"We appreciate you taking us in. We're so sorry for this tragedy that you're experiencing. Diane and I have enjoyed being your guests these past several weeks. We have found a home here and will not go back to Houston except to get our belongings. We had only rented, so there is no problem with selling a house."

"We love this country," added Diane. "Prior to this terrible incident that your family has experienced, I have never enjoyed myself so much, thanks to Lexie. We have nothing to keep us in Houston. I can work here, and Jake has consented to opening up an office for Carl in Ruidoso."

"Bo, we will get our own place immediately when we return so as not to be an imposition to your family," Carl explained.

"You've been anything but a problem for us. We couldn't have done without you through this ordeal," I said. "When are you going back?"

"Jake is leaving tomorrow, and we'll go with him. We can finish our business in Houston in a few days. We plan on being back here within a week. We've never done anything like this. We're beside ourselves with excitement and eager to begin this new adventure!" Carl said.

I informed the rest of the family about Carl and Diane's plans, and my mom immediately insisted they stay with them when they returned from Houston.

"You'll want to find a nice place to live and that will take time. We would love to have you stay with us. After all, how many people can say they have their very own doctor living with them?" Mom stated.

"That would allow us to take some time in looking for a house. We would like to buy rather than rent," Diane said.

"It's settled then. We look forward to having you stay in our guest suite," Tom replied.

We didn't leave Mom's until 10:00 that evening. Jake, Carl, and Diane, were going to stay with us, allowing them to get an early start the next morning. This announcement by them was something positive, since we had just been through another terrible day.

After our guests had retired for the night, Lexie and I had some time to ourselves.

"Bo, it was a nice service. Pastor Stevens did a wonderful job. I'm glad to be home and away from the crowd. People try hard to say the right thing and most of them fail. If they would just say, I'm sorry."

"We've been together so long, Lexie, we think alike. That same thought has been on my mind."

"Are you glad Zack is staying home?" she asked.

"I know it's selfish of me, but yes."

"I am too, Bo. It's going to make it easier on us. Having Tommie Rose here is going to be a tremendous help, also."

"Did you know she was the reason we left the cemetery?" I asked.

"Yes. I saw her whisper something to you. You've never liked anyone telling you what to do," she said.

"I know. It's strange, isn't it?"

"Did you know that she had become friends with Dr. Adders?" she asked.

"No. Of course not!"

"Well, it may be more than that," she hinted.

"What's that mean, Lexie?"

"She spoke highly of him to me. He was there for her when she was notified about Jack passing. They spent most of the day together. Tommie said she would have had a hard time making it if not for him."

"I don't like it."

"Tommie's thirty years old, Bo. Dr. Adders is older and the most respected neurosurgeon in the country. We should trust them to know what they want."

"I'm stubborn and the older I get, the worse I become. I know that. It's hard for me to imagine Tommie being that old."

"She is though. I'm glad she's interested in someone, and I would like to have grandkids before I'm too old to enjoy them."

"If that pretty little nurse in Colorado Springs who was always bringing Zack food and coffee had her way, we would have grandkids in no time."

"Zack wasn't interested. I could tell."

"Can you sleep tonight?" I asked.

"Maybe. I hope. I need to be up early and cook breakfast so Jake and his passengers can get on their way."

"I have a suggestion. Let's go for a long ride tomorrow after they leave. We'll take the horses over to the home ranch and ride."

"Okay. That sounds good," she said.

We rode several hours each morning for the next five days. Our starting point was the North Ranch. After the first day, Zack, Lacy, and Tommie joined us. It took some convincing to get Lacy to agree, but Tommie was able to get it done. We rode in the sunshine, in the cold, and even in the snow. We never got the horses out of a walk.

Maybe it was therapy or it could have been that we wanted to be together. Probably both. It didn't matter… it helped us begin healing. We would make a point to be back to my mom's for lunch each day. She had frozen most of the food people had brought so we had a feast every day. With the family together, we had moved a step beyond surviving.

On the fifth day while we were eating, Zack made a shocking announcement. "Dad, I want to start roping again. If you'll get us some calves, I would like to start right away."

Surprised, I said, "Sure, that's no problem. What size calves do you want?"

"What they're roping now, small," he said. "I'll use Cotton. I think Jack would like that."

"I'll help you," Tommie announced.

"Okay. I'll get right on it," I said.

We finished the meal in silence.

When Lexie and I were alone, I asked, "What's going on?"

"I don't know, Bo. Maybe it's his way of dealing with losing his brother. They were close. You know he was good, even better than Jack. I believe it will be positive for the family."

CHAPTER 21

Zack

HEALING WAS GOING TO TAKE a long time. Riding helped us the first few days after Jack's funeral; however, the nights proved the worst for us, especially Dad and Lacy. Sissy (I couldn't bring myself to call her Tommie) continued to stay with Lacy, telling us that some nights Lacy didn't sleep at all. Dad was the same way and was up every morning by 4:00.

I was comfortable with my decision not to return to school. I drove back to Houston and picked up my personal belongings. The owner of the apartments, after hearing what happened, consented to cancel my lease without a penalty.

I chose to rope again to honor Jack and to provide my dad with something in which to look forward. I believe it was the right decision and did not consider it a sacrifice on my part. I looked forward to getting back in the arena after being absent for years, believing I would rope better now because of my maturity. My main obstacle was going to be the physical part because of not being active. Hopefully, the work on the ranch would take care of that.

A week after the service, Dad bought twenty calves. Every day that the weather permitted, and some days it didn't, we were at the arena. The first few days we practiced, Lacy refused to come. Sissy would leave her and come join Dad and me. I assume, after several days, she tired of staying alone and came with Sissy.

I would use the good horse to rope six or so calves and then change to one of the other horses to continue. Dad had seen to it that my brother had several practice horses. Sissy would rope a few calves, also, but spent most of her time at the loading chute. When Lacy started coming, she worked the gate. Mom helped wherever she was needed. It meant that our family was together, at least two to three hours most days.

On the cold days, we would take a break occasionally and huddle in the tack room beside the wood burning stove to get warm. We always had a pot of coffee on.

After we had finished in the practice pen, there would be work that needed to be done on the ranch. Me, Dad, and Roany, would stay busy feeding, doctoring cattle, repairing equipment, and whatever other chore that needed attention.

Roany was never far from me. She was staying in the house at night and, of course, sleeping with me. It was obvious that I had taken my brother's place.

Jimmy, my dad's friend since childhood, was still stove-up from his horse incident. He would go with us occasionally but couldn't do much. He was still 'Uncle Jimmy' to me. With his guidance, I had been riding the race filly that had bucked him off. I was aware of his knowledge and followed his instructions. My dad was curious if Jimmy was going to train the filly when she raced, something that he hadn't done in twenty years."

I had attempted several times to talk with Lacy about Jack. She refused to enter into any kind of discussion about him. I know it would have helped if she would open up and talk about her feelings. Maybe it would come later.

Sissy was having the same experience with her. One positive was that she had indicated an interest in a prosthetic.

Thanksgiving came exactly three weeks from the time of Jack's funeral. Holidays are a difficult time for families that have experienced the loss of a loved one, especially so soon. This was no exception as the mood of everyone deteriorated. We had Thanksgiving dinner at Mia's. She had prepared her usual abundance of food with turkey and a dozen side dishes. She had become renowned for her dressing, which was loved by everyone.

We had just sat down and Sissy was in the middle of the blessing when the doorbell rang. She finished and Mom went to the door. I heard her say, "What a nice surprise. Let me get Tommie."

Sissy left the kitchen and went to the front door. I heard whispering and then she came back saying, "I have an announcement. We have a guest for dinner and it's important to me that you welcome him." She went back and returned with a frightened Ted Adders.

I immediately rose and shook hands, "We're glad to have you."

Mia said, "Welcome to my home, Dr. Adders. We are pleased you could join us."

Mom followed with a similar statement. We all looked at Dad…silence.

Sissy found another chair, set another place at the table by her, and guided Adders into it. "Now, I'm hungry and everything looks wonderful, as usual. Let's eat."

What happened next was amazing. The atmosphere and mood improved, with each of us having questions for Dr. Adders. The exception, of course, was Dad. He remained silent, pouting like a twelve-year-old. He knew better than to say anything negative. Mia, his mother, had emphasized "my home" when she welcomed Dr. Adders.

Dr. Adders explained that he woke up at 1:00 this morning and decided to come to New Mexico. He drove straight through and arrived in Capitan, where he asked directions to the ranch. Of course, everyone knew we were eating at Mia's. Even though my dad would not agree, Ted, as he insisted on being called, saved Thanksgiving for our family. It was a blessing, which we needed.

Ted stayed three days, spending the days with Sissy, and the nights at Mia's. Sissy took the day after Thanksgiving to show him around both ranches. On Saturday, we were back in the arena, with Ted watching and Dad still pouting. Sissy showed off her roping skills which impressed the doctor, as if he needed any more incentive to be impressed with her.

After he left on Monday, I had an opportunity to talk with Sissy alone. "Did you know he was coming?"

"No idea. We had talked several times on the phone, and of course I had invited him, but he never said he'd come," she answered.

"Were you glad to see him?" I asked.

"Yes. I'll admit it. We all needed an outsider to take our minds off our sorrow," she replied.

"Ah, come on, Sissy. You're talking to your brother, not your dad. You don't have to explain with an excuse that it was good for the family. Were YOU glad to see him?"

"You're tenacious, Little Brother. Yes, if you must know. I was glad to see him. He was there for me when Jack passed. I also enjoy his company. There's more to him than I originally thought. Now, are you satisfied that you got it out of me?"

"Not quite. Is it serious?" I asked, with a smile.

"Definitely not. I may not ever hear from him again," she answered.

"Watch out, Sissy. You're on the verge of an untruth. You don't believe that."

"That's all the questions, Little Brother."

"One more thing, Sissy. I'm glad he came. It was good for all of us, even Dad. Of course, he doesn't know it. I like Ted. He's okay."

"Will Dad ever get over his anger?" she asked.

"Sure, in time. He's stubborn, but he has enough respect and love for you to accept whatever you want. Plus, the rest of the family has already accepted Dr. Adders."

"Something else, Zack, on another subject. I've been thinking about taking Lacy to the Finals in Vegas. What do you think about that?"

"Awesome. If you can convince her to go," I said.

"Would you go with us?"

"No. I wouldn't leave Dad, not this early anyway. Besides, I need to rope every day it's possible."

"You're planning on going professional, aren't you? I leveled with you, now it's your turn."

"Yeah. I tell myself it's for Jack; however, I'm beginning to think it's for the both of us as well as Dad. I'm excited about the competition."

"I'll share something with you, Little Brother, since we're being honest with one another. You remind me of Dad when you rope. I'd never noticed it before. You're much better now than when you competed in high school rodeo. Now, that's the truth, and it's definitely a compliment."

Beginning on the evening of December 4 and continuing the next two days, Sissy and the rest of us encouraged, insisted, and pleaded with Lacy to go to the Finals. I think she just gave up and agreed to go with Sissy to stop us from nagging her.

Houser, the nurse, at the hospital in Colorado Springs had called me several times. She kept asking me when I was coming back to Colorado. I wasn't that interested in her, saying it might be years before I was back in that area. The last time she called, she put me on the spot, asking if she could come to New Mexico for a weekend. Declining as politely as possible, I told her that would not be a good idea. I hadn't heard from her since.

My plans were to start making some jackpot ropings as soon as possible. I was shooting for early spring, maybe March or April to attend my first professional rodeo. I knew the competition had become fierce from looking at the winning times. I was roping good but needed groundwork, if I was going to compete. One thing was going to be difficult. The calves were small and many of the cowboys were now saving time by taking only one wrap and a hooey. Dad had never allowed us to do that.

Dad continued to be upset over the 2000 Presidential election held last month. It wasn't so much that he disliked Bush but that he was a Republican. B-Boy, his granddad and my great granddad, had influenced him to not trust Republicans. Good or bad, he was firm in his political beliefs. When we were growing up, he wasn't that interested in politics but that had changed. He watched the news every day and kept up with national and world events.

Mom could care less about politics, but was thrilled that he had finally acquired a cell phone. He constantly complained about it and threatened to throw it away. Each time he left the house, she reminded him to take it. He complied if he could find it.

As the days moved closer to Christmas, I felt a dread that once again we would become more sensitive to our loss.

CHAPTER 22

Tommie Rose

THE FINALS STARTED ON DECEMBER 7. Dad had friends in the team roping who made the finals. They were able to get us tickets for the last three nights of the rodeo. We drove to Lubbock and caught our 4:00 P.M. flight on Wednesday the 13th, which would allow us to be there for the Thursday, Friday, and Saturday performances. Lacy remained reluctant to go, but hopefully she would feel different when we were there. I'm sure that she was embarrassed by her handicap and didn't want to be in public. The iWalk was an effective means for her to move, but she took her crutches, also.

Our plane landed at 4:00, due to the two hour time difference. We had booked a room at the Hyatt Place, which was less than a half mile to the Thomas and Mack Center where the rodeo was held. After finding our room, I asked Lacy, "Would you like to get something to eat? It's already five o'clock at home."

"No, I'm not hungry. Have you noticed how people stare at me like I'm a freak?"

"That's only human nature, Lacy. They mean no harm."

"I want to scream; I can't help it!"

"I'll order us a pizza from room service. Would that be okay?" I asked.

"I guess so. I may not leave the room while we're here. It wasn't my idea to come in the first place," she said, beginning to cry and going into the bathroom.

I ordered the pizza and turned on the TV. I didn't know what to say. She was right. It wasn't her idea to come and maybe it was a mistake. A few minutes later, someone knocked. That's quick service, I thought. Opening the door, two girls were standing there.

"Is this Lacy Skinner's room?" one asked.

"Yes, it is."

"Could we see her?" the other one asked.

"Sure, come in," I replied. "She's in the bathroom."

"Lacy Skinner, you get your skinny butt out here right this minute!" one of the girls exclaimed.

The door opened and the crying commenced, along with the hugging. All three girls were trying to talk at once, which was impossible. They would get a word or two out and then start sobbing again. This went on for several minutes until they finally were able to talk.

"Tommie, this is Shasta and Trina. They're my friends," she said, breaking down again. After that, more hugging and crying. I began to think it wasn't going to end; however, it did and we were able to have a conversation.

Shasta said, "We've been to a dozen hotels looking for you. One of those old team ropers told us you were coming. He'd talked with your father-in-law. When we found you here, the hotel wouldn't give us your room number. Trina had to use some of her charm on one of the bellboys, and he was more than glad to help us."

"There are some advantages to being a female," Trina said. "Now, we have a lot of catching up to do. We have about two hours until we have to get ready for the rodeo."

I knew it was time for me to leave. "Ladies, I'm going for a walk. I may even try some of the slots."

I guess they heard me, but I received no response. They were busy trying to all talk at once. I walked around for the next hour before going back to the room. Lacy had left me a note saying she had gone to eat with her friends. I took a deep breath and said aloud, *thank you, Jesus, for looking after us.* I sat down in one of the chairs and enjoyed the cold pizza.

When she returned to the room on her crutches she was a different person.

"Tommie, we have to go down to the lobby and watch the rodeo tonight on the big screen. This is Shasta's first time at the Finals. She just squeaked in at number 15. We competed in high school rodeo together. Trina is sitting 11th but she's ahead in the average. I can't believe they found me. I'm so excited for them. Aren't they something?"

"Yes, they are. Did you eat?"

"We ordered but had so much to talk about I didn't finish. Is there any pizza left?"

"Yes, but it's cold."

"No problem. I'm starved."

We spent the evening in the lobby watching round seven on a huge screen. No way would we have this good a view tomorrow night; however, there would be something special about being there in person.

Shasta had a good run but didn't place. Trina didn't have that good of a run but kept them up and continued to lead the average. The times in the calf roping were awesome with a 9.0 not even placing. Zack was going to have his work cut out for him.

The next day we stayed around the hotel, with a steady stream of Lacy's friends coming to see her. Each new visitor brought hugs, tears, and then more hugs. I stayed away as much as possible. We left for the rodeo at 7:30 that evening. It was only a short walk, but I knew we had to get a taxi. Arriving at the Thomas and Mack Center, I asked the driver what I owed him.

"Nothing, ma'am. I would drive this pretty young lady with you anywhere without a charge."

Entering the coliseum, I started looking for the handicapped seats on the lower level. I found them and directed Lacy there on her crutches. They were all filled, but I noticed several of the seats were occupied by people who didn't appear to be handicapped. In fact, I had witnessed one of the men get up from his seat and wave to a friend. I moved over to where he was sitting and asked, "Would you move so my friend can have a seat?"

"I was here first," he replied.

"Yes, but you're sitting in a handicapped seat," I reminded him.

"There're other seats available," he said.

Anger flew over me from head to foot, and I did a very un-Christian thing. I reached, grabbed his ear, twisted it, and with him squealing, guided him from his seat. That attracted attention and drew a round of applause from others in the handicapped section. He reeked of liquor and left the area cursing. After I had Lacy seated, I tracked down my reserve seat. I found it in the middle of an isle about half-way up behind the roping box. It wasn't the best seat but certainly not the worst.

The rodeo started on time with the grand entry, and a feeling of nostalgia swept over me. It had been years since I had participated in a rodeo. I didn't realize how much I missed it. It was a great rodeo, with outstanding stock and the best cowboys in the world. When the tie-down roping started I heard the man sitting in front of me say to the man next to him who had on a cowboy hat, "Here's your favorite event."

His companion replied, "Yes, it is. It's a much different event than it was for a boy from Merkel who roped calves in the 50's."

The word Merkel caught my attention. Merkel is where my dad bought my beloved Flame 20 years ago. I didn't want to interrupt them during the calf roping. After it ended and the barrels were being set up, I asked the one sitting in front of me, "Do you live in Merkel, Texas?"

Looking surprised, he said, "No, I'm from Dallas. My brother here," indicating the man next to him, "does."

"I had this wonderful horse that we bought from a man in Merkel in 1980. The horse's name was Flame and he was awesome. I won state in the barrels all four years I was in high school," I explained.

"Who did you buy the horse from?" asked the one with the hat.

"His last name was Russell. I don't remember his first name.

Both men started laughing. The one wearing a cowboy hat said, "That would be Ralph Russell. He's our uncle."

"I can't believe this. We came to Merkel, ate at this wonderful café, and went out to his place. My dad had met his brothers at the café and visited with them. Because of them, I liked not to have gotten the horse. They gave my dad advice on what to pay. I remember us leaving without the horse, with me crying. I ended up getting the horse when Mr. Russell followed us and agreed to my dad's offer. By the way, my name's Tommie."

"I'm Jacky and this is Jerry," he said, motioning to the one with the hat. "The men who gave your dad advice were our dad, S.G. and our Uncle Jim."

"I've heard of you, Tommie. Ralph bragged about how good you were doing on the horse he sold you. He kept up with the horses he sold," explained Jerry, the one with the hat.

"This is amazing! What a small world! Did both of you rope?"

"He did, in fact, he was the Texas High School Champion Calf Roper in 1955," Jacky said, with pride. "We also have some barrel racers in the family now."

Before we could continue, the announcer asked for the attention of the crowd. When the noise continued, this time he was more firm. "Ladies and gentlemen, please listen to what I have to say. I believe you will find it worthwhile."

The crowd quieted and he continued, "On the 30th day of July, a young couple were on their way home from Cheyenne after she had won the barrel racing. These two members of our rodeo family were in a terrible accident. The young man, Jack Skinner, did not survive, but his wife did, after losing a leg. She is here tonight. Her name is Lacy Skinner and she was sitting number 2 in the world in the barrel racing at the time of the tragedy. I would like to direct your attention to the handicapped seating. Lacy, would you please stand up." The huge screen showed Lacy standing with the support of the arm rest. "Ladies and gentleman, please welcome this courageous lady to the dream house of all cowboys and cowgirls."

The crowd rose applauding for at least a minute. I couldn't hold back the tears. What a wonderful tribute and so well deserved. I'm sure her fellow barrel racers were responsible.

The barrel race started and I concentrated on that. Shasta placed high enough to get a check and Trina kept the barrels up again but did not clock good. She was still leading the average and with two more clean runs had an excellent chance to win it. Lacy was going to be excited for both. When the rodeo ended, I said to my new acquaintances, "I enjoyed meeting you. Is Ralph still living?"

"Yes. He roped at Stamford in the Old-Timer's this year," said Jerry.

"What about your dad?" I asked.

"No, he and Uncle Jim have both passed," Jacky answered. "Did you come by yourself?"

"No. I brought my sister-in-law, who just received the standing ovation."

"I remember seeing that on the news. Her husband must have been your brother," said Jerry.

"Yes, that's correct."

"We're sorry," they said, almost in unison.

"It's been a tough four months," I said. "I can't wait to tell my mom and dad about meeting you."

"I'll tell Ralph about our meeting, also," Jerry said.

We said goodbye, and I went after Lacy.

We flew home on Sunday morning and Lacy was in better spirits. I enjoyed the trip, realizing that it was worth the effort with the results that it produced. I also became aware that the competition had reached another level in all the events, especially the barrels and the tie-down roping.

We were back in Lubbock by noon and at the ranch by mid-afternoon. We stopped at my mom and dad's and visited about the rodeo. They had watched each night of the finals and saw the tribute to Lacy. I told them about seeing the Russells and them being nephews of the man who sold us Flame.

"Dad, there were 17,000 people in attendance and I had a seat behind them. Isn't that something?"

"It could be more than that," my mom said. "It seems that our families are somehow connected. Let me give you some background. Your B-Boy was a customer for years at Ace Package, a liquor store in Roswell. I was with him on one of his visits. The proprietor of that store was Lucille Nunnely, who was a sister to the three Russell brothers. Your B-Boy made the Post Rodeo most years and was the flag man for the roping. He talked often of the Russell brothers who would be there. Of course, that was Ralph, S.G., and Jim. The two men you met at the finals were sons of S.G. Somehow, we ended up in Merkel, buying a horse from Ralph."

She continued, "My dad, Mia, and you were on your way home from Lubbock years ago when my dad's car broke down. A trucker stopped and helped get them started. His name was Johnny and his wife was a sister of the three Russell brothers. I don't know, it seems more than a coincidence."

"I remember that day. I was only ten at the time," I said.

"Doesn't matter," said my dad. "Every time our paths have crossed something good has happened. Remember, that day we had lunch with them, they told me about the man at Post who sold us Bear, the boys' first roping horse."

For the next hour, we talked about the rodeo. Zack had gone into town and wasn't present. Dad did comment on how stiff the competition was in the roping. We were all thinking the same thing; Zack had a lot of work to do in order to compete.

CHAPTER 23

Lexie

It was Monday, December 11 and only two weeks until Christmas. Bo had been unusually quiet the last week, and I know he was thinking of Jack. I doubted if it would do any good to attempt a conversation about his mood. One problem was the weather, which had turned bad. The days had been overcast and cold all week, with the temperatures remaining below freezing. We had tried to rope on two of those days and gave up after Zack had run a couple of calves. We froze out and ended up in the warm room. That's what we had named the tack room during cold weather. We weren't as tough as we used to be when the kids were small.

Zack had bought a travel trailer and put it next to the barn. We had argued against it, but to no avail. His excuse was that he needed the privacy. He still ate most of his meals with us. After giving it more thought, I realized he was right. Bo eventually agreed with me, also.

That afternoon, I went into the den to try talking to Bo but he wasn't there. I checked our bedroom and didn't find him. When I looked into the boys' room he was lying across Jack's bed, which we had not removed. He had his face buried in the bed and his body was shaking. I backed out of the door, leaving him to grieve the only way he knew, privately.

Christmas was going to be difficult, to say the least, this year. It had taken my dad years to enjoy Christmas after the death of my brother on Christmas Eve. I had tried to think of ways to make it easier on all of us, but nothing came to mind.

I left Bo a note on the table that I was going to see Tommie and Lacy. Maybe they would have some ideas about how we could make Christmas easier this year.

Being forced to stay inside added to the challenge of dealing with our sorrow. I was going to invite Tommie and Lacy to stay with us a few days. I found Tommie working on a sermon she was going to deliver this Sunday, giving Pastor Stevens a day off. Lacy was reading *The Horse Whisperer,* a book that had been made into a movie.

"How're you doing?" I asked

"We're making it okay," Tommie replied. "Mia brought several books over here for us to read. Lacy tells me I'll like the one she's reading."

I told Tommie and Lacy about Bo and asked if they had any suggestions that might help.

"Mom, I've got news that's going to do more harm than good. Ted has asked to come for Christmas this year. I was about to call him back and tell him it would be okay."

"Oh, me, Tommie, that's not good. Bo will throw a fit. Maybe, you should tell him not to come."

"I think she should allow him to come. I've tried not to think about Christmas without Jack. It's going to be a horrible time. Ted was a distraction at Thanksgiving, maybe that helped. I imagine the same could be true for Christmas. He couldn't make it any worse," said Lacy.

"Are you going to tell your dad, Tommie?" I asked.

"I thought you would do that. You have a way with him that nobody else does," she said.

"I came over here to ask for suggestions to help Bo's mood, and now I have to go back and tell him Dr. Adders is coming for Christmas. I should have stayed home. Maybe we should all go over to break the news. My other reason for coming was to invite you to spend a few days with us. I was hoping that would improve the atmosphere for all of us."

"We appreciate it, Mom, and that was thoughtful of you; however, we're doing fine here. Do you agree Lacy?"

"Definitely. This is a good book, and I'd rather stay here and read in my own house."

"Well, I'll go on back home. I'm not telling Bo the news until you're sure Dr. Adders is coming. Maybe a storm will come in and prevent travel."

"Thanks Mom. It'll all work out. I'll pray about it."

"Now, that's what I call blind and total faith," I said, going out the door.

The weather improved a little the next day. It was still cold but the sun was shining. Bo announced that they were going to rope and asked me if I was helping.

"Not today, it's too cold for me. I might come down later and sit in the pickup with the heater on and watch."

"Not a problem, we're only going to run a dozen or so calves. Tommie and Lacy aren't coming either. I can load and work the gate. We've already missed too many days and Zack needs the practice."

After he left, feeling guilty, I commenced to make chili. It was one of Bo and Zack's favorites. It took about an hour and when it was almost finished, I received a call on my cell phone.

"Mom, don't panic, but Dad's been hurt. It's not serious, but you need to come help us."

I don't remember if I said anything or not. I was out the door and there in minutes. Zack had his arm around Bo and he was hobbling out of the arena.

"What happened?" I asked.

"A calf kicked him on his leg that was broken," Zack replied.

Bo was grimacing in pain and had to stop every few steps. I told him to put his other arm around me and we would get him in the pickup.

"I can't believe he kicked me right in the spot I broke my leg. It hurts like hell," Bo mumbled, as we loaded him.

We finally got him in the house and on to the couch. I told him I was going to call the doctor.

"No. Just let me sit here awhile. It already feels better." I knew better than to try and argue with him. It would have been easy to get him in at the clinic in Ruidoso. Diane was already working there and would have seen him immediately.

Diane and Carl were living in Ruidoso now. My dad had offered to rent them his house. They wanted to buy it, but he refused to sell even thought it was vacant. It had been in our family for fifty years.

Carl had found a vacant building on the north side of Ruidoso and was having it remodeled for his office. It would be open within a couple of months. Todd, my brother, had been introducing him to prospective investment clients and had recruited him into the Lions Club. He and Diane were beginning their new adventure, proceeding full speed ahead.

The next morning, after a sleepless night, Bo agreed to a doctor's appointment. Diane got us right in and after X-rays informed us of her opinion.

"You have a severe bruise on that leg. Also, you have calcium deposits that will start bothering you soon, if they don't already. I would recommend that you let me make an appointment with a bone and joint specialist in El Paso. I'll give you a prescription for pain pills and recommend that you stay on crutches for at least two weeks."

"How soon can you get him in?" I asked.

"I'll need to check. It may be after Christmas. Do you want me to proceed?" she asked, looking at Bo.

"I guess so. I need to get something done," Bo said.

"I'll let you know when your appointment is," she said. "On a personal note, I want to thank you again for all you've done for us. We are excited and happy with our move. We love Ruidoso."

We thanked her and left, with Bo on crutches that Diane had furnished from the clinic.

On the drive home, Bo said, "I guess it's about time I started having problems with my leg. It's been almost thirty years."

"I imagine that calf kicking you had a little something to do with it," I reminded him.

"Yeah. Now you're going have to toughen up and help Zack."

"On another matter, Bo. It's time to get a Christmas tree. Let's all go look tomorrow. We'll get one for our house and for your mom's.

"I don't want a tree this year. Besides, they're no little ones around."

"Let's get one for your mom, anyway. We'll have Christmas over there," I suggested. This time he didn't answer.

This was just a hint of how difficult Christmas was going to be this year. I wish a few magic words would allow us to skip Christmas and go right into a new year.

Zack was waiting on us when we arrived at home. I told him what the doctor had said and suggested, since the weather was warmer today, that he could rope. I would call Tommie and Lacy to come over and help.

We spent two hours in the practice pen that afternoon, with me, Tommie, and Lacy working the loading alley and the gate. I had brought a chair for Bo, and he sat over by the fence giving us orders.

On Wednesday, December 20, Bo announced while we were eating breakfast that he wasn't using the crutches any more. I reminded him it hadn't been two weeks.

"You're still trying to be my nurse, like you did when I broke my leg all those years ago. Remember that?" he said.

"Yes, and you're even more stubborn now than you were then."

"I called you Nurse Goodbody. Remember that?" he asked.

"Sure. That's when you thought I was hot."

Smiling for one of the few times in the last three months, he said, "I still think you're hot. You age well, Little Girl."

Maybe, with his good mood, this would be the time to break the news. It was only five days till Christmas, and I had put it off as long as I could. I had watched the weather last evening, and I wasn't going to get any help there.

"We may have a guest for Christmas," I announced.

"Who?"

I could tell by the tone of his voice he knew the answer. "Dr. Adders," I said.

"I don't want him here Christmas. It's going to be hard enough anyway."

"I don't see how he could make it any more difficult," I said.

"It puts me in a bad mood to be around him."

"Well, Cowboy, you're in a bad mood most of the time."

"I'm going to tell Tommie that he's not welcome on this ranch and to stay away," he said, in a stern voice.

"Other people live on this ranch, too, Mr. Boss."

Silence.

I got up, moved over and sat down in his lap, putting my arms around him. I leaned down and bit him on the ear.

"What're you doing?" he asked gruffly.

"What do you think, Cowboy? I'm buttering you up to get my way."

"It's not fair," he muttered, in a much softer voice this time.

Two hours later we picked up Tommie and Lacy on our way to find a Christmas tree for Ms. Nancy's house. We found one in the same area that Bo and I had found a tree in 1970.

We had all agreed not to buy presents this year for one another. Instead, Todd had an Angel's tree in his bank with the names of needy children and each of us had taken the name of a child.

The next day we all went into Ruidoso, including Ms. Nancy and my dad, shopping. It was fun and good for our spirits. Todd joined us for lunch at one of our favorite eating places in town. All things being considered; it was a good day for us.

I stayed busy cooking the next three days to help Ms. Nancy. Dr. Adders arrived on Saturday, December 23. I was still somewhat confused about his and Tommie's relationship. When he was here Thanksgiving I didn't witness him showing any affection toward her; however, the same could be said of her.

Bo had accepted the fact that he was going to be on the ranch but said he wouldn't be welcome in his house. When I reminded him it was my house, also, he went silent. He always did that when he knew I was right.

Preparation for the holiday hadn't kept us out of the practice pen. With Bo able to help, Zack was roping every day. Bo had told me on more than one occasion that he was amazed at how well he was doing.

Dr. Adders stayed with Ms. Nancy and my dad. They admittedly enjoyed him, saying he was a delight to have in the house. Of course, my dad would have done anything for Tommie. She had always been his favorite.

Bo had stayed away from Dr. Adders, but was forced to eat Christmas dinner at his mom's. He didn't participate in conversation at the table and as soon as we finished he left. It didn't seem to bother the rest of us. The mood was better than I expected and, once again, Dr. Adders gets the credit.

On Tuesday after Christmas, I spent a good part of the day arguing with Bo. Dr. Adders was leaving the next day, and I wanted to do something together as a family. I had to use all my persuasion, but he finally agreed to go out to eat at the Cattleman's in Ruidoso.

I thought he might back out at the last minute, but we left home at 6:00, giving us an hour before our meeting time. He was silent on the drive, still pouting because he was having to do something he detested. We arrived a few minutes early, but Tommie and Dr. Adders were already there. We secured a table and didn't have to wait long until my dad, Ms. Nancy, and Lacy arrived. Zack wasn't going to be with us. He had left early this morning for East Texas to try out a horse.

We tried to include Bo in the conversation, before and during the meal, but had little success. One or two word answers were all we received in response to questions. I had noticed a Mexican family at the table closest to us that were enjoying themselves, laughing constantly while eating. Evidently, they didn't have a Bo at their table.

Just as we rose to leave, a loud commotion drew our attention. One of the men was choking and another was behind him attempting to dislodge the obstruction by administering belly thrust. A woman began screaming and I noticed several people using their cell phones, I assume, calling 911.

The choking man was turning blue and was dropped to the floor, unconscious. The person performing the procedure starting talking in Spanish and wringing his hands.

At this point, Dr. Adders, went over to the man, examined him and said, "We have to act. There's not much time. Somebody, get me a straw. A stiff one, not paper. I need a sharp knife that is clean. Hurry!"

"Bo, is your knife clean?"

"Yeah. I keep it that way."

He stepped forward and gave it to Adders. Adders asked Bo to clear the crowd away from the patient and to hold him in case he became conscious.

What happened next was gross, amazing, and unbelievable. Dr. Adders took Bo's knife and made an incision above the Adams Apple, with blood going everywhere. He took the straw and placed it in the incision. The ambulance didn't arrive for several more minutes. When they saw what had happened they loaded the patient on a stretcher and asked Dr. Adders to go with them to the hospital.

We followed the ambulance to the hospital, where we waited for the next three hours for Dr. Adders. When he came out, he was smiling.

"We were able to do the tracheostomy which was successful. The straw gave us enough time."

We were interrupted by the family of the patient, speaking Spanish and trying to hug Dr. Adders. I asked Bo what they were saying?"

"Lexie, it's all good. Believe me."

CHAPTER 24

Bo

I WAS RELIEVED THAT CHRISTMAS was over. It was supposed to be a time of joy and celebration, instead it came as a reminder of what we had lost. There were days like those before, on, and after Christmas, I thought it wouldn't be possible to go on, due to the grief that consumed me. Because I was suffering, everyone should be. When I saw people enjoying themselves, it made me angry. That way of thinking was selfish, which I knew, but I couldn't help it. That magnified my depression even more.

I had focused my anger on Adders, whom I continued to despise. Last night, at the Cattleman's, I witnessed the most amazing feat I'd ever seen. He saved the man's life. Not maybe, he did it, and that was a simple fact. The man was going to die before they transported him to the hospital. When we got home that evening, I had Lexie look up the procedure that he performed in the restaurant. It was called a cricothyrotomy, but the article said the success rate was not good. It was only effective for a short time, the article stated. Its purpose was to allow the patient to live until he arrived at the hospital, where a tracheostomy would be performed.

Adders was calm while performing the procedure even with all the noise and commotion around him. He told us later that if his malpractice insurance carrier found out they would drop him immediately. He was scheduled to leave the next morning but decided to stay another day. It had been after midnight before we were able to get home.

I called Tommie the next day and invited her and Dr Adders for supper that night. Knowing that he ate many of his meals at restaurants, Lexie had a home cooked meal, including chicken fried steak with cream gravy and mashed potatoes. She raided the deep freeze for black-eyed peas that she and my mom had put up. She made an apple pie that we decorated with ice cream.

Ted (he had insisted that I drop the Dr. Adders) had several helpings, showering accolades on Lexie, between servings. It was a successful evening, with me and Lexie sharing stories about Tommie when she was growing up. Ted was a good listener, only interrupting when he had a question.

I had paid little attention to Ted's appearance, and looking at him during this conversation, I became aware of several things. His hands were almost feminine, with long, slender fingers. He had blond, medium length hair to go with his light complexion. He was slender to the point of being thin, and because of this, he seemed taller than he was. In fact, Tommie was about the same height. He had blue eyes, a wide mouth, and admittedly, a nice smile. You wouldn't call him handsome, but after visiting with him, I could see why Tommie would find him interesting. I heard a tiny voice in my head say, *stupid, it's more than interesting and you might as well admit it.* The phone rang, interrupting us. Lexie answered and indicated it was for me. I took the call in our bedroom and it was Zack.

"Dad, how is everything at home?"

"Okay. How're you doing? What about the horse you tried?" I asked.

"Good. Probably even better than good. I roped on him the last two days, and he's everything and more than expected. The only drawback is the amount they're asking. It's too much for any roping horse, especially for me."

"How much?" I asked.

"Twenty-five thousand," he answered.

"How's he different from the horse you're using now?" I asked.

"Speed. He can put you on a calf without pushing the barrier. He works a lot of rope, also. He's eight, which gives him a lot of years."

"Tell me what you think, Zack."

"It's a lot of money," he said again.

"You have the money, with the trust your mother set up for you. I bet you haven't used any of it, except for college. You're too much like me. With your brother's horse and this one, you would be in a much better position to compete, in case one was injured. Plus, you'll be able to have two good horses to practice on."

"I don't know, Dad. It's too much money."

"Buy the horse, Zack, and come on home, so we can go to work."

"Let me try him one more time," he said before hanging up.

I had always though Jack was more like me. Now, this made me wonder. When I returned to the table, Lexie asked me if it was Zack.

"Yeah. He likes the horse," I answered.

"So, he bought him?" she quizzed.

"No. Not yet."

"Too much money. Right?" she asked.

"What makes you say that?" I asked.

"Because he has so much of his daddy in him." she said.

"There's nothing wrong with being thrifty," I stated.

"Thrifty! You're so tight you squeak when you walk, Bo Skinner."

That brought laughter from the others at the table, which had been in short supply the last three months. It was a good way to end the evening and as they were leaving, Tommie hugged me, saying, "Thank you, Dad."

It was after dark the next day before Zack was home. I saw his lights when he drove in and was at the barn when he unloaded his new horse.

"Long drive, huh?"

"Twelve hours. I left this morning after I'd run half a dozen calves," he said.

"Let's move inside the barn, so I can see what kind of horse you bought."

"They wouldn't budge on the price. I paid too much. I regretted it all the way home," he stated.

The horse was ordinary in every sense of the word. He was sorrel with a streaked face and some white on his legs, probably less than fifteen hands, with conformation that would not place in a show. I walked around him, looking closely, and could not see $25,000. I dared not say that because I remembered all too well my grands being upset when I brought the boys' first roping horse home. Anyway, Zack didn't buy him to show. Before I judged him, I needed to watch him work. I looked at Zack and asked, "What's his name?"

"Scooter," he replied ducking his head.

"My college roommate's nickname was Scoot. If he can run like him, he'll be okay. Don't be hard on yourself, Zack. You bought yourself a good horse, I'm confident in that. Put him up and then come to the house. Your mother has supper for you."

The next morning, we were at the arena by 9:00. Zack insisted I run the first calf on Scooter. By now, we had roped the calves enough times to know them, and the fastest calf in the bunch was loaded when I rode into the box. I nodded and the calf flew out of the chute. I said to myself, *oh no, I'm going to get outrun.* I put the reins forward on Scooter and he lunged forward, throwing me back in the saddle. By the time, I had regained my balance, we were on the calf, with me not ready to rope. I roped the calf halfway down the pen and Scooter's stop threw me forward. Once again, I was off balance, but at least didn't fall off. By now, I was laughing when I dismounted and took the rope off the calf. When I rode back to the front of the arena, Zack asked me, "What do you think?"

"I think you bought yourself a scorpion, Zack. He's the closest thing that I've roped on to Clay Cade's horse, Smokey, who went on to be voted a World Champion Roping Horse. I think you did good. I know several men who'd give your money back if you want to sell him. Scooter is going to be a welcome addition to the Skinner family." Zack beamed. At that point, for the first time, I realized how important it was to him that he had my approval. I would make a point never to forget that fact.

Zack roped a dozen calves on Scooter, and it was obvious he was worth every penny of what he paid. They fit together and that morning I realized just how good Zack could be.

After we had finished, we went to the tack room for coffee. I told him about the incident at the Cattleman's. He was amazed at Dr. Adders' action.

"Dad, most doctors wouldn't have attempted that procedure. They would have been afraid of a malpractice suit. Adders did a very courageous thing. I had suspected there was much more to him than what we thought. Sissy has the best judgement of anyone I know."

"Is she going to marry him?" I asked.

"Who knows. She has a mind of her own. I'm glad she found someone she cares about and that's not intimidated by her. You must admit, Dad, he's an amazing person. I've spent a lot of time around doctors, especially the last couple of years, and he's in a class all by himself. He's fascinated by Sissy, and there's no reason to believe he will change. That's not hard to understand because Jack and I were fascinated with her, also. I believe we all are, even you."

"Yeah, you're right. The last three months she's taken over the leadership in this family. I've come to depend on her, without realizing it."

"She's also been a tremendous help for Lacy, Dad. I hate to even think what she would've done without Sissy. After she gets her prosthesis, I believe she'll start riding her barrel horses again."

"Do you think she'll be able to compete again?" I asked.

"I haven't known of anyone who's competed on a professional level in her situation; however, she probably could attend local barrel races. You know, they have started this 4D business, which allows almost everyone to compete."

"Zack, are we ever going to get over losing Jack?"

"We won't, Dad. They say that 'time heals everything', but we will always feel his loss. Maybe one day we can talk about Jack and remember him without grief, only cherishing the memories."

"On another subject. When are you going to start making some rodeos?"

"Since I only have a permit, I'm going to be limited on the rodeos that will allow me to compete. Most of the big shows don't allow permits. Lubbock has a rodeo the last of March and they do. Maybe something will come up before then. It takes winnings of $1,000 to get a PRCA card."

"I need to get some fresh calves. I'll take these to the sale in Roswell Monday and get a new batch for you," I stated.

"Uncle Jimmy hasn't been around lately," Zack commented.

"No, he's still recovering from that spill he took. We've neglected the filly he was riding, the last few days. You need to ride her this morning. I have a strong feeling that he'll take her to the track this year. That's something he hasn't done in twenty years; however, I believe he's realizing that physical work on the ranch is becoming more difficult with each year."

"I can't do nearly as good a job as he does," Zack said.

"Nobody else could either. He's the best with a young horse. He always has been. You were just six when we won the All American with Malo. He was a difficult horse to train, and if not for Jimmy, we might not have had the success we did. Of course, Tommie had a lot to do with Malo's success, also. She could do things with him that no one else could."

"Did Malo really pay for this ranch?" he asked.

"That's right. When we syndicated him, my half was enough to pay for this ranch. He's not had the success as a sire that we expected. He's had some runners but not enough to call him a great sire. In fact, this filly you're riding is not by him. Her sire was Mr. Jess Perry."

"How did the family get into racing?" Zack asked.

"Grands and Lexie's dad formed a partnership in 1971. Grands had the knowledge of horses and Tom had the money. It was unbelievable the success they experienced."

"Gramps is rich, isn't he?"

"Yes, your mom's dad is probably the wealthiest person in the state."

"That's why they kidnaped Sissy, isn't it? I still remember it even though I was just six or seven."

"Yes."

"I can't believe mom shot that lady."

"Your mom is a much stronger person than most realize."

"We better get busy if we're going to get that filly ridden by lunch," Zack said.

CHAPTER 25

Tommie Rose

LACY WAS DOING BETTER; HOWEVER, she continued to have spells of depression that would come on without warning. She had told me that her tears would build up until they became a bucket full. They did occur less frequently. I'd stopped having the prescription for anti-depressants filled, realizing that the busier we stayed the better she was. Recently, that hadn't been a problem. With the beginning of 2001, winter had come to New Mexico, along with the flu. We had one cold spell after another with either snow, ice, or both. Jesse and his boys had been sick, unable to do much, so the feeding fell to me and Lacy. Bad weather meant more feeding, and even with the range cube dispenser on the pickup, it still took most of every day.

Gramps also had the flu, which frightened all of us. After three days with no improvement, Diane put him in the Ruidoso Hospital. Mia would stay with him in the morning but came home in time to cook lunch for us. There were days, however, in which she wasn't able to get into Ruidoso because of the icy roads.

Mia was able to take him home after six days. He was too weak to walk and had to be transported in a wheelchair.

Mom and Dad didn't get sick, but Jimmy, Felicia, and their son, Poco, came down with the flu. Mom, besides having to help feed, had the additional responsibility of looking after them.

On a brighter note, Lacy had decided to go ahead with being fitted for a prosthetic. Diane, who had turned out to be invaluable to our family, made us an appointment for February 20 with a clinic in Houston. She also put her in touch with several people who had gone through with the procedure. After talking to them, she was more positive about getting her artificial leg.

On Monday, February 5, I received a call from the hospital administrator in Colorado Springs. When I answered, there was a sound of desperation, when he spoke.

"Miss Skinner, have you talked to Dr. Adders recently?"

"No, as a matter of fact, it's been a week since he called. That's unusual."

"Dr. Adders lost a patient last Thursday and we haven't seen him since. I thought maybe he had been in touch with you," he explained.

"No. What happened?" I asked.

"A sixteen-year-old girl was in an accident with similar injuries to your brother. Dr. Adders performed surgery and she died. He was visibly upset when he left the hospital and has refused to return. The first several times we spoke to him, he told us he didn't deserve to be a physician. I went to his house, but he refused to let me in. Now he has stopped answering his phone. We are worried sick about him. Would you try to get in touch with him?"

"Certainly. I'll call you with any information that becomes available," I said. After hanging up, I felt a sense of panic. That was not like Ted in the least. He had been calling several times a week. It was strange that a week had gone by without talking to him. I immediately called his cell number, but it went directly to voice mail.

I still hadn't been able to understand my feelings for him. Maybe I felt sorry for him, or it could be that I wanted to provide whatever was missing in his life. He certainly wasn't the masculine hunk that described some of the cowboys who had been interested in me. He admitted to being an atheist, and the thought had occurred to me that I just wanted to convert him. Finally, an inner voice answered my question, *you like him, how complicated is that?*

After trying to call him at least ten times that day, I made a decision to go to Colorado Springs. The first flight from Lubbock to Denver left at 6:00 the next morning. Lacy was not interested in going and assured me she would be fine at home.

I packed and left for Lubbock in the late afternoon, stopping at Mom and Dad's to explain the situation. They were understanding and supportive. Even Dad expressed his concern about Ted.

After spending the night at a hotel close to the airport, I boarded my flight at 6:00 and was in Denver two hours later. I rented a car and was at Ted's house an hour and a half later.

I knocked on the door and nothing. Next, banging, but nothing. "Ted, it's me, open the door!" I yelled.

Through a crack in the door, he said, "I'm sorry Tommie. Please go away."

"No. You open this door, right now! You need help!" I yelled.

"No. You can't see me like this," he replied.

"Ted. Listen to me. Open this door or I'll break it down," I said, in a calm voice.

When he opened the door, I was amazed at what stood before me. Evidently, he hadn't shaved since leaving the hospital. He looked like a skeleton, with his clothes hanging on him. His eyes were bloodshot, which a whiff of liquor explained. He stepped back and going into the house it smelled terrible.

I followed him into the den and sat down after removing several liquor bottles. They were everywhere and the stench proved to be vomit.

"What's going on, Ted?"

He shrugged before answering, "I killed a girl. A beautiful sixteen-year-old girl. I killed her," he repeated.

"Tell me about it. Just tell me what happened," I said.

"I-I was exhausted. I had not slept in twenty-four hours. It-it was one surgery after another… nonstop. When she was scheduled, another doctor should have performed the operation. I was too stubborn and egotistical to admit that. Halfway through the surgery, it was evident that I could not continue, but it was too late. Another surgeon finished, but she died on the operating table. I hope the parents file charges against me. I should go to prison."

I didn't know what to say. It was impossible to imagine the agony he was going through. It had to be every surgeon's nightmare. One thing was evident, we had to get out of this house.

"Ted, listen to me. Go take a shower, put on clean clothes, and we're going out. Don't even consider arguing with me. Just do what I say." Somewhat surprised, he rose and left the room without saying a word.

While he was in the shower, out of hearing distance, I called the hospital and asked to speak to the administrator. When I told them my name, they put me through immediately.

"I'm with Ted," I explained. "I need some information about the last surgery. He's blaming himself for the girl's death."

"Thank you for calling. We're desperate. I wish I could help you with information about the surgery. The problem is that the surgeon who finished the operation will not comment one way or the other. He despises Ted, as most of the doctors do. His only comment has been, 'He got what he deserved'."

"That's horrible!" I exclaimed. "Surely, the man is more decent than to say something like that. Ted is suffering terribly. Do you believe he caused the girl's death?"

"Absolutely not. He would be better than most surgeons, performing blind. I believe it's only a case of revenge and jealousy. Everyone knows Ted is treated differently because of his skills. He is responsible for this hospital receiving a great amount of publicity."

"Can you give me the name of the surgeon who completed the operation?"

"I'll do better than that. I'll give you his name, phone number, and home address. Don't expect much cooperation from him."

"I'll see what I can do. Thank you."

While waiting for Ted to finish, I called the number of the surgeon, whose name was Dr. Loughton. He picked up on the fourth ring and immediately ended the call when I identified myself. This was not going to be easy.

When Ted came back into the room, he looked like a different person. He had shaved, put on clean clothes, and looked like his old self. I asked him, "When was the last time you had something to eat?"

"I don't remember. I've been drinking my meals."

"I can see that. We'll go out to eat and then come back here and clean up this mess," I said.

We ended up at the restaurant where he had taken me on our first date. He ate a decent meal, during which

I told him about life at the ranch. His response was polite but limited. I stayed away from his grief over losing a patient.

After finishing, we drove around, much like we did after Jack died. Again, the conversation was sparse, and we stayed away from the surgery. I did get some response from him, when I asked, "Are you coming back to the ranch for a visit this spring?"

"Would you allow me on your property after this?" he asked.

"Ted, that's ridiculous. Of course you'd be welcome. We're going to work through this, one way or the other. Right now, it's one thing at a time. We're going back and do some housecleaning."

Ted dropped me off at the hospital that afternoon. I wasn't going to leave him at home by himself. After he refused to accompany me inside, he agreed to drive around for an hour before he returned to pick me up.

I was able to catch Dr. Loughton after a nurse pointed him out to me. I walked up to him and introduced myself. "I need to talk with you a few minutes," I stated.

"I'm busy. I don't have time. I know what you're here about, and I have nothing to say on the subject."

"Are you willing to ruin a person's life?" I asked.

Without answering, he turned and walked off. On the way to the administrator's office I spotted a familiar face. "Hello, Nurse Houser."

"Tommie, what're you doing here?" she asked hugging me. "That's a dumb question. Of course, you're here for Dr. Adders. We've all heard about the trouble he's in. It's too bad, he's a different person after he met you. He's actually very likeable."

"Can you tell me any details about the surgery?" I asked.

"Not really. I get off in another thirty minutes. If you'll meet me in the lobby, we can visit with more privacy," she stated.

"Thank you," I responded.

While waiting for Nurse Houser, I had some time to think about what had occurred. It was strange that no one would speak up on Ted's behalf. Everyone agreed that he was a brilliant surgeon. Even if he did make a mistake, it would seem there would still be some empathy for him. The only explanation would be that he had created so much resentment and anger over the years that others were not willing to help him.

I had to wait the half hour plus another fifteen minutes for Nurse Houser. She arrived apologizing for being late.

"I'm sorry. My replacement was late and I couldn't leave. How is Dr. Adders doing?"

"He's suffering. Blames himself for the girl dying," I said.

"I'm not surprised. The nurse that was in the operating room heard Dr. Loughton say to Dr. Adders, 'It was your fault. You waited too late and botched the surgery. Now live with it.'"

"Did the nurse hear any kind of explanation from him about what Dr. Adders did wrong?" I asked.

"If she did, she didn't say?" she answered.

"Do you know Dr. Loughton?" I inquired.

Rolling her eyes, she responded, "Yes, most of the younger nurses know him well. He's married with three children, one of which is still at home. His wife is sweet."

"What do you mean when you say most of the younger nurses know him?" I asked.

"He's propositioned most of us and been turned down. He's constantly finding excuses to put his hands where they don't belong. Also, he's known for his off-color jokes. We all avoid him whenever we can."

"That's sexual harassment in the workplace. Why hasn't he been exposed?" I asked.

"He's a doctor. People around here think they're God. It would be his word against ours. It's easier to tolerate the harassment."

"Amazing. Would you consider filing a grievance?" I asked.

"Maybe, if some of the other nurses would also. Not by myself. I wouldn't have a chance."

"What kind of reputation does Dr. Adders have among the nurses?" I asked.

"Good. Especially since you came along. Of course, the single nurses are interested in him since he's an eligible bachelor; however, he shows no personal interest in the ladies that work here. It will be a great loss to this hospital and society if he doesn't practice again."

"How many nurses are you talking about that have been harassed?"

"I would say at least four for sure and maybe more." she said.

"Would you speak with them and see if they would join us? Be honest and tell them that we're trying to help Dr. Adders."

"I won't promise anything, but I'll try and see what can be done," she answered.

"I would appreciate that. This may be the only way we can find out the truth," I said.

Ted was waiting for me in the parking lot. On the way back to his house, I told him about talking to Nurse Houser. He was surprised when I explained Dr. Loughton's actions toward the nurses.

"I would never have guessed that. He has a wonderful family. I have met his wife and kids. He dislikes me, that I am sure of, but I've never done anything to him."

"Did he really tell you it was your fault the girl died?" I asked.

"Yes. He didn't mince words. On another matter, don't you need to get a hotel room for the night."

"Nope. I'm staying at your house. I'm not about to leave you by yourself," I stated.

"That will not look very good. People might talk."

"So? Let them talk. I can't believe you're in this situation and worried about what people will think about a lady staying at your house. You do have an extra bedroom. I'll just make myself at home there."

"I'm hungry again," he announced.

"We'll order pizza when we get to the house. After that, we'll find a movie on television and get your mind off your troubles."

I was up by six the next morning and had to make a run to the grocery store for breakfast items. When I returned, Ted was up and had made coffee.

"How do you feel?" I asked.

"I slept for the first time in a week."

"Here's your instructions this morning. I'm going to cook breakfast while you gather up some warm clothes. You're going to take me skiing today. I understand Loveland Ski Resort is less than a two-hour drive. We can make it easily by the time they open and be back by six this evening. I need to get some enjoyment out of this trip."

"I haven't skied in at least ten years," he said.

"No problem. You can stay on the bunny slopes."

"Is there any room for argument?" he asked.

Smiling, I replied, "What do you think?"

We had a large breakfast, consisting of bacon, eggs, and potatoes. We left immediately afterwards, and were at the ski area by 9:30, in time to rent our gear. An outfit to ski in was no problem for me. The boys and I always skied in our jeans, just spraying them with Scotch Guard. I had brought plenty of warm clothes, anticipating cold weather.

There has always been something about skiing that allowed me to put everything out of my mind. It was a gorgeous winter day with temperatures in the 20s and sunshine. Ted was truthful about not skiing for ten years. That was evident from the beginning, but he improved throughout the day and by evening was doing much better. We tried a black on our last run but halfway down Ted took a terrible fall, rolling over and over. When I reached him he was laughing. When I asked him if he was hurt, he replied, "Only my pride." Lying in the snow, laughing at himself, was just too much for me. Helping him up, when he was eye level, I kissed him. It surprised both of us.

"I need to fall more often," he said laughing again.

We made it down the mountain and called it a day. Both of us were exhausted, but on the way back to Colorado Springs, Ted was more talkative.

"I almost forgot my problems. I had also forgotten what it was like to have fun. Is there anything you can't do? You can ski with the best of them."

"Growing up with boys, I always did everything they did. Also, my dad was a gifted athlete and expected us to be as well. Thank you for the kind words," I said.

When we arrived in Colorado Springs, rather than going to Ted's house, we went directly to the hospital. He let me off at the door and said he would return in an hour.

Nurse Houser was working and it was no problem finding her. My first question after our greeting was, "Did you talk with the other nurses?"

"Yes. Three agreed but one refused, saying she didn't want to get involved. We're going to the hospital administrator in the morning. If you like, you're welcome to attend the meeting."

"Thank you. I'll be there. I appreciate your help."

The meeting was at 9:00 the next morning, but I was at the administrator's office an hour before that. He welcomed me and said we had time to visit before the meeting. He thanked me again for coming and looking after Ted.

"Are you aware of the purpose of the meeting with the nurses this morning?" I asked.

"Yes. Houser told me when she asked for the meeting. I had suspected this of Loughton but there wasn't any proof."

"Did you know that he told Dr. Adders that the girl's death was his fault? That's what upset him."

"No. I thought Adders was just blaming himself since he did the surgery."

"Dr. Adders started the operation but couldn't finish because of fatigue. Dr. Loughton finished the surgery," I explained. "Dr. Adders believed what Loughton told him."

"Well, I don't believe it. I would never believe Adders caused her death. We'll have an autopsy report soon, and I doubt if Loughton knew they were performing one. Most times that is not the case in an accident involving a teenager."

"We need to get the truth out of Loughton if it's possible," I said.

"Let's proceed in this manner. I'll talk to the nurses and then ask Loughton to come in. If what I suspect is true, I can pressure him into telling the truth about the surgery."

"Sounds good," I said.

The morning couldn't have gone any better. I left the hospital at noon, anxious to get back to tell Ted the news. Dr. Loughton had panicked when confronted by the nurses and the fact that an autopsy was going to be available. He admitted that the girl had died of a blood clot and had nothing to do with Dr. Adder's surgical procedures.

When Ted drove me to the airport the following morning, I was leaving a much happier physician, who was anxious to get back to work. He kept thanking me and finally, as I was about to go through the security check, I told him to stop.

"I saw you laugh on the slopes, and when I told you the good news, I'm sure there was a tear. That's all the thanks I need. Now are you going to kiss me bye or stand there looking like a school boy?"

CHAPTER 26

Zack

WITH SISSY HOME, I COULD rope again. The weather was still not agreeable, but it was less than a month until my first rodeo. It really put us in a bind when she was in Colorado Springs. We were already short-handed, and with her gone, it forced Mom to help Lacy on the North Ranch. The other hands continued to be down with the flu.

We would be through feeding by three in the afternoon and go to the practice pen. I didn't feel guilty about receiving help, knowing it was good for us to spend time together as a family. Scooter was proving to be awesome. I realized how fortunate I was to be able to afford a horse like him. My dad or my B-Boy could never have owned a horse like him when they were roping.

I was still, after all these years, awed by my dad, watching him rope. There is not a doubt in my mind that he could have been a world champion. I had mentioned team roping to him several times but he showed no interest. Maybe later he would reconsider.

Not an hour went by that I didn't miss Jack. A simple reminder, such as coming across one of his possessions in the tack room, would bring sadness and memories. Sometimes, especially around the barn, it seemed that I could feel his presence. It had been four months now since his death and waking up in the morning, but still being half asleep, I would think that he was still with us.

I never doubted that coming home was the right decision; however, at times, the idea of not pursing my dream of becoming a doctor would bother me. I would immediately put that aside, repeating to myself, *I did the right thing.*

What really frightened me was my feelings for Lacy that had never gone away. Jack being gone had nothing to do with it. From the time I was a small boy, I had adored her. Without doubt, she was meant for Jack and I had accepted that. The fact still remained, after all these years, that I cared deeply for her. I had never been in a serious relationship, blaming it on how busy I was, which I now realized was only an excuse.

I arrived in Bay City, Texas on Thursday, March 1, for my first PRCA Rodeo. They allowed participants who had a permit along with ones who already had their card. Being close to the Texas Coast, it was warm and humid, unlike the climate I had left. I found a place that had a hook-up, unloaded and tied my horses to the trailer, and went to enter. I didn't see anyone that I knew, which didn't surprise me. I let Roany out of the pickup when I took the horses to their stalls. She stayed right beside me.

That night, I didn't sleep much because of being nervous. I finally gave up and got up to make coffee at 4:00. While the coffee was making, I went to check on the horses. The stalls were empty, with both gates closed. I thought, this can't be right. I must have come to the wrong stalls; however, with both of their halters hanging on the fence, that was not the case. Panic hit me! Somebody had turned out my horses!

The barn had rows of stalls, and I started going up one and down the other. They were not in this barn! Who would have turned my horses loose? I didn't know anyone here. I went back to the trailer, realizing it would be futile to continue looking in the dark.

Daylight seemed to take forever to come. Taking Roany with me, we started scouring the grounds when first light shown. When the sun was full up, I started asking some of the people if they'd seen any loose horses. Everyone was nice, but their replies offered no encouragement. Suddenly, Roany took off in the direction of the entrance to the rodeo grounds. I followed at a run and what I saw literally scared me out of my wits. Both horses were in sight, but they had gone through the gate and crossed the highway. They were grazing in the ditch like they didn't have a care in the world.

I didn't breathe easy until I had them haltered and back across the busy highway. It was a miracle that one or both of them didn't get hit crossing. Back at the stalls, I realized that the slack would start in an hour, without even knowing my draw.

I went to the office immediately, discovering that my draw was number two. This time, when I left the stall riding Scooter, Roany remained with Cotton, my other horse.

When they called my name to rope, I thought, what will happen next? I had a little Brahma calf, and when I nodded for him, he left fast and immediately turned back, without giving me any chance of a loop. I rode out of the arena feeling discouraged and angry. When I arrived at my stalls, more trouble was waiting.

"Your damn dog bit me!" shouted a man who was accompanied by a lady, who I presumed was his wife.

I didn't respond immediately and he shouted again, "That dog bit me on the leg. I want something done to him!"

"Where were you when it happened?" I asked.

He didn't answer for several seconds. "I was looking at your horse."

"He needs to be put down. He's a dangerous animal!" the lady said.

"I'm sorry. She's protective of the horses. Can I see where she bit you?"

He pulled up his breeches leg and sure enough, teeth marks were evident; however, no blood was visible. "Has he been vaccinated for rabies?" he asked.

"Yeah. she's had all of her shots," I answered. Roany was lying in front of the stall, looking innocent.

"I tell you what. I've had a terrible day. Somebody turned my horses out last night. I found them across the highway, which still frightens me to think about it. I drew a bad calf that turned back on me. Now I come back to my stalls and my dog has bitten someone. I haven't had breakfast. Please go with me and it'll be my pleasure to have your company and pay for the meal."

Looking confused, they didn't answer. In a strict voice, I told Roany, "Get over there and apologize for biting this man!" She got up, with her tail between her legs and eased over to him. He held out his hand and she licked it. That was the game changer.

"We've had breakfast, but we'll let you buy us a cup of coffee. Maybe your day will get better," he said.

Their names were Allen and Janice and they lived in Matagorda. He was a fishing guide and she was a third grade teacher. Allen explained how they loved horses and planned on getting one soon. Janice wanted to learn to ride, and he was looking for a gentle horse for her to learn.

I, in turn, told them about the ranch and my goal to make it to the finals. We had a nice visit and when we were back at the stalls, I asked Janice, "Would you like to ride some today?"

"Oh, my, I'm not experienced at all. Is your horse gentle?" she asked.

"Cotton is gentle as they come."

"I would love to ride!" she said.

I went to the trailer, getting Lacy's barrel saddle for Janice. I saddled Cotton, and after she mounted, had her ride up and down the alley where our stalls were located. She did fine, and I told her to go wherever she wanted.

Allen and I visited while she rode. She would check by with us every hour or so, but she rode most of the day. I had never seen anyone so excited about riding a horse. It was something I had always done and taken for granted. When she finally was ready to quit, she thanked me over and over.

"We have this favorite seafood place. We would like for you to be our guest tonight," Allen offered.

I accepted the invitation and enjoyed the meal immensely. Of course, fresh seafood was not available in New Mexico, and the shrimp platter was delicious. When parting company, they assured me they would be at the slack the next morning.

The next day was much better. I drew a good calf that was fast but was no problem for Scooter. I was 8.5 and could hear Janice screaming encouragement. That was good enough to win the go-round and a check for $728, which surprised me. I was not disappointed in my first PRCA rodeo, even with some things going wrong. After all, new friends were made due to Roany, and I had won

$728 toward my card. Allen also invited me and my family for a fishing trip on the coast. I was going to make every effort to take him up on that offer.

It was a twelve hour drive back to the ranch. It was a long trip, but necessary, since there were few rodeos out my way this time of year due to the weather. After getting my card, I could attend some of the larger shows that didn't allow permits.

It was too late when I got home to go visit with Mom and Dad; however, I was there for breakfast the next morning.

"How did your horse work?" Dad asked.

"Great. He's awesome. Some guy wanted to buy him. I told him he wasn't for sale. You were right in telling me to buy him."

"Cotton was just along for the ride, I guess," he said.

"No. Not really." I then told him about Allen and Janice.

"Zack, you should be a politician," Mom said. "Who else could have made friends with someone their dog bit. Plus, you received an invitation to go fishing. Now, that's amazing."

I also told them about someone turning the horses out and finding them across the highway.

"Did you tell the officials in the office?" asked my dad.

"Yes. They said it was unusual but had happened before. They had no idea who would have done it."

"From now on, you better put locks on your stalls," Mom stated.

"On another subject, how are Sissy and Lacy?" I asked.

"Lacy's getting around better everyday on her new leg," Mom said. "Balance is still a problem but she's determined. She still hasn't gotten back on her barrel horses yet. Tommie thinks that will happen soon."

"Where are you going next?" Dad asked.

"Lubbock is the last of this month. There's several rodeos in East Texas and other states but that's too much travel. Maybe I can win enough in Lubbock to fill my card. This summer I can make some of the bigger rodeos up North. What chance is there of you making some of the shows with me?"

"The older I get, the less time I want to spend away from home," Dad said. "We might go with you to some of the closer ones here in New Mexico."

"Did you meet any girls at Bay City?" Mom asked.

"No. I wasn't really looking for any."

"You're not getting any younger, you know," she said. "It looks like, with all your free time between go-rounds, you could have met someone. You can't keep making the excuse of being too busy."

"Be patient, Mom. Somebody will come along eventually."

CHAPTER 27

Lexie

AFTER BO AND ZACK LEFT to feed, I thought of what Zack had said about someone coming along. Mothers know their children better than anyone and he wasn't fooling me. He hadn't shown interest in any girl because he had never gotten over Lacy. Now he was struggling with the fact that she was single again and feeling guilty for even thinking about her. He would never express his feelings toward her. I felt sorry for him. What a dilemma he faced.

Tommie had asked me to come to their place today. Lacy was going to ride for the first time with her prosthetic. She hadn't wanted Zack or Bo to be present, which was understandable.

When I arrived, they were saddling one of her barrel horses. I asked Lacy, "Shouldn't you start on something else that was more gentle?"

"That was my recommendation," Tommie stated.

"I'll be okay," Lacy announced.

She was able to mount by herself, and as she rode off toward the end of the arena, Tommie observed, "She lived with Jack long enough to inherit some of his stubbornness."

"We can hope for the best," I said. That didn't work out. The mare that Lacy was riding started acting up, and trying to control her, she lost her balance and fell off. By the time we reached her, she was up and crying.

"It's no use. I-I'm a cripple. I a-always will be."

Tommie grabbed her by the shoulders and shook her. "Listen to me! You need to be able to get your balance and use your prosthetic. Now, we're going to Mom's, and you're going to ride Cotton."

She continued to cry but didn't object. Tommie got on her horse and loped her around the arena until she calmed down. I was always amazed at how Tommie rode and could handle a horse. They seemed to know she was the boss.

After Tommie finished, they followed me to our place and for two hours Lacy rode Cotton around the arena. She trotted and then galloped and was able to stay on. By the time we unsaddled Cotton, she was all smiles, saying, "Both of you were right. I rushed it. I need to go slower until I get my balance. It's going to take time."

That day marked the beginning of an unbelievable recovery for Lacy Skinner. She never looked back, riding Cotton for a few weeks and then getting back on her barrel horses. One month later she won a 4-D barrel race in Andrews, beating a number of professionals. She had mastered the prosthetic and her balance had returned. Now, it remained to be seen if she would go back on the pro-rodeo circuit.

Zack was winning also. He gained his card by winning a go-round and placing in the average at Lubbock. He made several more rodeos in Texas and New Mexico before preparation for a pro tour that would take him all over the country. He planned to leave on the first of May and be gone for three weeks.

On Sunday, before he was to leave on Tuesday, we were at the barn helping him load his trailer when Tommie and Lacy drove up.

"Did you come to help us load?" I asked.

"No, not really," Tommie replied.

"You just came to watch?" I asked.

"Not really," Tommie repeated.

I stopped what I was doing and looked at her. "Well?"

"We want to go with him," she replied. "Winter's over and you can do without us. Lacy thinks she's ready to compete. I kinda agree with her. We'll just have to wait and see."

Everybody stopped what they were doing, with Zack asking, "Are you sure?"

"I'm positive," Lacy said. "That's what Jack would have wanted. If I fall off, I'll get back on. I want to make a run at it."

Nobody knew what to say. We remained silent until Bo spoke. "I'm proud of you, Lacy. Jack would be, also; however, it's up to Zack whether he lets you ride with him."

"Sure. You and Sissy are welcome company. I haven't been on the circuit before, and it will be good to have someone along who has," Zack said.

"It's settled then. We need to go home and start packing," Tommie said.

"We'll leave Tuesday morning. I'll pick you and your horses up at 8:00 and we'll head for Guymon, Oklahoma. The trailer only has so much room so pack light," Zack instructed.

Laughing, Tommie replied, "You're kidding, aren't you? What woman ever packed light for a three-week trip?"

We were at the barn when Zack pulled out Tuesday morning. Seeing him leave, I wondered how Bo and I were going to make it without Zack, Tommie, and Lacy here with us. As if reading my mind, he put his arm around me, saying, "We'll be okay, Little Girl. This is the best thing for them. Here at home, they're constantly reminded of Jack. On the road, their minds will be on the rodeos. It won't be easy but we'll get by. After all, we have each other."

Maybe that's why I loved him so much. He was always in control and most of the time, right. "Well, Cowboy, we've been through some tough times together and survived. I'm sure this time will be no different."

"I have a suggestion. Trout fishing is usually good at Bonita Lake this month. Let's see if we can have fish for supper tonight. What do you say?"

"I say that's a wonderful idea."

We left immediately, but the fish weren't biting and we spent the day lying in the sun on a beautiful spring day. Bo took his shirt off and suggested that I do the same, but I declined. He could have still been a model with his small waist, wide shoulders, and flat stomach. It seemed unfair that he still looked the way he did at fifty years old. It was a wonderful day, and since we didn't take a lunch, we were starved when we had supper in Ruidoso.

We arrived home to an empty house, with the realization that it was going to be that way for some time.

Beginning the next morning, I went with Bo each day, since Jimmy had decided to take the filly to the track. It was a wonderful time of year to be on the ranch. The cows were calving and each day we witnessed new life. I'd never become accustomed to how beautiful baby calves were. It was neat to see one cow with half a dozen calves around her because she was the designated babysitter.

One morning while we were on a tour of the ranch Bo asked me about the plans for the new house on the North Ranch. It was the first time we had spoken of it since we lost Jack. I think that we had both associated his death with the idea of moving back to the old place. Because of this, we hadn't mentioned it.

I don't know, Bo. I've put it out of mind. Do you still want to move?"

"I would like to if it's okay with you?" he answered in the form of a question.

"Sure. It's fine with me. We would be closer to Ms. Nancy and my dad. They'll need us eventually. I was thinking that Zack might move into our house after we leave. Do you think that's a possibility?"

"I have no idea. He hasn't mentioned going back to school, but it's not like him to quit anything. I can't see him spending his life here on the ranch, unless..." he stopped in mid-sentence.

"Go ahead and finish," I said.

"I can't. I can think it but I can't say it," he said.

"Okay, I'll complete the sentence for you...unless he marries Lacy," I said.

"It makes me feel bad to wish it would happen, Lexie."

"You shouldn't. We have to move on. I believe, in time, it might happen. Who knows? They're going to spend the next three weeks together."

"They may not be gone as long as we think. They were shut out at Guymon. Zack broke out both times and Lacy hit a barrel on her run. Funny though, when Zack called he didn't seem disappointed," Bo stated.

"Where's their next rodeo?" I asked.

"They're in Jasper and then they go to Crockett in East Texas. Texas has a number of the smaller rodeos this time of year. That's good for them before they make the big shows up North," he answered.

Several days later when we were finishing breakfast, Felicia called and wanted to visit. I knew what that meant. She needed me to do something, or she had a problem. My college roommate never called anymore just to visit. As the years went back we became farther and farther apart. I can't put my finger on the reason for this; however, Felicia had always been self-centered and instead of getting better she became worse with age. My only explanation for us becoming more distant was that she had her life and I had mine.

I told Bo to leave without me and come back by the house in a couple of hours. Surely we would be finished by then.

Felicia showed up shortly after Bo left. She probably watched for him to leave before coming. She was not his favorite person, thinking that her treatment of Jimmy could improve. Bo didn't hide his feelings well, and she was aware of them.

She came into the house talking, which was normal. "Lexie, I need to talk to you about several things. You always give me good advice."

"Sure, Felicia. What's on your mind?" As if I had to ask.

"Jimmy's going back to the track to train a horse. That means he will be gone most of the time. I don't like that one little bit. I told him so and he ignored me. Didn't even answer me. It made me furious. Now, I want to know what you would do in my situation."

I sat there a full minute, trying to get ahold of myself before responding. Jimmy was a wonderful husband and had done everything he could to please her for twenty-five years. He had forgiven her for having an affair and put up with her complaining all these years. He was a good provider, mainly because of his hard work and knowledge of horses. Now, here she was asking me what I would do. What infuriated me the most was she didn't even know what kind of person I was or she wouldn't ask me in the first place.

"Felicia, do you enjoy the house that y'all built several years ago?"

"Yes. I love my house. What's that got to do with my question?"

"Where did you get the money to build such a fine home?" I asked.

"Jimmy. We could never have built the home with the salary I make," she replied.

"Where did Jimmy get the money?" I asked.

She didn't answer immediately, looking confused. "He made good money when we first married," she finally answered.

"And that money, Felicia, came from his ten percent of the purse money that he received training my dad and Bo's horses. His share of the purse for the All American was $70,000. Now, you're complaining because he wants to go back to the track again. Bo's been good to Jimmy. They've been friends most of their lives. He pays him very well, and lets him run some cows of his own; however, even thought Bo wouldn't admit it to anyone, Jimmy is an employee of this ranch.

I had to take a deep breath before I could continue. "Jimmy was hurt when that filly bucked him off. Bo told me later that he expected Jimmy to go back to the track. He's fifty years old, Felicia, and ranch work is hard work. I doubt if Jimmy wants to be doing that kind of work ten years from now. Maybe when he didn't answer you he expected you to understand. Now, I told you what I think and you probably don't like it. The most fortunate day in your life is when you married Jimmy Light."

"So, that's your advice?" she said.

"I'm not finished. Think about Jimmy for once. Go with him to the track occasionally. Spend the day with him. See what a gift he has with horses. Encourage him, praise him, and be interested in what he's doing. If he goes to Sunland for the Fall Meet, go with him. You have nothing to keep you home."

"That's not what I expected you to say," she said, looking at the floor.

"Look, Felicia, we've been through a lot. You were there for me when I messed up, and I was there for you when my brother was killed. We've been friends too long to lie to one another. I told you what I believe, not what you wanted to hear."

"This is too much for me now. I have another problem I wanted to ask you about, but it can wait until later," she said, getting up and leaving.

CHAPTER 28

Bo

THE KIDS CAME IN FROM their trip on May 21. I still thought of them as kids and always would. It proved to be a long three weeks without them. While they were gone, I tried to stay busy, and a good result was that me and Lexie spent a lot of time together. Jimmy had taken the filly to the track in Ruidoso and was away from the ranch most days. Lexie filled in for him, and we had no problem looking after things since spring was here. With the winter moisture, we had early grass, but we still needed to put out feed since the cows were calving.

They returned in good spirits and it was evident that the trip had done them good. Zack had limited success but was able to make the short go in several rodeos. Lacy was a different story, winning several shows and placing in all of them but Guymon. Lexie had them over for supper on the Monday they returned. They had good stories, and we seemed to be healing as a family. Tommie gave us her description of the trip before anyone else was able to talk.

"Dad, you wouldn't believe how well Lacy did. She was amazing. Her horses worked well and it's hard to imagine, but she only hit one barrel the entire trip. Zack was another matter. I tried to help him, but he didn't listen. He relied too much on Scooter's speed and didn't push the barrier. He made good runs, but he roped too far down the arena. A time or two, I thought he wasn't coming out of the box. Maybe he'll listen to you. Now, do you have any questions?"

I couldn't help but laugh at the conversation. It seemed that we had turned the clock back at least fifteen years. Tommie had always wanted to coach the boys whether they wanted it or not.

"Would it be all right, Sissy, if I said something in my defense?" Zack asked.

"Sure, but you know I'm right," she replied.

"I didn't draw well, Dad. It just seemed that I always had the fastest calf in the pen. Scooter has tremendous speed, and I kept thinking I didn't need to push the barrier."

Lexie entered the discussion saying, "Zack, I believe this family calls that 'scared money'." That brought another round of laughter.

"I'll take up for Zack. He didn't draw well," stated Lacy.

"Who did the cooking on the trip?" Lexie asked.

"Sissy did most of it. Since we're critiquing the trip, let me say the food was mediocre at best," Zack said. "I got tired of Hamburger Helper and Sloppy Joes. Sissy didn't get her cooking talents from Mia or Mom."

It was wonderful to hear the back and forth banter between Tommie and Zack. The conversation turned more serious after that.

"Did you have any problems?" I asked. Both Lacy and Tommie looked at Zack.

"Well, let's hear it," Lexie demanded.

Silence followed, until Tommie finally said, "We had one bad experience. It happened at a rodeo in South Texas. Zack had helped Lacy in the alley, since her horse always acted crazy. After the run, Lacy was riding back to the trailer and a cowboy made a terrible remark to her.

Zack was following and heard the comment. It took three of the cowboy's friends to pull Zack off him. Do I need to go any further?"

"I can take up for myself," Lacy said. "It wasn't necessary for Zack to get involved. He thinks I'm an invalid because I only have one leg."

"That's not true. He said something horrible to you. J…Dad would have done the same thing I did if he had been there," Zack exclaimed.

I didn't like the direction this was going, so I said, "If that's the only problem you had during the three weeks, then you were fortunate."

I continued, "We'll go right to work on scoring calves and getting out. I bought fresh stock while you were gone. How long do you have before you leave to go up North?"

"A couple of weeks," he answered.

"That'll give us enough time. The weather has been nice so we can get a lot of work in," I said. "Tommie, are you and Lacy going with him?"

"I don't know, Dad. I enjoyed the trip and was able to stay busy. I held an early Sunday morning service at each of the rodeos, and after word got around, the attendance was good. Many of the families told me they missed going to church at home and appreciated this opportunity."

She continued, "The problem is that Zack sleeps in the pickup. I told him there was room in the trailer, but he wouldn't listen. It makes Lacy and I feel bad."

"I do fine in the pickup. The seat leans back and I sleep fine. Besides, I have Roany with me and she sleeps good too," Zack said.

Zack continued, "I'll be gone the month of June and July and it would be nice to have company. After all, who's going to coach me if Sissy's not along."

"I'd like to go if Tommie does," Lacy announced.

"I guess that settles it. Maybe Zack can take a cot this time and sleep in one of the trailer stalls since it will be warm weather," Tommie suggested.

It was a pleasant evening and besides the awkwardness involving Zack's confrontation everything was positive. Zack almost slipped and said Jack would have done the same thing as he did. He caught himself in time, which was good.

I didn't know what we would do without them for two months. One thing for sure, we would make at least one of their rodeos and maybe more.

The next day I drove into Ruidoso to visit with Carl. He was set up in his new office and Lexie had been one of his first customers. I had remained determined not to use Lexie's money for the ranch. I had been able to make it profitable, due to the fact that I didn't have any land payments. We still argued about it occasionally but not as often as we used to. I was happy with my life and had everything I wanted. My pickup was four years old but still in good condition.

Lexie had set up trusts for Jack, Zack, and Tommie that had become available when they reached twenty-one. Of course, Jack's went to Lacy after his death. I wasn't sure how much money was involved but it was considerable. The further I stayed away from it, the better, was my thinking.

My reason for visiting with Carl was purely personal. I enjoyed reminiscing about our college days and football. Anticipating the kids being gone for two months motivated me to think I needed a distraction.

Going through the front door of Carl's office, I was greeted by the secretary. "Mr. Skinner, how are you today?"

"Good. Is Carl busy?"

"Mr. Skinner, I like my job. If I didn't interrupt him immediately to see you, I would be unemployed mighty quick."

Carl and I visited for an hour and then went to lunch. The change in him was amazing. Even his appearance conveyed more confidence and self-assurance. He was more talkative, and we actually had a two-way conversation. We replayed several football games that occurred thirty years ago, and it was surprising how much detail we remembered.

I left the restaurant feeling better about everything. The more time that elapsed, the more I enjoyed the memories of my years at Texas State. I assume that was something that just goes along with age.

On the drive home, I thought about what Lexie had told me about her visit with Felicia. I would never understand her and why she couldn't appreciate Jimmy for the good husband that he was. After knowing him all these years, he was still one of the best men I'd ever known.

Poco, their adopted son, was a good hand and had proven to be a valuable asset to the ranch, splitting time between the North and South Ranch. Lexie had been determined that he attend at least two years of college but neither Jimmy or Felicia would force the issue.

Their daughter, Jolynda Kay, was in college, but from what Lexie said, was not doing well. She was the image of her mother, not only favoring her in appearance, but talking constantly and being dramatic.

I was glad Jimmy had gone back to the track. He was a gifted horseman, and this filly had shown great potential. I was convinced that no one could do as good with her as Jimmy. Tom and I still were partners in the racing even though we had tapered off the last several years. He still enjoyed the racing and was excited about Jimmy taking over the training.

When I was alone, I couldn't help thinking of Jack. A kind of deep sadness would come over me and depression would set in. The only cure was to be around other people and stay busy. I had talked with Lexie about it, and she assured me the same was true for her. I usually felt better after sharing my feelings. I continued to hope that it would be possible to recall memories of him without sadness. Maybe with time that would happen.

For the next two weeks we roped every day, even on Sunday after church. We used the barrier, which we had not been doing previously. We moved the score from short to medium to long, since at most rodeos it would be different. I emphasized to Zack that the competition, at this level, would force him to push the barrier. Certainly he'd break out occasionally, but that was part of it.

During breaks, I had the opportunity to talk with him about his future plans. On one occasion he was especially talkative.

"Do you plan on going back to school and finishing your medical degree?" I asked.

"Probably. I'm not sure when, though. It's been good taking some time off. The last six years have been hard, and it's been positive to be relieved of the pressure that pre-med majors are constantly under. I haven't lost the desire to become a doctor. I think often of Dr. Sadler and what he meant to this family and community."

He continued, "I'm still amazed at Sissy and how she finds ways to help people. She not only did a devotional on Sunday mornings at the rodeos we attended, but also, people continually came by our trailer to share their problems with her.

I feel guilty, Dad, but I had fun on the trip. Lacy appeared to enjoy herself, also. Maybe that's not right;

however, that's being truthful. It would be hard for me to imagine Jack not wanting us to enjoy ourselves. She's awesome, even with her handicap. There's no doubt in my mind that she will be back at the finals next year. Of course, she got too late a start this year and missed some of the big shows."

I listened without interrupting. It was obvious that Zack was facing a tough dilemma. Lexie and I had visited about it more than once.

"Do you have any advice for me?" he asked.

"No, Zack. I'm proud of you. Whatever you do in the future, I'll support it. You've always made good decisions. I've never told you, but I appreciate you taking time off to come home. It's been hard, but having you and Tommie here has made it bearable."

"Changing the subject, Dad, but I thought you might take up team roping. It has become immensely popular."

"No. Probably not. I should never have talked it down to you and Jack. It's a good sport for those that enjoy it. I just happen to be one of those people who don't care for it. I won't give you a hard time if you decide it's something you would like to do," I said.

"Well, anyway, Dad, I would like to rope just half as good as you do."

Laughing, I said, "Now you're just trying to make an old man feel good."

CHAPTER 29

Tommie Rose

THE TRIP TO TEXAS HAD been a success, as far as I was concerned. Lacy had done well, becoming more confident with each run. Zack would do better with the work that Dad had been providing. I was glad that Zack wanted us to go with him on the next trip. Of course, it was because of Lacy. I didn't know if she was aware of that or not.

Ted had continued to call me several times a week. He was doing well and wanting me to come to Colorado for a visit. I told him we would be in his vicinity within the next few weeks. I still didn't have a grip on my feelings about him. I enjoyed his company and respected his ability as a surgeon. I kept thinking that maybe I was only impressed with his reputation and the fact that he was attracted to me. Was he attracted to me? Maybe......maybe not? He hadn't made any physical advances indicating that he found me desirable. What if he only wanted a female friend? That might explain why he never touched me, appropriately or inappropriately. The only time he kissed me, I told him to. Now I sounded like a junior high girl. Smiling, I thought maybe George Strait would be my only true love.

I had been spending more time at Mia and Gramps' place. I asked him how he was doing on my last visit, like I always do.

"I'm doing okay, Tommie. It's not possible to do much now, in my condition. I watch a lot of television, especially the news programs, which is depressing. There's some bad people out there and it worries me. Of course, the media reports on all the terrible events that happen."

As he talked, my heart reached out to him. It was evident that he wasn't doing well. After his bout with the flu, he remained weak and was on oxygen twenty-four hours a day. Mia was still able to take care of him. There would come a day when she would need additional help. He was still alert, and his mind was as sharp as ever.

"How long are you staying before returning to Africa?" he asked.

"I had only planned to stay one year. Now, I don't know. I feel bad about leaving to go on this trip with Zack and Lacy; however, she's still fragile and, of course, wouldn't go without me. Mom and Dad seem to be doing better. I guess that's my justification for leaving for two months. I may extend my stay on the ranch past the one year. I've spent five years caring for others and neglecting my family. They need me now, and I won't leave until they have at least partially recovered from losing Jack."

"Bo and Lexie will be fine while you're gone this summer," Mia said. "It's Lacy I worry about the most. You're dong the right thing."

"I hope so," I replied.

"Tommie, I've not known you to make a wrong decision many times in your life. In fact, I can't think of one," said Gramps.

"Changing the subject, Gramps, but tell me about your race filly that Jimmy is training."

"She's beautiful, Tommie. She's a granddaughter of the first mare that Bob and I purchased. She has all the attributes of a runner. Jimmy thinks so, too. I'm pleased that he's agreed to train her. Nobody can get as much out of a horse as he can. We're not going to start her until the trials for the All American. Racing has been one of the joys of my life, and I owe it all to your B-Boy, who I still miss."

"Maybe we'll be home to see the trials," I said.

"When are you leaving?" Mia asked.

"This Friday we're going to make the Pioneer Days Rodeo in Clovis, but we'll come home after the weekend. Mom and Dad are going to Clovis to watch the rodeo. They're excited about getting to watch Zack and Lacy compete. On Tuesday, we're headed for Reno to one of the largest PRCA Rodeos in the country. It's the second week in June, and Zack has our schedule all planned. Before we leave, I'll get you a list of the rodeos we're going to make. He's picked out the ones that have the largest payout. Of course, the competition will be stiff."

I stayed and visited awhile longer, and leaving, promised to see them before we started our trip. It was Wednesday, and we were leaving for the Clovis rodeo on Friday. We wouldn't be back until late Sunday, which meant I would only have Monday to pack for the two-month trip. I should start now to give me plenty of time. I would try to prepare a more diversified menu this time since my chef marks had been low on the Texas trip.

We left for Clovis after lunch, since Zack was up in the show that night. He would rope again in the slack Saturday morning, and if he made the short go, in the Sunday afternoon performance. Lacy only received one run in the barrels and that was in the Saturday night performance. Mom and Dad assured us they would be there to watch Zack Friday night.

On the drive to Clovis, I asked Zack, "How do you think you'll rope tonight?"

"Better," was his short answer.

"You going to get out good?" I asked.

"You just watch and see," he replied sharply.

"How do you feel about your run tomorrow night, Lacy?" I asked.

"Okay, I guess. It's a big pen, so I'll ride Jazzy. My mom and that man are coming. I wish she'd leave him at home. When I lived with them, all he did was lay around, watch television, and eat. I guess that's the reason he gained so much weight."

"Your mom will enjoy watching you ride," I stated.

"I guess so. I should have more patience with her. She does care about me, but it's just that Roy is always with her."

The three-hour drive seemed short, with all of us sharing stories about our high school rodeo days. Lacy actually opened up and talked about some of her experiences. I was pleased that she was able to talk about the past. That was a step forward in the mourning process.

We arrived, found a place to park our trailer, and while Zack and Lacy went to check in and pay their entry fees, I unloaded the horses.

They came back talking about some of their friends they had seen. "How did it go?" I asked.

"Good. There are only ten roping in the show tonight and I drew the fourth slot. Lacy is running tomorrow night. She's running second with nine other entries."

"The saddles are beautiful," Lacy said. "I'd like to take one home with me."

"We have stalls, so let's go put our horses up," Zack suggested.

We had only brought two horses. Zack was going to ride Scooter and Lacy, Jazzy. Personally, I liked her other horse better. He was a gelding and wasn't as fast, but he had a lot more sense. Also, he was beautiful, with four stocking legs. His name, Chrome, fit him perfectly.

Mom and Dad arrived before the rodeo began, and she called me to find out where we were parked. When they exited their car, I thought, what a beautiful couple. My dad had on his jeans and his usual white shirt and black hat. Mom had on jeans, also, and a red western shirt with white fringe. I had no doubt but what my dad could enter and win the roping.

"Mom, you look gorgeous," I said.

"Thank you, Tommie. I feel younger when I come to a rodeo. That's strange, isn't it?"

"Dad, you look handsome," I stated.

"You wouldn't be a little biased, would you?" he asked.

"No. Not one bit. How was your trip?"

"It was okay, after we got off. I had to wait on your mother. I thought we might miss the rodeo," he said.

"Are you going to ride in the grand entry?" Mom asked.

"Yes, I think both of us will," replied Zack. "In fact, we need to go saddle our horses."

After they left, Mom asked me, "How's Lacy doing?"

"She's doing great, Mom. She looks beautiful, doesn't she?"

"Yes, however, I was afraid attending a local rodeo might bring back memories that would be difficult for her," she replied.

"That doesn't seem to be the case at all," I responded.

"Let's go get a seat and watch the grand entry," Mom suggested.

Of course, we found them in the grand entry and Lacy was having problems controlling her mare. Zack riding close to her, grabbed the bridle and snubbed the mare up to his horse until she settled down.

My dad didn't join us in the stands. He was hanging out at the roping chute to push Zack's calf for him. The tie-down roping was the third event, following the bareback bronc riding and the steer wrestling.

By the time they were loading the calves, Mom said, "Some things never change, Tommie. I'm a nervous wreck. I would like to hide my eyes and let you tell me what happened. I hope Zack has a good run."

She had nothing to worry about. Zack got out good, roped his calf, and was 8.8, which took the lead. Both of us were jumping up and down, screaming. That was one reason Dad would never sit with us. We watched the last five ropers and the second best time was a 9.5. We left the stands and met Dad and Zack at the trailer.

Bo was beaming and Zack was all smiles. "What'd you think, Sissy?"

"Little Brother, you did good. For once you listened to me."

"Zack won the first go. I checked on the morning slack and his time was better than any of them. Now, if he has a good run in the morning, we'll make the short go," Dad said.

Zack's time the next morning was 9.2 which was good enough for a third and assured him a spot in the short go. It was nice weather, and we spent the day sitting outside the trailer visiting with friends who came by. It was amazing how many people we knew from high school rodeo and even before then.

Lacy decided not to ride in the grand entry that night. I offered to warm up her horse but she declined, saying she would be fine. She did say her mom and Roy had not shown up, which didn't bother her at all. The barrel race was the next to last event, and she had drawn the two spot.

When it was time for the event, Zack went to the alley to help her with the mare. When her name was called, I could see that she was going to have trouble. The mare refused to go in the alley. Zack would try to lead her in and she would whirl and not face the barrels. Zack finally got her turned toward the barrels and let her go. She reared straight up on her hind legs before leaving the alley. My breath caught in my throat, as I noticed that Lacy had lost her right stirrup. I yelled as loud as I could, *pull him up, pull him up! Stop your run, Lacy!* Of course, she couldn't hear me and it wouldn't have made any difference if she had. She made the first barrel, and I could see she was trying to find her stirrup with her foot. On the second barrel her weight would be shifted to her artificial leg. She made the second barrel and I prayed, *just one more.* Her mare was flying when she reached the barrel, and it was just too much. She fell off as the mare was turning. Mom screamed and I was out of the stands, over the fence, and running to her. Zack beat me and was bending over her when I arrived.

"Lacy, Lacy, can you hear me?" he asked.

She opened her eyes, looking confused, and said, "I fell off, Jack." Then lost consciousness.

By this time Dad was there, yelling, "Bring an ambulance."

The ambulance was there quickly and within ten minutes, we were in the emergency room at the hospital. She was still not conscious when she was taken in on a stretcher.

Several other friends of ours had followed us to the hospital and were in the waiting room. One of them asked, "Is that mare always that crazy?"

"Sometimes, sometimes not," I responded. "You never know what she'll be like. I should have insisted that she let me warm her up."

A doctor came out after twenty minutes or so and said, "She's going to be fine. I don't think she has a concussion. She has no broken bones, but it would be a good idea to leave her overnight. She should be fine to leave in the morning. She's a brave lady to ride with a prosthesis. You can go in and see her if you like."

We gathered around the table she was lying on and I said, "We're thankful that you're not hurt badly."

"I fell off. It's no use," she said with tears rolling down her checks.

"Any of us would have fallen off with only one stirrup," I said.

"No. I need two legs, not only that, I was in front of all my friends. I don't want their pity. Now, please leave. I just want to be alone."

Mom, Dad, and I told her we loved her and left. Zack stayed behind, and we waited for him in the lobby.

When he came out, he said, "She doesn't want any company but I'm staying. When they move her to a room, maybe she'll let me stay with her. She needs somebody. Maybe I'll do. She called me Jack when she was still out of it. I know she misses him terribly, just like all of us."

The next morning when I returned to the hospital, Zack was in her room and Lacy appeared to be asleep. "How'd it go?" I asked.

"Okay. They gave her a sedative and she slept. I don't know if she even knew I was here."

"Yes, I knew you were here," Lacy said, evidently not being asleep after all. "I'm ready to leave this place."

A doctor came in before we could respond. "You ready to go home?" he asked.

"Definitely," she answered.

He did a quick examination, including a blood pressure check, and released her. Zack waited outside while she dressed, and after checking out and paying the bill, we were back at the trailer by 9:00. I was scheduled to conduct a devotional at 10:00 but had prepared my presentation the night before.

Lacy informed us she was staying in the trailer and not attending my devotional. I was disappointed but didn't respond. Zack, Mom, and Dad did attend, and it went even better than I expected. I talked about my experiences in Africa and the many needs that were not being met. Some of my stories were sad but some encouraging and uplifting. Before I finished, I asked that an offering be taken up to be given to the mission that I served in Africa. I was surprised that the offering amounted to over $900. Several people came up after the service and asked for the address of the mission to enable them to make further donations.

When I returned to the trailer, Lacy was still there. She informed me she wasn't attending the rodeo that afternoon. I didn't press the issue, but of course, Zack would be disappointed. I didn't know what to do. All the progress of the last several months had been eliminated with one incident.

The rodeo started at 2:00 and the roping was the third event. They had taken the top eight to the short go, with Zack having the second best average on two calves. He was roping next to last. Mom was keeping track of the times, and when his name was called, she said he needed a really good run to win.

Zack had drawn a good calf that ran straight but was fast. He got out good and Scooter's speed was amazing, putting him on the calf quickly. Zack's loop was true, and he was down the rope and tied the calf in 7.9. We celebrated; then held our breath as the last roper rode into the box. He made a nice run but was not fast enough to overcome Zack.

"Tommie, if I had not known it was your brother, I could easily have taken him for Bo. They move so much alike."

"I know, Mom."

We were waiting on them at the trailer when they arrived, with Zack carrying his new saddle. We hugged and congratulated him, with there being no way he could hide his excitement. Dad didn't try to hide anything, reminding me of B-Boy when he was excited.

Lacy didn't come out of the trailer, and when we loaded the horses and prepared to leave, she announced she was riding home with Mom and Dad.

On the way home, Zack and I talked about our problem. "We can't leave for Reno Tuesday," I stated.

"No way," he replied.

"What do you suggest?" I asked.

"Postpone our trip, at least until Lacy recovers, if she does. We might want to consider making the smaller rodeos in Texas this summer. There's a slew of them during July. We could even come home in between rodeos. That would also allow Mom and Dad the opportunity to attend a number of them. Were you surprised at Lacy's reaction?"

"Zack, I was more than surprised. I knew she was fragile but didn't expect that kind of setback. I don't know what to expect next. Your suggestion about the change to rodeos in Texas is realistic under the circumstances."

I continued, "Something else has come up. I received a call on my cell yesterday from Daniel Lester. Getting me on my phone was a miracle in itself. He oversees the mission I served in South Africa. Maybe it was more than a coincidence that it came before my description of the time spent in Africa. He has two new missionaries, and they are experiencing all kinds of difficulties. The people aren't accepting them, and they're frustrated. He's afraid of losing both of them."

"What does that have to do with you?" he asked.

"Simple. He begged me to come back for a couple of weeks to help them adjust and get acquainted with the population. I told him it was impossible to leave now. He was disappointed but said that he understood."

"Now, you're thinking that it might be feasible?" he asked.

"Right. I would be back in time for the July rodeos."

"What about Lacy?" he asked.

"That's the problem. I'll need to think on it some more before I make a decision.

Nothing was simple. Zack had a good weekend and Lacy's reaction to falling off her horse had diminished it. Hopefully, when we were home, and I had a chance to talk with her, the incident could be put in its proper perspective. Surely she would realize it was only a setback.

CHAPTER 30

Lacy

NOBODY REALLY UNDERSTOOD. I WANTED to be left alone, and they kept trying to say everything would be okay. It was not going to be okay and never would be. I would never get over losing Jack and yesterday brought it all back. I needed him and no one could take his place. I fell off my horse in front of people who had been my friends since starting to rodeo. They probably laughed at how ridiculous it was for a one-legged person to run barrels. If they didn't laugh at me, they felt sorry for me, which was worse.

On top of that, my mother didn't even come to watch me. I didn't like to admit it, but I loved her. After all, she was my only family. I expected her to be there with Roy, who I detested. He had made improper advances toward me during my junior year in high school. I never told anybody but instead gave him a good cussing.

I rode home from Clovis with Bo and Lexie, not wanting to hear a lecture from Tommie. They took me home, and when Tommie came in, I was already in my room. She didn't attempt to talk to me and I went to bed early, wanting to put the weekend out of my mind.

The next morning Tommie didn't mention the rodeo. She asked me what my plans were for the day. "Just stay home and maybe read a book. I still have some of the ones Mia gave us."

"I have a suggestion, Lacy. Zack and I agreed that the trip to Reno is off. Let's take off for a couple of weeks and not ride. In fact, I've decided to go on a trip, and I would like you to accompany me. We wouldn't be gone but a couple of weeks, and it would be interesting for you."

"Where?"

I described the call from Daniel Lester asking me to come to Africa for two weeks to help two of the new missionaries adjust to their responsibilities. I assured her we would return in two weeks.

"First of all, I don't plan on running barrels again. I would rather just stay here at home and maybe help out on the ranch. If my mother cares for me at all, I would probably go home. Why would I want to go to Africa?"

"It would be a great trip. You would see a country which is fascinating, and people who live differently than we do. Plus, I would like your company on the trip. You would be doing me a favor by accompanying me."

"I'd like to think about it."

"That's fine, but I need to know something by Wednesday."

I went back to my room to find a book to read and was startled when my phone went off. I saw the call was from my mother. Taking a deep breath, I answered, "Hello."

I couldn't understand what she was saying. She was crying and trying to talk. "Mother, calm down. What is it?"

"I'm hurt. I need help. Come home, please," she begged.

"What's the matter? Tell me what's wrong!"

"Please, Lacy. I need you."

"Okay, I'm leaving now."

I caught Tommie before she left and told her about the call. "I'll go with you to see about Alejandra," she said.

We stopped in front of the ranch house two hours later, and Tommie went with me to the door. I rang the doorbell and she opened it quickly. If I had not been expecting my mother, I wouldn't have recognized her. Her face was bruised and swollen. She had the beginnings of two black eyes and her lip was busted. She was wearing a housecoat and her hair was a mess. Her eyes were red and filled with tears when she told us to come in.

We sat down in the den and she said, "Thank you for coming. I look terrible as you can see. I'm sorry for having to call you. I have no transportation and there was no one else to ask for help."

"What happened to you?" I asked.

"It happened Saturday. We had planned on coming to the rodeo to watch you that night. Roy started drinking that morning and continued throughout the day. He decided we weren't going to the rodeo. I told him that I was going by myself and he went ballistic, accusing me of wanting to see Bo. When I tried to leave he stopped me. I tried to get away from him but he hit me, more than once. I thought he might kill me. He finally left, taking the keys to the other vehicle, so I've been here ever since. I hope he's left for good."

"Can you tell how badly you're hurt?" Tommie asked.

"I'm in constant pain, especially my side. It hurts me to take a deep breath, also. I have at least one broken tooth. I know I look terrible," she said again.

"Lacy, if you'll help her get cleaned up, I'll call Diane and we'll take her to Ruidoso. She can examine her injuries and determine how serious they are."

"Okay," I said. "Mother, is that what you want to do?"

"I have no other choice," she replied.

It took an hour to help her shower, fix her hair, and try to cover up some of the bruises with makeup. I kept insisting that we needed to get to the doctor and she didn't need to worry about how she looked. My argument was futile and when we left, she did look much better.

The shortest route back to Ruidoso was through Cloudcroft. On the drive, she apologized several times for not coming to the barrel race. When she asked me how I did, I told her what happened. As I was describing my run, it didn't seem as devastating now. Maybe seeing what my mother had gone through was the reason. Roy was the scum of the earth, which I already knew. This only proved it further.

I asked her if this had ever happened before. She hesitated before replying. "Not this bad." I didn't know whether to believe her or not. It dawned on me that Roy was the reason Mother and I had drifted so far apart. It made me feel better knowing that she had planned on coming to the rodeo.

Arriving, we only waited a few minutes in the doctor's office before Diane was able to see Mother. Tommie and I remained in the waiting room until summoned a half hour later. Diane asked to talk to us in her office while Mother waited in the exam room.

"Alejandra took a terrible beating. She has bruised ribs, facial bruises, and will need to see a dentist as soon as possible. It's hard to believe a man would do that to his wife. She doesn't need to be alone for a few days. Is there anywhere she can stay?"

"Sure. She can go home with us," Tommie said.

"What about Lexie?" I asked.

"Mom will understand," she replied.

I wasn't so sure about that, I thought.

There was a pickup in front of my house when we arrived at home. Mother announced that it was Roy. He came over as we were getting out and told Mother he needed to talk to her. I expected her to refuse; however, she motioned for us to go inside and she stayed behind. I watched through the window for an hour as they exchanged words. It was evident Roy was doing some fast talking, many times making hand gestures to emphasize his point. The longer the conversation went, the calmer it became.

Mother came back in the house, informing us she was going home with Roy. Shocked, I responded, "You're not serious? After what he's done to you?"

"I have no choice, Lacy. You know how Lexie feels about me. I can't stay here and cause trouble for you. Roy is all I have. That's sad, but true. My choice of men has been terrible and no one is to blame but me. Roy has promised that it won't happen again."

"Mother, you're a beautiful lady. Surely you could find someone that treats you with respect and affection."

"I've made other bad decisions, also. I didn't have Roy sign a prenuptial agreement, and he wouldn't leave without a major battle."

"Give him enough money to agree to a divorce," I suggested.

"Oh, me, Lacy. Another problem is the ranch. Roy's treatment of our ranch hands caused all of them to quit. After that, we sold our cattle and now have little income. I promised Mom and Dad to keep the ranch intact, so selling a part of it is out of the question. We're going to have some income next year. I leased the hunting rights to a group out of Dallas."

"Mother, Granddad and Grandmother would understand. Sell part of the ranch and get rid of this bum before he hurts you again or worse. Ask him how much it would take for him to agree to a divorce and get out of your life."

"You believe that my mom and dad would be okay with breaking my promise?" she asked.

"Without doubt. At least go see a lawyer and tell him your situation."

"I'm going to give him one more chance before doing that," she said.

There was not any use in arguing. She had made up her mind, and all I could feel was pity for her. She left, and as they drove away, I thought, Roy will never change.

I agreed to go on the trip with Tommy. I couldn't refuse after she had helped me with my mother. It wasn't something I looked forward to but more of an obligation to Tommie.

We left Thursday morning, June 7, and drove to Lubbock. From Lubbock, we boarded a flight to Denver. From Denver, we flew ten hours to Munich, arriving on Friday. The flight to Johannesburg was another ten hours, and we arrived on Saturday. I hadn't considered how long we would be in the air, and was a nervous wreck when we arrived. Compounding the frustration was that at each security point I had to remove my prosthesis because of the metal. I hadn't flown in years and was amazed at the security in the airports.

We were met by Daniel Lester at the Johannesburg airport. He was a small Black man with a huge smile. He hugged Tommie and shook my hand as he greeted us. He spoke with an accent but was easy to understand. "Thank you for coming, Missy Tom. We are in need of your services." I would not hear her addressed any other way except Missy Tom while we were in Africa.

He showed us to a parking lot where his twenty-year-old pickup was parked. After seeing it, I hoped we weren't going far. It was only a single cab, so we crowded in and began our trip. Driving through the city, I was surprised at how modern everything looked. Nice cars were abundant, and people didn't seem that much different from a city in the United States. Most were dressed neat and some of the men were wearing suits and ties. It was winter here and Tommie had warned me to bring warm clothes even though the climate was mild. Today, it was cool but comfortable with my long sleeve blouse and a light jacket.

I'm not good with directions, but we seemed to be going northwest when we left the city. We were on a paved road for half an hour, then turned more west on a dirt road. Tommie and Daniel were talking about the mission, and I was left out of the conversation. Finally, I asked Tommie how far we had to go.

"Lacy, it's a rural area about 150 miles from Johannesburg. We'll be driving at least five hours, so get as comfortable as possible."

Five hours, I thought! I can't ride cramped up for that long. Of course, I was in the middle, and it was impossible to relax. I kept being afraid of touching Daniel, with the pickup bouncing around on the rough road. Now, I regretted ever accompanying Tommie on this trip.

The scenery had changed since leaving the city. Poverty was evident everywhere, with occasional shacks along the road and people dressed in rags sitting beside them. We saw a lot of goats and a few cattle with their hides stretched over bones, looking like they hadn't eaten in days. The country had little grass, and if water existed it was not in sight.

After two hours, I was about to panic, with my leg cramping and needing to go to the bathroom. Just as I was about to speak, Daniel pulled the pickup off the road in front of one of the better houses I'd seen since leaving the city.

"Time for a pit stop," he said, smiling.

Thank goodness, I thought. Getting out, I could see it was also a little store with various groceries and other items. I rushed ahead of Tommie to get to the restroom. Opening the door, there was only a white pot on the floor. Suddenly, I realized there was no running water. This trip was going to be something to remember…or forget.

I was leaned back against the seat, half asleep, when I heard Daniel say, "There it is." I opened my eyes and saw lights in the distance. Surprised, I said, "There's electricity."

"Yes. Electricity but no running water," Tommie said.

We stopped in front of a small house and before we exited a crowd was gathering around the pickup. When Tommie got out, she was greeted with a chorus of "Missy Tom, Missy Tom, Missy Tom." They came closer, some hugging her and others just touching her. She was laughing and greeting each of them by name. I stood back and watched, amazed at the love they showered on her.

We finally were able to get in our residence. It was a small two room house with maybe 600 square feet. One room had two chairs and two small beds and the other room was a kitchen with a stove and refrigerator. A table with four chairs took up most of the room. A light hung from the ceiling with a string to turn it on and off.

Alone, I was able to ask questions. "Why electricity and no running water?"

"The government, under Mandela, has been able to get electricity to most rural areas; however, the water is another matter. Wells are scarce and water hard to find. There is a well six miles from this village. Women leave each morning after our devotional and take donkeys to get water from the well. It takes most of the day. The only days they don't go is when it rains enough to catch water in barrels."

"Why do they live here like this?" I asked.

"It's all they've ever known. They have nowhere else to go. There are many hardships, but you'll see they're a very happy people. When I came here, probably as many as twenty percent of the population went hungry. That has changed, as government is providing more food and supplies to these areas."

"I'm hungry. Is there something to eat?" I asked.

"The fridge probably has been stocked for us," she replied.

Tommie took out cheese and some kind of bread, along with rice. It was not something I was used to eating, but after she said the blessing, I had my first meal in rural Africa. The best I could say was that it was filling.

Both of us were tired and went to bed early. I woke up some time during the night freezing. I got up, put on another layer of clothes, and went back to bed. The next time I woke up, Tommie was cooking something. I could tell it was not light outside. "What time is it?" I asked.

"Five. It'll be light in another half hour. One thing you learn about this country. It goes from dark to light quickly. Another is that it gets cold at nights, because of the arid climate. Coffee is about ready. Daniel knows how much I like coffee, so he stocked us with a good supply."

We had coffee and something similar to grits for breakfast which Tommie said was made from maize. She was right about it getting light. By the time we walked outside there was activity throughout the village. It took almost an hour to walk the quarter mile, with people greeting Tommie every few minutes and stopping us to visit. Daniel met us there with the two other missionaries that Tommie had been asked to help. He made the introductions. One of the ladies was young, the other middle-aged.

There were about twenty gathered inside for the devotional. Daniel acted as an interpreter since many couldn't understand English. The devotional lasted less than half an hour, with the group being very attentive. Surprisingly, they clapped when she had finished. Several stayed to visit with her, standing in line waiting their turn.

After the building cleared, we were left with the two ladies. Tommie asked them if they would like to visit about their experiences so far at the mission.

"Yes," said the younger one, who had been introduced as Samantha.

We sat down in chairs that formed a small circle, with Tommie saying, "Tell me about your experiences so far."

"Disappointing," replied the older lady, who had been introduced as Doris. "We're not accepted here. They treat us like we have some kind of disease."

"How long have you been here?" Tommie asked.

"A little over a month," Samantha replied.

"It was not what we expected. We had no idea it would be this primitive. We don't have toilet facilities. It's not sanitary," explained Doris.

"Don't you see the need of the people for your help?" asked Tommie.

"Yes. I see that plainly; however, the people here don't seem to want our help or guidance," said Samantha.

"Do you love these people?" Tommie asked.

Silence, followed by more silence. Finally, Doris said, "How can we love them when they detest us?"

"Do you ever touch them?" Tommie asked.

"Seldom. They smell awful," said Doris.

I said to myself, *how terrible. I didn't notice any smell. They are wonderful people. Besides, they can't waste drinking water on bathing. What's wrong with this woman?*

"You must touch them and show them you care. They are smart people, and seeing that you love them, will return that love. If you don't understand that then you don't need to be here," Tommie said, in a stern voice.

"I understand," said Samantha.

I looked at Doris, expecting her to respond, but she said nothing.

Our next stop was the clinic where a long line of patients waited to see the doctor. Tommie introduced me to Dr. Zaragoza who came from Cape Town and was dedicating two years to the mission.

We spent three hours at the clinic, with Tommie helping administer medicine and assist the doctor in treating his patients. Several patients were bedridden and Tommie asked me to help in feeding some of the ones who could not feed themselves. It was truly a humbling experience. They were a pitiful group but were smiling throughout the meal. Looking into their eyes, I could see the appreciation for my help. It was all I could do to keep from crying when they attempted to thank me but didn't have the strength to do so. Later, Tommie told me they were in the final stage of AIDS and would die soon. I cried when she told me.

CHAPTER 31

Tommie Rose

I HADN'T BEEN BACK IN Africa but a few days before realizing how much I loved and missed the work at the mission. My subjects were amazing, countering their hardships with a joy for life. They smiled more than any people that I had known and had less to smile about.

The problem with the two new missionaries was solved in three days. Doris was able to ride back to Johannesburg on a truck that had delivered supplies to the village. Samantha was a different person immediately, going everywhere with me and being a willing learner.

The surprise was Lacy, who had pitched right in with enthusiasm for the jobs I had designated for her. She had become attached to an orphaned five-year-old boy who had been bitten by a poisonous snake. His right leg had to be removed to save his life. He used crutches which were too small to get around and throughout the day was never far from Lacy. He followed her everywhere, reminding me of a little puppy. After we had been there a week he was eating with us and sleeping in our house. Lacy had fixed him a pallet on the floor beside her bed. His parents had both died of AIDS and he had no other relatives. They were Christians and had named him Mark. Another family had agreed to let him live with them, which was not uncommon in these situations.

Lacy spent most of her time at the clinic assisting with whatever task needed to be done. They ranged from helping feed the patients, changing the bed covers, to even empting bedpans. When I complimented her for her work at these difficult jobs, she had replied, "It reminds me of when I was taking care of Jack."

After ten days, Samantha had taken over for me and was performing her duties faithfully. Very few of our patrons spoke English, with Zulu being the most common language of South Africa. It was a difficult language, but I had gained a fairly large vocabulary during my five year stay. In time, Samantha would be able to communicate enough to make herself understood.

There was a small hill outside of the village where we could get a signal for phone service. I had called Ted twice and checked to see how he was doing. Each time he insisted that he wanted to come to New Mexico when we returned. He was disappointed that we had cancelled our rodeo tour and would not be coming to Colorado. He sounded good, and I assured him it would be fine for him to come for a visit. He actually told me that he missed me the last time I called.

Two days before we were scheduled to return to Johannesburg, Lacy hit me with a bombshell. We had finished eating supper, and without warning she said, "I want to take Mark home with us." I thought maybe I had misunderstood her.

"What do you mean?" I asked.

"I want to take Mark back to New Mexico with us. He needs me. I want to get him an artificial leg, like mine."

"That's commendable, Lacy, but complicated."

"Why?"

"We would need to get a Visa and approval for him to leave," I replied.

"He has no parents. Who would give approval?" she asked.

"I don't know. This is sudden. Let me talk to Daniel. Maybe he can answer that."

"I'm not leaving without him. He needs me," she said.

The next day, after a sleepless night, I sat down with Daniel and told him about Lacy's idea. Idea is not a strong enough word...demand was more like it.

"It may not be as difficult as you think, Tommie. The family he stays with is crowded and they struggle to have enough to eat. I'm sure they wouldn't object. Mark has tested negative for HIV on two occasions so that is encouraging. The problem might be a Visa; however, you could probably get a temporary one and go from there. Has Lacy talked to Mark?"

"I'm sure she has. They adore one another. Mark is fascinated that Lacy only has one leg, also."

"It was a miracle he didn't die from the snake bite. The doctor here took his leg off. You may remember it."

"No. I must have just left when it happened."

"Mark is a brave little boy. He has been through so much," he said. "Let me make some phone calls and see what I can find out."

We left the village on Friday, June 22, for the five-hour trip to Johannesburg, with Lacy and Mark riding in the back of Daniel's pickup.

On Monday, June 25, after a weekend of paperwork in Johannesburg, we boarded our flight for Munich. Little Mark, had a new pair of crutches that fit him, and he was all smiles. Lacy was already acting like a mother, looking after his every need.

We landed in Lubbock the following Wednesday and started our drive to the ranch. Lacy was in good spirits and talkative.

"I feel good, Tommie. The first thing I'm going to do is contact the clinic that provided me with my prosthetic. I've always had everything I needed or wanted. I took that for granted, never realizing that millions didn't have that blessing. Now, I have a chance to help someone and the means to do it."

Without giving me a chance to respond, she continued, "I'm going to start riding again immediately. I gave up too easily, Jack would have been disappointed in me. Do you think we have time to make some of the rodeos in Texas during July and August?"

"Sure. Zack will be pleased."

I had called Mom and told her about bringing Mark back with us. I didn't want it to be a surprise. Of course, she had been positive. Mark could already say and recognize a few words of English. The Zulu greeting was not hello or hi. Instead Mark would greet Lacy first thing in the morning with, "I see you, Acey." He had trouble pronouncing the L. He still called me Missy Tom. He was a darling little boy, not weighing over thirty pounds and being three feet tall. He could get around on those crutches at an amazing speed.

When we arrived in Roswell, I called Mom and told her we would be there in less than an hour. She must have notified Mia and Gramps because everyone was there when we drove up, including Zack. It was quite a welcome home gathering, with everyone going on about Mark and how precious he was. Even my dad carried on like a new granddad. Mark hid behind Lacy at first but eventually realized no one was going to harm him. We had to tell them about our stay in Africa, and Lacy spent much of the time describing her tasks.

Finally, I told them we were exhausted and needed to get home for some much needed rest. Before we left, I told Zack that Lacy wanted to start riding again. He was pleased, responding that he was ready to go to Texas for some rodeos.

The next day, Lacy announced that she was going to get an appointment with Diane for Mark to have a complete physical. There was not any waiting period when our family asked to see Diane. She had us bring him in immediately.

She did a thorough exam, with blood tests and X-rays. She was patient and caring with Mark, going on about how darling he was. "Everything looks good, but it will be a few days before I have the results," she said. "Mark is a beautiful little boy. I would like him to meet Carl."

"That won't be a problem. When we come back for the results of the tests, we can all have lunch together," I suggested.

"Wonderful," she responded.

The first thing we did when we were back at the ranch was to ride. I suggested to Lacy that we might use rubber bands to secure her feet to the stirrups. I'd never used that technique but knew girls who had. She agreed and hopefully that would be an advantage, ensuring that she did not lose a stirrup on a run. I was amazed at how well she did, being off over two weeks. Her horse had profited from the time off and was sharper than ever. She only rode Jazzy, but it was evident that she was ready to compete.

I rode her other horse, Chrome, but didn't make a run. I did let Mark ride with me and he was excited, talking Zulu the entire time. When Lacy made her run he squealed and clapped.

When Lacy came back from her run, she said, "Two weeks made a big difference. I feel great. What happened?"

"I believe that you now realize there is much suffering in the world. You witnessed it first hand, along with the extreme hardships that many have to endure. You saw how those people still enjoy life and find joy and happiness even in a difficult life."

"I'll never feel pity for myself again," she answered.

"I see you, Acey," said Mark with a huge smile.

That brought laughter from the both of us.

Two days later, Diane called and said the results of the tests were available and could we come in to visit with her. I told her that Lacy and Mark would meet her and Carl for lunch at noon, but I had promised my dad to help with moving cattle from one part of the ranch to another pasture and couldn't come.

I was at my mom and dad's by 9:00 that morning. Zack was going to help us also. We assembled at the barn before beginning our day's work, and Zack asked me what I thought about Lacy bringing Mark home.

"It's been good for Lacy. She's a different person. She insists that Mark needs her, but she needs him just as much."

"Is she going to take him with us to Texas?" he asked.

"Oh, me. I don't have a definite answer to that. We'll just have to wait and see; however, right now, it appears that he'll go with us."

"Will she ever get over losing Jack?" he asked.

"I can't answer that, Zack."

"I still have feelings for her," he said.

"I know, Zack. I'm sorry, but right now, she's still suffering, and it's not a good time to ask that question."

"I need to just stand back and see what happens?" he asked.

"Yes." I replied.

We spent the day horseback moving cattle and it was wonderful. I was exhausted when we returned to the ranch, but it was a good feeling. Before I left, Zack and I agreed that we needed to leave immediately for Texas to make as many rodeos as we could in July.

Lacy and Mark were home before me, and she met me at the door, saying, "You missed it. It was something else."

"What did I miss?"

"Let me start from the beginning. We met Diane and Carl at a restaurant in town. We had a nice meal and Mark was on his best behavior. Several strangers came by to comment about how cute he was. He put on quite a show, saying to each of them, 'I see you' but of course they didn't understand the greeting. We finished our meal and went outside to our vehicles."

"It must be quite a story, Lacy. You sure are stringing it out," I said.

"Just be patient, I'm getting to the good part. We were standing there visiting when these two guys across the parking lot began making terrible comments. They were standing by a pickup with a confederate flag in the back. One of them, talking loud enough for us to hear, said, 'Looks like they got them a little darkie. Old Grandpa there couldn't have produced anything like that. His woman must have a black man in the woodshed.'

Lacy hesitated, then continued, "Before I knew what was happening, Carl started running toward them. I thought he was going over there to talk, but instead he got faster, never slowing down, and running directly into the chest of the one doing the talking. I tell you, Tommie, he knocked this guy flat on his butt. He was on him in a second, flaying away at his face. The other man just stood there stunned. Carl had broken his glasses and the impact had given him a nosebleed, with blood all over his shirt. Thank goodness two policemen who had eaten there came out and pulled Carl off the guy."

"It must have frightened Mark out of his mind," I said.

"Not hardly. He was clapping and screaming something like 'Ibutho'. Do you know what that means?"

"Yes. It's a Zulu warrior."

"The police questioned us and when we told them what the guys said, they laughed, commenting they picked on the wrong people. When we left, the man he attacked still hadn't recovered and they were taking him to the hospital."

"Was Carl injured?" I asked.

"He insisted that he was fine. Diane applied pressure and stopped the nosebleed. I would never have guessed he was capable of anything like that."

"Dad had told us that he was a fierce hitter on their football team."

"Well, I believe it. I'm now a witness."

We had planned to leave for Texas on Monday, July 2. Late Saturday night, Mark woke up crying, holding his stomach. We immediately thought appendicitis, taking him to the emergency room in Ruidoso. Diane met us there, and after doing a blood test, she assured us it wasn't his appendix.

"I have a theory, and I'm pretty sure it is accurate. His diet has changed drastically these last ten days. From the time he could eat solid food most of his diet has been heavy fiber. Now he is eating our food, which is not nearly so healthy, and his little body cannot adjust to the change. He's probably eaten more meat the last ten days than he has for several years. He's going to be fine, but we have to change his diet gradually. Let's keep him in the hospital tonight, and we can see if my diagnosis is correct. I'll stay with him since it's only a few hours until I go to work. In fact, tomorrow is my day in the ER."

"You're sure he's going to be okay?" asked Lacy.

"Positive. Go on home and come back tomorrow around noon. I'm going to call Carl, and he can come up and sit with us. He was awake when I left home," she explained.

"Will you call us if there's any change?" Lacy asked.

"Of course," she replied.

"Lacy, we do have to get ready for our trip. We can be back in less then an hour if Diane needs us," I said.

We left, after telling Mark bye. He was relaxed and smiling, after being given medicine for his stomach and a pain pill. On the way home, Lacy told me she wouldn't leave Mark if he was still sick.

"He's going to be fine, Lacy. Worrying is not going to help him."

"Do you think he'll enjoy the rodeos?" Lacy asked.

"He'll like being with us. I'm sure he'll become tired of being around the rodeo arena all day with nothing to do. Of course, we can trade out keeping him entertained."

We heard nothing from Diane the next day and we were at the hospital an hour before noon. She and Carl both were in the room with Mark.

"How's he doing?" I asked.

"Good. Oatmeal agrees with him more than a hot dog and fries. He just needs a little time to adjust to our unhealthy lifestyle. Carl has something to ask you."

It took a few seconds for him to get started. After clearing his throat, he said, "Diane and I would like to keep Mark while you're gone. We'll take good care of him, and Diane can make sure he eats healthy. We'll call you every day and let you talk with him. We can work on his English. We've already found a website that translates Zulu to English. We would like very much to keep him."

I held my breath, while Lacy hesitated before speaking. "I don't know. He might not want to stay. He's attached to me."

"Lacy, it might work out. He's going to get awfully tired of waiting around on us," I said.

"He may not be willing to stay," Lacy repeated.

I looked at Mark and said Uhlale (stay in Zulu) and pointed to Carl.

He immediately started clapping and saying, "Ibutho! Ibutho!"

"Carl, I believe you have a fan. He has named you a Zulu warrior," I said laughing.

"Okay, we'll give it a try," Lacy said frowning; "but I need to talk with him every day."

"We promise," said Carl.

CHAPTER 32

Zack

I WAS RELIEVED THAT LACY had agreed to let Mark stay with Carl and Diane. It would prevent us from having to keep him occupied during the long days and nights at the rodeos.

I was frustrated about my feelings for Lacy and didn't know what to do. One minute, it was guilt, and the next, indecision about what to do. Sissy had told me it was not a good time to approach her, but it was difficult not to let her know how I felt. Maybe she already knew, and was waiting for me to tell her; however, it could be that she had no idea.

Of course, the guilt came from me wanting to replace my brother. I kept telling myself that Jack was gone and we needed to move on. I truly believed that he would not have an objection, in fact, he would be pleased that Lacy had someone to look after her. At least, that's what I wanted to believe. She had not given me even one indication that she considered me anything other than a brother-in-law and friend.

We left on Tuesday, July 3, for Stamford. I had always wanted to go to that rodeo. It was one of the oldest in the country, and I had heard about it for years. The saddles they gave were said to be the best of any of the rodeos, large or small. Lacy would only get one run unless she made the short go. I would get two calves and another if I made the short go.

It was about a seven-hour drive, and we were at the arena by three in the afternoon. We found the most level place we could and parked our trailer. Tommie unloaded our horses while we went to the office and entered, also getting stalls. I asked Lacy if she'd like to check out the arena.

"Sure. We can saddle our horses before we stall them and ride for a while since it's early."

Riding through the alley, I was surprised at how long it was. The score would be long, which would be an advantage for me, riding Scooter. The arena was in a large bowl shaped hole.

"Zack, can you believe how big this pen is. The sand's deep and the last barrel is uphill. It's going to be a long and tough pattern."

"Which horse are you going to run?" I asked.

"Chrome. It's a long way between barrels. He listens better and is less apt to break the pattern and turn before he reaches a barrel. He doesn't have the ability of Jazzy, but he has a lot more sense."

"It's plenty hot down in this hole," I observed.

"Well, there's no breeze, and if there were, it couldn't get down here," she said. "I'm up in the morning and it should be cool."

"I'm roping Thursday afternoon in the slack and it'll be plenty warm." We rode for about thirty minutes before putting the horses up. The stalls looked like they'd been built for the first rodeo, which was held in the 30s. I had just taken Scooter into his stall when Lacy screamed in the one beside me.

"Snake! There's a snake in here! It's bit Jazzy!"

I dropped the halter shank and was beside her in a few seconds. Sure enough, a large rattlesnake was slithering off into a corner of the stall. We backed out, found a hoe and killed it.

"Where did it bite her?" I asked.

"On the front right leg. I think she stepped on it."

I found the fang marks just above the ankle. "Let's take her back to the trailer."

Tommie said immediately that we had to get her to a vet. An older man who had heard us talking came over to offer help.

"Snakebite, huh? Not surprised. Those stalls are not used except during this rodeo and there's lots of snakes in these hills. You need a vet. Let me give you some advice. Take her to Colorado City. It's less than two hours. There's a vet there who you can depend on. I have the phone number if you want to call."

"Let me have the number," Sissy said. She punched in the number and waited. She explained our situation, hung up and asked, "How's the best way to get to Colorado City?"

Within a few minutes we were on the road toward Abilene. From there, we hit Interstate 20 and were in Colorado City an hour and twenty minutes later. We unloaded Jazzy and were met by a young man who looked to be in his late 30s or early 40s. His hair was longer than you would expect, and he had a smile that said welcome.

After introductions, we put Jazzy in the stocks, and the vet gave instructions in Spanish to another young man who had been introduced as Louie. After the instructions, he walked off mumbling.

"What did he say?" asked Lacy.

"I couldn't understand him," I said.

Louie began washing the snakebite with antibiotic soap and when he finished, he took a razor and shaved the hair around the injury. A little while later the vet came back, saying, "She should be fine. What we have to prevent is an infection. I need to keep her here a few days if it's possible."

"We're at Stamford until Saturday," Tommie said. "Could we pick her up Sunday?"

"Sure. Before 10:00 or after 1:00. I'll be in church during that time. You're welcome to go to church with me," he offered.

"We'd take you up on that, but Sissy is holding a service at the arena for anyone who wishes to attend. We'll pick him up after 1:00."

"Is Sissy this tall lady that you introduced as Tommie?" he asked.

"Yes. I've always called her Sissy. Can't break the habit," I explained.

"Goodness, a woman minister. A pretty one at that. What church?"

"Methodist," Sissy replied.

"What's your favorite scripture?"

"1 Corinthians 13:13," I replied without hesitation.

"And now these three remain: faith, hope, and love. But the greatest of these is love," he quoted.

"I'm also partial to Matthew 28:19," she said.

"Go thee therefore, into all nations, making disciples and baptizing them in the name of the Father, Son, and Holy Ghost. That's from the King James Version, which I hope you use."

"I do."

"My daddy was a Baptist preacher. Nothing wrong with Methodist. We're all trying to get to the same place," he said.

We were interrupted by one of his hands who spoke to him in Spanish. He walked off mumbling, and the only thing we could understand was that he would see us Sunday.

"The Spanish is easier for me to understand than the mumbling," Zack said.

On the drive back, Lacy said, "I can't believe it. What a way to start a rodeo!" she said.

"It could've been worse. What if you hadn't seen the snake and left Jazzy in there with him?"

"I don't want to even think about that."

Both of us had good first go rounds. Lacy had the second best time out of the 35 that ran the next morning, and in the Thursday afternoon slack, I tied my calf in 10.1, which was good, considering the long score.

Tommie and I went to the Thursday night performance and were impressed with the rodeo. A band was there from one of the colleges in Abilene, providing lively music, and it was obvious that the rodeo was seeped in tradition. We visited some of the inside exhibits, looking at rodeo pictures dating back seventy years. Several of the pictures included Will Rogers.

Lacy found us, accompanied by a man.

"Zack, you and Tommie remember Raleigh Dumont?"

We shook hands, and I did recall him from our high school rodeo days. "Good to see you, Raleigh. It's been a long time."

"I'm sorry Raleigh, I can't recall you," Sissy said.

"I remember you. All the young boys thought you were beautiful, but we were afraid of you," he said smiling.

"Raleigh and Jack were good friends," Lacy said.

"I was sorry to hear about Jack. He was a special guy," he said.

"Tommie, there's a dance after the rodeo and Raleigh has invited me to attend with him. I don't know about dancing, but it might be fun to give it a try," Lacy said.

"That's great, Lacy. Have fun."

Suddenly, I had a sinking feeling in my stomach. I didn't expect this. I lost interest in the rodeo and went back to the trailer. Now I was angry with myself. You sat around without expressing your feelings, and here she is going to a dance with someone else. I said out loud, *you have to be stupid, Zack Skinner.*

It wasn't long before Sissy came into the trailer, saying, "I'm sorry, Zack. Maybe she's ready to move on with her life. It looks like I gave you bad advice."

"I'm confused, Sissy. How could she be moving on this quickly, especially with someone who she hardly knows? I was giving her more time and now this."

"Zack, there are dozens of girls here that would jump at the chance to go out with you. Look around and stop waiting for something to happen with Lacy. She's a strong willed young lady, and if it's meant to happen it will. If not, move on."

"I wish it were that easy, Sissy. I've loved her as long as I can remember."

"Well, I'm going back to watch the rodeo. Are you going with me, or will you sit here and feel sorry for yourself?"

That stung, but she was right, as usual. We returned and watched the remainder of the performance before going back to the trailer. I slept very little on the cot in the trailer stall, listening for Lacy to return from the dance. I heard her come in at 1:30 and still didn't go to sleep until after 3:00.

I was up at 6:00 the next morning and went to feed the horses. Hard as I tried, it was not possible to get my mind off Lacy and Raleigh. How in the world could this happen? I wait around, giving her time, and now another man steps in. I made a mistake and now I had to do something about it. I would talk with her today and find out where I stood. One way or another, I was going to see if she had any feelings for me.

I wandered around until 8:00 after feeding the horses and then returned to the trailer. Sissy was up and had made coffee, but Lacy was still sleeping. We took our coffee and went outside to sit in our lawn chairs.

"Feel better today?" Sissy asked.

"Not really. Didn't sleep much. I need to get my mind off her. I'm up in the show tonight, and I need a good run to make the short go."

"Right. I saw the saddles and they're beautiful. It would be nice for you to take home the one that says Champion Calf Roper 2001."

I didn't comment on her statement. My chances, with my present attitude, were not good. Instead, I changed the subject, asking her if Ted had called recently.

"Yesterday. He's doing good and plans to come to the ranch when we get home. I'm looking forward to seeing him. Isn't that strange?"

"Not at all. I like Ted. I wouldn't mind having him for a brother-in-law."

"Not so fast. Nothing was said about marriage. He's only kissed me twice. I may turn out to be an old maid."

"That's a sad thought. We're all going to be old one of these days and we need someone to accompany us when we get there."

"Well, Little Brother, if Ted and I are going to have a future together, he's going to need to get more aggressive."

"Just you wait, Sissy. It's going to happen."

After a long day, it was finally time for the Friday night performance. I didn't have a chance to talk with Lacy.

Every time I saw her, Raleigh was by her side. I rode in the grand entry, mainly because my dad had always encouraged us to participate. Lacy didn't ride with me but instead was next to Raleigh.

When it came time for me to rope, I blanked everything out of my mind, thinking only of getting out good. I drew a good calf, making my best run since I had started back roping. I was 9.2, which took the lead in the second go round.

Sissy and I stayed for the remainder of the rodeo. Lacy was going into the short go with the fourth best time. I was sitting third in the average and was going to have a legitimate chance of winning, being only .05 seconds off the leader.

I waited up again for Lacy and heard her come in sometime after 1:00. I went to sleep thinking that maybe I would have a chance to talk to her the next day.

The next morning, with nothing else to do, I watched the Old Timers roping. The breakaway was limited to the 70 and over. One of the last ropers was Ralph Russell, who had quite a fan club in the stands. He caught his breakaway calf in 5.2. I hustled down to the back of the alley and found him leading his horse up the steep hill.

"Mr. Russell, wait up a minute. You probably don't remember me. My dad bought a horse from you twenty years ago at Merkel. My name is Zack Skinner. My dad's name is Bo."

Smiling, he replied, "Sure, my brothers framed me and I sold the horse too cheap. They told me, after the horse was gone, that they told your dad not to give my asking price. They got a big laugh out of that and cost me several thousand dollars."

"You made a nice run," I said.

"Probably my last one. I guess it wasn't bad for an 80-year-old."

"You had quite a group of supporters," I said.

"Several of my family members came. Did you rope?"

"Yeah. I made the short go," I answered.

"Good. Maybe you can win the saddle. I've tried for years and haven't been successful. I can win everywhere else, but I seem to be jinxed here at Stamford."

"My sister is here that rode Flame. I know she'd like to see you. She loved that horse and was virtually unbeatable on him."

"Let me take my horse to the trailer, and then I'll go with you," he said.

Sissy was delighted to see Ralph, and sitting outside the trailer, we visited about horses, especially Flame, for the next half hour. Finally, he left, saying he needed to find his family and thank them for coming.

Lacy was not around and I assumed she was with Raleigh. It was going to be a long day. Added to that discouraging observation, by noon it was looking like we were in for a storm.

The lightening and thunder had begun by 5:00 and the sky opened up during the grand entry, which I chose to skip. I wanted my clothes and gear to be dry when I roped. When the rodeo began it was still raining, with the arena turning into a sloppy mess resembling a pigpen.

The barrel race was the second event, following the bronc riding. Raleigh led Lacy's horse into the alley, which was a joke. Chrome was calm as always and never gave her any problems. The sorrel gelding amazed me once again. He was not a typical, high strung barrel horse. He handled the pen well and made a nice run with a time of 18.7.

The condition of the arena gave most of the contestants' problems, with one horse falling and three hitting barrels. Tommie and I were under the awning on the east side of the arena. She was writing down times and figuring the averages. When the event was over she announced that Lacy had finished second, getting beat by .02 of a second. There went the beautiful saddle, I thought.

It was still raining when the tie-down roping started. I roped third from last and had been giving myself a talking to since the first contestant. *The pen is the same for everybody. You're supposed to resemble Dad, who was great under pressure. You're riding the best horse on the grounds. Concentrate on getting out good. Don't rush. Slow down and be fast.*

I had drawn a black white-faced calf, larger than most in the pen. I didn't figure him for a runner, especially in the slop. For once, I was right, and the extra second hesitation kept me from breaking out. I made a good solid run, tying him in 11.8. The guy who roped next, and was sitting second, broke out. The last roper, who was leading, got out late and was 13.4. That moved me to first. I felt good about my effort and patting Scooter on the neck told him, *we did good, boy.*

Sissy met me coming out of the alley with a big smile, saying, "You looked like your daddy tonight, Little Brother. I'm proud of you. I've already called Mom and Dad and told them you won."

After the rodeo, when I picked up my saddle, Lacy and Raleigh were there also. Lacy had finished second, but a strange rule caused her to win a saddle also. It seems that you could not win the saddle but one time. The lady who beat her had won the previous year. The result was that both of us were taking home saddles.

Sissy and I went back to the trailer. I assume Lacy and Raleigh went to the dance again. I called my dad and his effort to hide his excitement was futile. Of course, Mom didn't even attempt to hide her feelings.

It was a good weekend, and now all that was left was to talk with Lacy when she came in. I lay in my cot rehearsing what I would say. Finally, after almost giving up, I heard her come in at 2:15. I still had on my clothes, and I knocked on the door immediately after she went in. She opened the door, probably expecting Raleigh, and looking surprised, said, "Oh, Zack. What do you need?"

"Could we visit? We can sit in the pickup."

"It's late, Zack. Can it wait until morning?"

"No. I've waited for you, and we need to have this conversation," I answered. Without commenting, she came out of the trailer, and we got into the pickup.

"What's so important that it can't wait until morning?" she asked.

"I need you to know something, and I've waited long enough. Probably too long. I care about you, Lacy. I always have, but Jack was your choice. Now he's gone. I still care about you. In fact, more than care. I wanted to wait a respectable time, but now, when I see you with Raleigh, maybe it was too long." I hesitated, and she remained silent. I started to speak again, and she raised her hand for me to stop.

"Don't say any more. I know. I have for a long time. I like you, Zack. You're a special person in my life. I'll never love anyone like I did Jack. You look so much like Jack, which you should since your twins. But looks is as far as it goes. You're so different and I could never accept that. I loved Jack for the way he was, not for his looks. Of course, most girls wouldn't believe that. Maybe in time someone will come along. I don't know. It's certainly not Raleigh. I just needed to see if I could enjoy someone's company again and he was handy."

"So you knew how I felt?" I asked.

"Only for twenty years. After Jack passed, I knew this day would come. I dreaded it with a passion. I wouldn't trade our relationship for anything. I need you to be there for me, just not in the way that you want. Please, please, don't let this interfere with our being friends and family."

"No. I won't let that happen. I'll never be angry with you. I'm disappointed but I understand."

That ended the conversation and I went to my cot in the trailer stall and spent another sleepless night.

CHAPTER 33

Lexie

BO COULDN'T CONTAIN HIMSELF OVER Zack's success. He seldom showed emotion but in this case he made an exception. We talked with them daily on the phone, and after making four rodeos in Texas, Zack had won two and placed high in the other two. They were smaller rodeos, but Bo had said that sometimes they were the toughest to compete in. Lacy had done equally well, and Jazzy had made a complete recovery from the snakebite.

It was already the first week in August. They had been home once for a few days since leaving the first of July. Zack was quieter than usual, especially considering how well they had done. When I asked Tommie about him, she explained what had happened with Lacy. My heart reached out to him, but I knew better than to mention it. Every time I felt concern for my children the memory of Mr. Bob telling me about the mother cow protecting her calf from the mountain lion came back. His words, *there is no greater love than a mother for her child*, will always remain with me. We want what they desire, but sometimes, many times, that does not happen. I have to believe that usually it works out for the best.

I had only talked with Felicia a few times after she became upset with my advice about Jimmy. It's amazing that we lived only a few hundred yards apart and our relationship had become so distant. I was determined to do something about that. I had Bo invite Jimmy and her to supper after they had finished working the calves. It was on a Friday, August 10. I told Bo it would be necessary for him to insist that they come. He could make it seem like a celebration of sorts after working hard for the past five days.

Bo suggested that we invite Carl and Diane also, saying it might help an awkward situation with Felicia. Maybe a chocolate cake would put Felicia in a good mood, since it was her favorite. We had been friends too long to let one conversation interfere with our relationship.

On the day I had selected for the supper, I spent most of it cooking. I made cheese potatoes, which was a favorite of Jimmy's to go with the ribs that I had cooked. The ribs were one of Bo's favorite meals. Carl and Diane didn't get many home cooked meals and would appreciate anything. I also made vegetable and fruit salads. At the end of the day, I was pleased with my efforts, thinking how far I had come since Bo and I married thirty years ago. Ms. Nancy was the primary reason for my improvement.

Carl and Diane arrived early, saying they had left Mark with a babysitter. The times we had been around them, most of the conversation centered around Mark. They adored the little boy and the feeling was mutual. Bo and I had talked on more than one occasion about the possibility of Lacy allowing them to adopt Mark. We agreed that would be best for him. Diane had already taken him to Houston to be fitted for his prosthetic.

Diane was talkative from the time they came in. "Lexie, can I help you with anything?"

"No, thanks. Everything's ready. All we need is for Jimmy and Felicia to show up."

"Mark wanted to come; however, he didn't fuss. He's the sweetest little boy. I can't believe how he has taken up with Carl. He follows him everywhere he goes. Carl is doing great with his business. Your investments in his firm are one of the reasons. Jake has insisted that he go to New York in September for a five-day conference. The major investment companies in the world will be making presentations. Carl hates to be away from home, but it doesn't appear that he will have a choice. I would go with him, but Mark is starting school this year."

"When will Lacy be home?" Carl asked.

"Probably the last of the month. They have several more rodeos to attend," Bo answered.

"We would like for Mark to attend school in Ruidoso. There's an elementary right down the street from us," Diane said.

"You'll have to talk with Lacy about that," Bo stated.

I knew where this was headed. She was hinting that we speak on their behalf about Mark. Thankfully, before any more could be said on the issue, Jimmy and Felicia arrived.

"Sorry we're late. I didn't get home from the track until after 6:00," Jimmy said.

"No problem," I responded. "Sit down and visit while I get it on the table."

"I'll help you," Felicia added.

While we were putting food on the table, I asked Felicia how things were going.

"Okay, I guess. Jimmy comes home as often as he can. Jolynda continues to be a problem in college. She's not making her grades and complains constantly. She wants to change her major to theater. I've told her it's not a good field to make a living, and we would be wasting our money."

"Kind of sounds like someone I knew in college," I said.

"I know. Don't think that hasn't crossed my mind."

"Have you made any progress in changing her mind?" I asked.

"Zero. She's more determined than ever after attending a summer theater camp in Texas. All she talks about now is some instructor at the camp. I've heard Kelly this and Kelly that until I'm sick of it."

"The last time you asked me for advice you didn't like what I said."

"I'm desperate, Lexie. Tell me what you think I should do."

"Let her pursue her dream. Just like you did. She's so much like you and that's not bad. Right now, it's important for you to have a positive relationship with her. That means giving her your support."

"That means she'll want to change colleges. This Kelly is an instructor at a college in Texas."

"So? We went to school in Texas and turned out okay," I said.

"I'll talk to Jimmy and see what he thinks," she said.

What a joke, I thought. She won't listen to Jimmy. She'll do whatever she decides. At least she asked me for my advice again and didn't get angry.

The meal was a success with everyone complimenting my cooking. Felicia ate two pieces of chocolate cake.

After everyone had left, Bo and I talked about the evening. "I thought I married you because you were beautiful but it may have been for your cooking."

Laughing, I said, "You must have forgotten that I couldn't boil water when we met. Your mother taught me how to cook."

"Anyway, the meal was great and a big success. Maybe your relationship with Felicia will return to normal," he stated.

"I hope so. We've been through a lot together over the past thirty years. Jimmy seems to be happy."

"He is. The filly has been somewhat of a disappointment so far. He said that she'd not come around like he thought, but he'd still run her in the trials this month for the All American. He's taken a couple of outside horses to train. He's excited about one of those."

"Jimmy never changes. It's easy to see why he has been your friend for all these years," I observed.

"Exactly. You always know what you get with Jimmy," he said.

"Can you believe the change in Carl and Diane?" I asked.

"Unbelievable. They're now acting like a normal couple. They were hinting that we convince Lacy to let them keep Mark."

"I know, Bo. I don't believe we should go there. That's a decision that Lacy needs to make on her own. However, I do believe it would be in Mark's best interest if they got their wish."

"Speaking of Lacy, we haven't heard from them today. That's unusual since they've been calling every day," he said.

Our land phone started ringing just as he completed his observation. He went into our bedroom to answer it since we had the television on. He came back a few minutes later, saying, "That was Tommie and she had more good news."

"Great! I always like positive reports."

"They're in Coleman and both had good runs in the short go. Zack tied his calf in 8.5, which won the go. Lacy had a 15.85 which also was good enough to win the short go. The big news, however, was that they will be home Monday, and we are having company tomorrow. Guess who's coming to dinner?"

"I hope it's a future son-in-law."

"Ted Adders will be here at noon. He's flying into Lubbock and renting a car. Tommie said she knew it was short notice but to please be nice to him. She had a heavy emphasis on 'please'. I told Jimmy that I would come in to the track tomorrow. One of his outside horses is running. That means you'll have to entertain the doctor."

"Thank goodness I have plenty of leftovers from tonight. I'm glad he's coming. If we're ever going to have grandchildren, Dr. Adders is going to have to move faster."

"I would prefer a cowboy or neighboring rancher. But, hey, any port in a storm, as Grands used to say."

The next morning, after Bo had left, I put my mind to work about what to do with Ted. By the time he arrived at a few minutes after 12:00, I had a plan. He seemed glad to see me and instead of shaking hands, which was his usual greeting, he gave me a hug.

"Have you eaten?" I asked.

"No, ma'am. Nothing since breakfast and that was early. Please don't go to any trouble."

I fixed him a plate of leftovers and wondered how he could be so thin after he had two and a half helpings, plus a third of a chocolate cake. Studying him as he ate, I noticed how delicate he was. In a dress with makeup, he could easily have passed for a woman. A very pretty woman at that. I did become aware of something that had gone unnoticed until now. When he smiled, his blue eyes seemed to sparkle. I imagined him with a tan and thought that would do wonders for him. All his work was indoors, which gave him an unhealthy look.

He was wearing dress slacks and a short sleeve Polo shirt with shoes that tied. A typical dress for a city doctor. Even though he ate a large meal, his table manners were perfect. It was not difficult to imagine him as a little boy in a boarding school, where other kids made fun of him. It wouldn't be hard for me to learn to be a mother to him.

"Mrs. Skinner, that was delicious. I embarrassed myself eating so much, but it was scrumptious and impossible to stop. Can Tommie cook like you?"

I couldn't keep from laughing, saying, "No, Ted, afraid not. In fact, she has never had the least bit of interest in the kitchen. The boys were actually better cooks."

Smiling he replied, "Well, she has many other wonderful attributes that make up for that."

"What do you like about my daughter, Ted?"

"She's not like anyone I have ever known. Of course, she's beautiful, but that is not all. She has so much self-assurance. Even when she walks across the room, it's obvious that she is on a mission. She is fearless in everything she does, from riding a horse to confronting an arrogant neurosurgeon. I know this sounds trite, Mrs. Skinner, but Tommie has changed my life. I discovered what it was to be human after I met her."

"Are you ready to go shopping?" I asked, moving to another subject.

"Shopping. What for?"

"Clothes. If you're going to be around this family, we need to dress you a little different."

"Sure. I'm willing to do whatever it takes to fit in," he said.

When he came out of the dressing room of the western store in Ruidoso, I was stunned at the transformation. He was wearing wrangler jeans, size 30, and a denim shirt that was a medium and still too large. But he still looked like a long tall Texan and Tommie would be surprised! He looked at himself in the full length mirror and smiled saying, "Not bad. I feel good in these clothes."

"Now, all we lack is the boots," I stated. We ended up getting him some ropers instead of dress boots. We didn't need to overdo it. *Less says more,* was one of Mr. Bob's quotes that fit the occasion.

He ended up buying another pair of jeans and two more shirts before we left the store. He wanted to get something for Tommie and asked me for a suggestion.

"She seldom wears jewelry, but when she does, it's usually turquoise. There's a nice store a couple of blocks from here that sells jewelry. We can look there if you like."

He ended up buying her a bracelet, necklace and a pair of earrings. All were beautiful and cost him more than Bo would have ever spent. Maybe I should have married a doctor.

CHAPTER 34

Bo

I WOKE UP AT 2:00 A.M. with my leg killing me. It had been keeping me awake for a month. With the pain and Lexie nagging me, I'd finally agreed to the surgery, which was scheduled for this coming Thursday in El Paso. I was to go in on Wednesday for my pre-op and a battery of tests and would be forced to stay in the hospital for a couple of days. Therapy was out of the question since that would require staying in El Paso for another two weeks. I'd put off the surgery for too long, thinking that the steroid shots would give me enough relief to get by. Just like Diane had told me, surgery was the only solution.

I finally gave up on going back to sleep and went to the den to sit in my recliner. Now my next problem confronted me. I didn't know what I was going to do with Ted tomorrow. Lexie had already told me he was my responsibility Sunday since she entertained him Saturday. I could insist that he go to church with us and that would take up part of the morning. We would go to my mom's for lunch afterwards and that would take up a couple of hours. It would still leave the remainder of the afternoon. Maybe I could show him some of the scrapbooks that Lexie had done for Tommie. He would be interested in that. Why was I even worried about him, anyway? He could entertain himself.

Okay, just explain that to Lexie, I said out loud. No way was I going there.

Suddenly, a thought came to mind. My grands entertained his guests by telling them about Lincoln County and this ranch. I could take him on a quick tour starting with the museum in Lincoln and then to the one in Fort Stanton. I would take him to the cemetery and tell him about Tommie's kin who were buried there. This might not be so bad after all.

The next day went much better than I expected. Of course, everyone at church was curious about our visitor, not being the least bit timid about asking questions. When they found out he was visiting Tommie, I thought we were never going to get away. She was everybody's favorite, including Pastor Stevens, who had as many questions as anyone. I finally took his arm and guided him to the car, saying lunch was waiting on us.

On the drive to Mom's, Ted asked, "Are people always this friendly?"

"Most of the time," Lexie replied. "Especially when Tommie's involved."

"Were you surprised that Tommie became a minister?" he asked.

"Not really. She always enjoyed church, even as a little girl. Pastor Stevens also had an influence on her. He's been an important part of this family for thirty years and been there for us through some difficult times."

"Her gramps is special to her, isn't he?"

"Yes, Ted. That could be an understatement. It's a long story, but he's adored her since she was a little girl. My dad would do anything for her. He has always been partial to her and didn't hide it well," Lexie explained.

Mom had lunch ready when we arrived. She asked me to say the blessing, which was a surprise. Lexie's dad or my mom usually did that. Without notice I did okay, attempting to be short and sincere. I had found out one thing about Ted Adders. That boy could put away the food. We had meatloaf, one of my favorites, with potatoes, fresh vegetables, and cornbread. Mom had made two pies with apples from our orchard. I swear, Ted ate half of one pie by himself, smothered in ice cream. He might be shy around Tommie, but he was plenty relaxed at the dinner table. Of course, my mother was pleased with his response to her cooking, soaking up the praise.

Every time I saw Tom, he looked worse than the previous time. With the least bit of exertion, he had difficulty breathing, even with the oxygen. Mom had told me that the doctors had done all they could for him. He was not a candidate for surgery and his medication could only do so much. He had suffered his first heart attack over thirty years ago and had undergone surgery after his second one ten years later. I never heard him complain, and he was always in good spirits. He and Mom had been married for twenty-five years, and to my knowledge, never had a cross word. So many good things had happened since Lexie asked me for a ride to Ruidoso during my college Christmas vacation in 1970.

Interrupting my thoughts, Mom said, "Bo, your mind looks like it's in another world."

"No. I was just thinking how fortunate our family has been. The more time that passes, the greater I seem to be aware of it," I said.

"I believe the older we get the more grateful we become for all of our blessings," she said.

"What time do you think they will be home tomorrow?" asked Ted.

"By noon," I said. They only have about 350 miles to come and will leave early. Plus, they gain an hour because of the time change." It didn't escape me that Ted changed the subject away from family. It must be difficult to hear about family when it was a foreign subject to him. The more I was around him, the more evident it became why Tommie was attracted to him.

"What's on your agenda this afternoon?" Mom asked.

"Local history. We're going to tour the museums at Fort Stanton and Lincoln. I know there's not much culture involved but Ted needs to be aware of this country where we live," I said.

"You sound like your grands, Bo. My dad would be proud of you," Mom said.

"We'll probably end up at the cemetery. I want Ted to know about our family, and there's no better place to start," I explained.

"What about you, Lexie. Are you going with them?" Tom asked.

"No, Dad. I'm going to let the boys have the afternoon to themselves. I've seen the bullet holes in the walls at the Lincoln jail where Billy the Kid killed two men while escaping. I'm going to take a Sunday nap and have a relaxing afternoon."

We weren't but a few miles from Fort Stanton so Mom took Lexie home. Ted and I were at the museum by 2:30. He was strangely quiet on the drive there. I asked him if he was feeling okay, thinking he had overdone it at lunch. After all, half an apple pie would make anyone feel bad.

"Sure. I feel great. It's hard to believe, but I know something about this place. I had a class at the university which focused on the most common diseases and treatments of the 20th Century. My professor was in his seventies and had developed an interest in tuberculosis when he was young. He was the go-to guy if anyone wanted history on the disease. He talked frequently about this place, saying it was the first TB treatment center in the country. He had visited it several times when he was younger. I can't believe this. Have you been through the Fort?"

"Yeah. Several times. When we have friends from out of state we usually visit this museum," I said.

"This is something else. We hear our professors talk about ideas and places but we seldom visualize them as real."

I had worried for nothing about entertaining Ted. We entered the museum, and for the next three hours, I waited, while he went through every detail. He must have read all the letters, descriptions and manuscripts that the place contained. Needless to say, we didn't get to see the bullet holes in the Lincoln county jail.

On the drive home, he talked about his day. "I enjoyed the museum immensely. It's much easier to imagine the work that was done there after you visit, rather than hearing about it in a classroom. It was wonderful that people could come to this high altitude and find relief from their disease. It actually gave them a longer and better life. My work and my studying has been about the future for the most part; however, I realize, also, how important it is to know about the past."

I listened intently without interrupting while he continued to express appreciation at what he had seen. Surprisingly, he also commented about the church service. "I enjoyed attending church today. Pastor Stevens had a good sermon. Maybe if I had attended a church with a pastor like him, I would have felt different about religion. The church we were forced to attend at boarding school was nothing like this. Most of the sermons were designed to put fear into us, threatening us, if we did or didn't do this or that."

We stopped by the cemetery on the way to the ranch. I asked Ted if Tommie had taken him up here. "No, we drove all over the ranch but didn't go to the cemetery. She showed me where it was and mentioned that it was important to her family."

We spent the last hour of daylight sitting in the chairs that had been placed there by my grands many years ago. I told him about my great-great-granddad coming to this country at the last of the 19th Century and buying this ranch. I tried to include information about each generation, including my Indian heritage. I told him about memories of my meme, grands, and of course, my mom and dad. I included the memory of that day, which is still clear in my mind, when Lexie and I told Jack and Zack that Sissy was their half sister. They had asked her if they could still call her 'Sissy' and she cried. I don't ever remember talking about it again. If anything, they became closer to her after that. Ted was a good listener and didn't interrupt until I paused.

"I envy you. Of course, as you know, I never had a real family. I guess my mom and dad loved me, in their own way. It makes me uncomfortable to even talk about family. Other boys had frequent visitors to the boarding school and I was jealous. When I left to attend college it was without regret and I never returned. Thank you for sharing the memories of your family. I have questions, but I prefer to save them for Tommie."

We returned to the ranch, to a supper of chicken and dumplings. I didn't expect Ted to be hungry. I was wrong.

The kids were home by early afternoon the next day. Lexie and I had discussed what type of greeting would take place between Tommie and Ted. She had bet me a thirty-minute massage that he would kiss her in front of everyone. I jumped all over that, telling her that wager was a lock.

We met them at the barn as they drove up. Zack had called from Roswell, so we were expecting them. Tommie exited the pickup, met Ted and kissed him. I nearly fell over. I could argue that he didn't kiss her, it was the other way around; however, I knew that wouldn't fly. Lexie nudged me in the ribs, saying, "That back massage is going to feel so good."

Lacy went to Ruidoso immediately to get Mark. After putting up the horses, the rest of us went to the house, settling down in the den to discuss the trip.

"I'm glad to be home," Tommie announced. "That trailer is a little crowded."

"Dad, I can't believe Scooter. He's a great horse. If you had roped on him nobody could have beaten you."

"Are you ready for some of the bigger rodeos?" I asked.

"I think so. You know, some of the professionals that made the rodeos we attended didn't do that well. The competition, for the most part, came from the local amateurs. That was strange, but exactly what you said."

"I have an announcement. Lacy doesn't need me anymore. I'm through traveling and babysitting these two. She'll be fine on her own. I'm sure she can find some friends to haul with," Tommie said.

"Where does that put me?" asked Zack.

"I would suggest that you get your own rig. Maybe you can find someone to haul with you. Mom and Dad might make some of the rodeos with you," Tommie said.

"What are your plans, Sissy?" asked Zack.

"I've been off a year. It's time for me to return to my mission work in Africa. I miss it. I've enjoyed being home, but I'm anxious to get back."

I glanced at Ted and he looked like he had been slapped away from the table. His mouth moved but nothing came out. Without doubt, the news was a shock to him. Give it to Tommie; she was anything but predictable.

"Don't looked so shocked. I'm not going tomorrow. It'll be a few weeks, at least," she said.

Silence followed the announcement until Lexie changed the subject to Lacy. "Is Lacy bringing Mark back to the ranch?"

"That was her plans," Zack replied.

"Diane and Carl will be disappointed," I said.

"That's something else I've given considerable thought to. I was part of bringing Mark to the United States so I have a responsibility to see that he has a good home. Lacy can't provide that on the rodeo circuit. I know that some families on the tour homeschool their children. I don't approve of that. Lacy needs to allow Carl and Diane to adopt Mark and give him a stable environment," Tommie said.

"Will she consent to that?" Lexie asked.

"I'm going to insist that she does. It's the right thing to do for Mark. I believe she'll agree when she's given it some serious thought. Lacy can still spend time with him when she's home."

We talked a while longer but Tommie's announcement had put a damper on the mood. I think the expression on Ted's face depressed all of us.

Ted stayed at the ranch for two more days, sleeping at our house, but spending the rest of the time with Tommie. By the time Lexie and I were ready to leave Wednesday for El Paso, Ted had gone back to Colorado Springs. Tommie was at the house to see us off.

"Dad, you be nice to the doctor and take care of yourself," she instructed.

"I'm nice most of the time, Tommie."

"What about Ted? He seemed depressed after your news," Lexie said.

"He's moving slow. No, that's not correct. Our relationship is at a standstill. It's like he's afraid of doing something wrong, so he does nothing. I thought my announcement might shock him into action. It didn't happen. He did hold my hand when we went to lunch yesterday in Ruidoso. Isn't that a hoot! Thirty years old and holding hands encourages you. Ted needs me, and maybe that's the reason I'm attracted to him."

"Have you talked to Lacy about Mark?" I asked.

"Dad, she said she would think about it. I'm going to bring up the subject again this week. Mark is still with Lacy but is wanting to go back to Ruidoso."

After the exchange about Mark, we said goodbye, and left for El Paso for my surgery.

CHAPTER 35

Lacy

MARK WAS GLAD TO SEE me but was reluctant to leave Carl and Diane. I had known this might happen, after being gone for several weeks. That's not long for an adult, but a child has a different perception of time. They had called most days and let me talk to Mark. His vocabulary had increased considerably, which was proof they had worked on his English daily. Each time I talked with him he would proudly have several new words.

Tommie's announcement that she would not accompany me on another tour did not surprise me, considering how much she loved her missionary work. I could never repay her for what she had done for me. My admiration for her had continued to grow during the last several months. I envied her strength and convictions.

I would never get over losing Jack. There were fewer days that I wasted grieving. That's strange to consider them wasted but that's the best description. I finally admitted that no amount of grieving and suffering would change the past. I was not interested in male companionship. The interest I had shown in Raleigh was intended to discourage Zack and nothing more. I cared for Zack but didn't love him. He was probably the most honest person I had ever known and was a wonderful man; however, he wasn't Jack, even though he looked so much like him.

Tommie had talked with me about allowing Carl and Diane to adopt Mark. I would do that, even though I didn't tell her at the time. It wouldn't be easy. I had imagined Mark as being my new family. I realized now that wasn't realistic and he'd be better off with Carl and Diane. They loved him and would give him a wonderful home.

I was going to continue to rodeo. Tommie's suggestion that I get someone to haul with me was good. That wouldn't be a problem. My horses were sound, and I'd give them some rest this fall to be ready the first of the year for the major shows at Fort Worth, Houston, and San Antonio.

It was Tuesday, August 14, and I was anxious to get back on the road. I planned to enter rodeos in Denton, Texas, Vinita, Oklahoma, and Pueblo, Colorado. I had everything ready to leave the next day. Suddenly, I had this great feeling of freedom and being able to take care of myself. Guilt followed at feeling good, but that passed quickly. I might only have one leg but I was in charge of my life and going after my dream.

I left early the next morning for the eight-hour drive to Denton. I was still feeling good and looking forward to my trip. I was up in the morning in the slack but should be in Denton by three in the afternoon.

Everything went good until I stopped at a red light in Decatur, which was only thirty minutes from Denton. My pickup sputtered, lost power, and when I accelerated to move through the light, it died. I tried to start it but was not successful. A strong smell of gas engulfed the cab. The car behind me started honking and suddenly, I panicked. What could I do? I had stopped traffic and now several cars were honking. I put my arm out the window and motioned for the cars to come around me. I couldn't decide whether to get out or remain in the cab. The light changed several times with a repeat of the honking and me motioning each time for them to go around me. The horses began moving around in the trailer, rocking the pickup. A voice in my head whispered, *you've got to do something.*

A man wearing jeans and a white shirt with a badge pinned to it came up to my window.

"Problem?" he asked.

"My pickup won't start. It just died. I don't know what to do."

"Release the hood," he instructed.

Looking under the hood, he returned, saying, "There's a gas smell. Probably a line broke. I'll call a wrecker to take you to a mechanic."

"What about the trailer and horses?" I asked.

"No problem. The wrecker can tow the entire rig. Just sit tight. He should be here shortly."

What a predicament. Why didn't this happen when Tommie and Zack were with me? That was a strange cop. His blonde hair was shoulder length and he had on jeans rather than a uniform. When he walked away, I noticed how broad his shoulders were. Oh, well, at least he was going to help get me to a mechanic.

Within fifteen minutes a wrecker pulled up in front of me and commenced to hook me up. A few minutes later we were on our way, arriving at a shop on the outside of town. I noticed the cop had followed us.

He met me as I was getting out, saying, "We'll need to unload your horses and unhook the trailer. That way, they can tow your truck inside the shop and take a look at it."

I followed his instructions, and after my pickup had been in the shop for a short time, a burly man smoking a cigar came out and said, "Injector went out. "I'll have to order one from the parts store. Hopefully they'll have it. Might have to send someone to Denton to get one." Without waiting for a reply, he turned and went back into his shop. I had tied my horses to the trailer and for the time being they were doing fine. I had forgotten about the cop who was standing by his car, smoking a cigarette. I looked in the trailer for a bucket to water the horses, found one, and when I came out the cop was gone. I didn't even get a chance to thank him.

Two hours later, Mr. Personality came out, saying, "Got it fixed. Here's your bill. Pay my wife inside."

When he turned to leave, I said, "Thank you. Could you tell me the name of the cop who helped me?"

"John," he said as he kept walking.

I went to the office, finding a woman who looked a great deal like her husband. I was hoping she would be a little more social. I had the bill in my hand, and asked, "Do you take credit cards?"

"Sure, honey. What kind do you have?"

"American Express."

"No problem."

"I appreciate your husband getting me fixed up. It was scary being stranded in town," I said.

"My husband doesn't talk much, but he knows his business. I do most of the talking. I noticed John brought you in."

"Yes. He's a strange cop. He doesn't wear a uniform. I didn't get a chance to thank him."

"Honey, he's a deputy sheriff and doesn't have to wear a uniform."

"I'm surprised they allow him to wear his hair that long. I would think they'd have a dress code."

"Honey, John can wear his hair anyway he wants in this county. People love him. Young, old, middle aged, men, women, and especially the single ladies."

"He doesn't even wear a gun," I said.

"Honey, John doesn't need a gun. Pardon my French, but John is a bad ass. No one knows his past except it was military, Special Forces. The only people in this part of the world that give him any problem are strangers. And they only do it once."

"He's not that big and he seems nice," I observed.

"He is. As long as you abide by the law," she stated.

"How long has he been a sheriff?" I asked.

"I guess about five years, give or take a few months.

I paid my bill, which I thought was reasonable, and was on my way, still thinking what a strange cop John was. I arrived at the arena, driving under a banner that read, *Welcome to the North Texas Fair and Rodeo.* I located the office, paid my entry fees, and was assigned stalls. They had hookups, but all were taken, which was not a problem since I had a generator.

My spirits were good again after resolving my pickup problems. I could handle things on my own, even though it might take me a little longer. I stalled Jazzy, and saddling Chrome, rode around the arena. It was a medium sized pen and would be a good fit for Jazzy. Chrome was more consistent but didn't have near the ability as Jazzy. When she made her run, I was going to win most of the time.

I was tired and went to bed early that night. My last thought before going to sleep was wondering if that cop noticed that I only had one leg.

The next morning, I had trouble getting Jazzy into the alley, but after several attempts was successful. She made a good run, with a time of 16.92. That was the fastest time of the other 29 in the slack. Ten more would run in the rodeo tonight and the top eight would go to the short go.

I had the remainder of the day with nothing to do. I had brought some books to read and that thought crossed my mind.

I was unsaddling Jazzy at the trailer when a voice from behind startled me. "You did really good."

Turning around, I was shocked to see the cop standing there smiling. "How did you find me?" I asked.

"It wasn't difficult. A lady with two horses going toward Denton would mean only one thing. I drove over this morning because you didn't get an opportunity to thank me yesterday."

"That wasn't my fault," I said.

"I know. I received a call and had to leave before you had the chance. I'm off today so here I am. Have you had breakfast?"

"No. Just coffee."

"There's an IHOP a few blocks from here. I'll let you buy my breakfast if you like."

I thought, this cop has a lot of gall. However, he did help me and that would be a way of repaying him. Suddenly, it dawned on me who he reminded me of. He was a replica of a younger and larger version of the vet at Colorado City.

"Okay, I can do that. Let me put my horse in the stall. I won't be but a few minutes."

"I'll go with you. I don't know the first thing about horses. Maybe I'll learn something."

As we were headed to the stall, I asked him, "How do you know that I'm not married?"

Laughing, he replied, "You would have told me right off. I read people pretty good. That goes with my job. You're not the kind of person that beats around the bush."

"Are all cops that perceptive?"

"Couldn't say. You know, some people consider the word cop a derogatory term. Fortunately, I don't. I would prefer deputy but it's not a big deal."

"Did you notice that I have a limp?" I asked.

"Yeah. Most people with a prosthetic do."

We had breakfast at IHOP and the pancakes were delicious. The conversation was good and easier than I thought. He told me that he had lost his wife after only being married a year. She had cancer, and after it was diagnosed didn't last but three months. It had occurred before he became a cop. I didn't tell him about Jack. I wasn't going there, not even sure that it would be possible for me to do so without breaking down.

We stayed an hour and visited after we finished eating. I went to the register to pay, reminding the cashier that I hadn't received a ticket.

"There's no charge. We're happy to have Deputy John eat with us. I assume you're his guest so there's no charge."

Going back to the table, where he had laid down several dollars for a tip, I said, "You fooled me. You knew they wouldn't charge you."

"Right. You enjoyed the breakfast though," he said.

"Yes. Thank you again. Me thanking you could get to be a habit," I said.

He dropped me off at my trailer, saying he would come back and watch the finals. I thanked him again, and as he drove off, scolded myself for repeating it.

My time held up that night, and I won the go round. Out of the 39 runners, I had the best time going into the finals. Now, if I could make a good run the next night in the short go, I would win the average.

I spent the next day with two friends, going on a shopping spree in Dallas. I had known both of them in high school and it was a fun day, plus it was a good way to spend the additional time before the rodeo.

I started getting ready two hours before the grand entry. I had lost some weight the past year. I bought several pair of jeans in Dallas that fit better. I had not paid much attention to my looks the past year but now felt a need to do so. Looking in the mirror, I approved of what I saw. I was a brunette with shoulder length hair that I usually wore in a pony tail, but tonight I had let it down. I was petite at 5 feet 2 inches but had a curvy figure as evidenced by the snug jeans and red plaid western shirt. The jeans that I had purchased in Dallas were too tight and I knew it at the time. I preferred loose jeans to ride in but something caused me to go against my better judgment. I had a black hat with buffalo strings that was several years old but felt good.

I rode in the grand entry and had two different cowboys try to start a conversation, but I let them know quickly I wasn't interested. I did catch myself looking into the stands for the cop who said he was coming to watch me.

The barrels were the second event and I was rider 8. I had decided to ride Chrome because of his consistency. I clocked a 17.02 which placed me third in the short go, but as I had hoped, was good enough to win the average. With the win in the first go and the average, I collected a check for $3200. I couldn't have been prouder of my horses. Two girls in the top ten were there and I beat them. That was encouraging for me.

I stayed the night in Denton and couldn't help but be disappointed that the cop never showed.

CHAPTER 36

Tommie Rose

I WAS SATISFIED WITH MY decision to send Lacy on her way. She was ready to be on her own and become independent. Ted had gone back to Colorado Springs without conveying interest in furthering our relationship. I had begun to think that he didn't want or expect it to go any further than it was.

It was Friday, August 17, and I had decided to leave for Africa around the first of next month. Dad should be recovered from his surgery by then. His operation had been yesterday, and he was coming home tomorrow. I had offered to accompany them but both insisted I remain at the ranch.

I was spending as much time as possible with Gramps and Mia. Yesterday, Mia had followed me to the car when I left, saying, "He gets worse by the day, Tommie. I don't know what to do. Surely, there's some kind of medicine that could help him."

"Let me talk to Diane and see what her thoughts are. Maybe she can refer Gramps to a specialist that could do more for him."

"I think that's a good idea. It's heart-wrenching to see him suffer day in and day out. He has such difficulty breathing, even sitting in his chair."

"I'll see what Diane thinks and get back with you immediately."

On the drive back to the highway, I realized Diane might be at home, since she didn't work Friday afternoons. I drove on into Ruidoso and saw that her car was home. She asked me in and said she was about to call me. Then she broke into tears.

"What's wrong?" I asked. She motioned me to sit down.

"Nothing. Everything's wonderful," she said, sniffing.

"Lacy called about an hour ago and told me she was going to allow us to adopt Mark. I can't believe it! It's a dream come true for me and Carl. We have prayed about it daily. I'm going to surprise him when he comes home. Oh, Tommie, I am so thankful."

"Where is Mark?" I asked.

"I take him to a day care center three afternoons a week to allow him to play with other children. He loves it. Carl will pick him up on the way home."

"I'm happy for you and Carl. Lacy did the right thing, and I'm proud of her. I know it wasn't easy."

"Carl had planned to take off work Monday morning to register Mark for kindergarten. He's going to be thrilled. I hope Mark will be happy also."

"I don't believe you need to worry about that," I said.

"Carl is going to a meeting next month in New York. He's dreading being gone and this will make it even worse. Jake has insisted that he go. Investment companies from all over the world will be present for seminars and lectures."

I did ask her about referring my dad to a cardiologist in Dallas where I thought he would be more comfortable. She said that would be a priority for her on Monday. She thought it was a good idea.

I left before Carl came home with Mark. I knew that was going to be a special occasion for their new family and didn't want to interfere. I was amazed at how things usually work out for the best.

Since Lacy was gone, I had the house to myself, allowing me too much time to think. I took my iced tea out on the front porch after eating supper and watched the sunset. I had my 30th birthday last month. Being so involved in my work, I had never given much thought to a family. That had changed since being back at the ranch with my family. Now, I felt a sense of urgency that was new to me. Previously, I had thought that my work and the people in the village receiving my ministry were my family. Realizing that I didn't feel that way anymore posed a major problem. Would it be necessary to sacrifice one or the other?

I love my ministry in Africa but coming back home for a year made me realize how much I loved this ranch. I had decided that the mission would have to do without me one month each year so that I could return to my family.

Like most, I had my demons that haunted me. The kidnapping, when I was ten definitely had an emotional impact on my life. The fourteen days I spent tied up in that basement would remain with me for the rest of my life. I still had nightmares reliving that horrible experience. My family and others have told me how strong my faith is. Faith and prayer are the only way that I was able to survive the hell those people put me through.

They left me tied up and gagged day and night. I was untied and allowed one meal a day and two trips to the bathroom, which was a pot in the corner of the basement. There were times I couldn't wait and soiled my clothes. When this happened the woman would pinch me as punishment. I knew their plan was to kill me.

I will never forget the shot, and a few minutes later, the basement door opening and my mother standing at the top of the stairs. When she took me upstairs and I saw that woman laying against the wall, I screamed, *I'm glad you're dead.* I've asked forgiveness many times for that statement. Of course, she wasn't dead. I've even tried to forgive them for what they put me through. Maybe, to some extent, I have. However, I hope they never get out of prison.

I saw my mom, after that incident, in an entirely different manner. My dad had always been the strong one, and even though we loved Mom, we would never have thought her capable of such an act. To this day, she wouldn't talk about it. The only comment I ever heard her make was *I'm so glad she didn't die.* To my knowledge, she has never touched a gun after she rescued me.

Recovering took time; my family was wonderful, and went to great extreme to support me and understand my fears. The most effective therapy came from Flame and rodeo. Flame seemed to understand how I needed him. I'll never own another horse like him. Dad called me the first year I was in Africa to tell me he had died and he had buried him in the apple orchard beside his friend, Bear. Sitting there watching the sunset, tears came to my eyes, as I thought of that call.

I've often wondered, if not for the kidnapping, would I have become a pastor. Each time, my conclusion is that it wasn't the decisive factor in me entering the ministry. Maybe my commitment became stronger, but I have convinced myself the decision was made even before that terrible experience. Pastor Stevens did have an influence on my decision. Not by what he said to me, but by his actions, as he ministered to this community. I had noticed, even from an early age, that whenever our family suffered a tragedy he was the first person we called.

I didn't know what Zack's future held for him. I couldn't see him remaining on the pro circuit indefinitely or staying on the ranch for any length of time. I had developed a whole new appreciation for my brother. Prior to this last year we had not spent much time together since I graduated from high school twelve years ago. He was a gentleman in every sense of the word, being courteous, respectful, and honest. My dad had always spent more time with Jack and, of course, Gramps was partial to me. Mom split the difference between them, but that still left Zack out.

Zack resembled our dad to an unbelievable degree when he roped. They favored one another anyway, and when he dismounted his horse and went to tie his calf, he was a replica of Dad. I had no doubt but what he was going to be successful on the pro tour; however, I didn't know how strong his commitment was going to be. I knew that it was not nearly so strong as Lacy's.

It was difficult to imagine any girl rejecting Zack, even Lacy. I know she was devastated at losing Jack, but with time I had thought she would see what a wonderful man Zack was and how much he cared about her. I still thought there might be a chance it would happen."

Jack and Zack, being identical twins and favoring our dad, had been downright good looking boys. With their dark complexion, black hair, and blue eyes they turned heads wherever they went. What continued to amaze me is that Zack showed very little interest in anyone except Lacy.

Being an eternal optimist, I thought, *someone will come along and will steal his heart before he even knows it.* My phone interrupted me before my next thought.

"Tommie, are you busy?"

"No, Mom. Just sitting outside, thinking too much."

"I have a problem. Maybe you can help me," she said.

"Sure, I'll try."

"It's my mother, Tommie, and your grandmother, who has never accepted either of us as her relative. She has refused to talk to me on every occasion that we were thrown together, most times by a funeral. Lord knows I've tried but to no avail. I received a call from one of our longtime family friends in Dallas this afternoon. My mother is ill, and from what I gather, it's serious. I can't decide what to do."

"What do you feel you should do?" I asked.

"Go see her. But what if she refuses to talk to me, like she has done in the past? I might do more harm than good."

"If she dies, Mom, without giving her one last chance, imagine how you would feel. Would you like for me to go with you?"

"Oh, Tommie, would you? That would make it much easier for me."

"Sure, but let's drive instead of flying. I can't leave until after church Sunday. I promised Pastor Stevens to allow him some time off. I'm going to do the service for the next two Sundays. The church can't afford a pastor to fill in for him, so the only way he has of getting time off is with my help."

"No problem. We can leave after church Sunday."

We packed the next day for the trip and left after church, August 19, for Dallas. Dad was apprehensive about us going, saying that there was no reason for her to be any different after thirty years. I had seldom ever referred to her, and when I did, I called her Grandmother.

Mother had hardly talked about her, but opened up more on the drive to Dallas. "My mother never gave me any indication that she loved me. She appeared to find me more of a nuisance than anything. She was partial to my brother, Todd, who could do nothing wrong. She treated my other brother, Zack, a little better than me, but not much."

"She didn't even talk to you when Uncle Zack was killed?"

"No. She was angry at the funeral and ignored me when I tried to make conversation. I've never known anyone as bitter as she is. She didn't contact us when you were kidnapped, and it was on the national news, so she was aware of it."

"Does she ever talk to Gramps? He never mentions her to me," I said.

"Probably. After all, she receives a large amount of money each month due to the divorce settlement. He hasn't said anything to me either about talking to her. My dad doesn't hold a grudge against her, in fact, he has always taken a share of the blame for her being the way she is. Your gramps is a very forgiving person."

It was a long drive, but the traffic was light until we reached Weatherford. We decided to stop in Arlington for the night and go on to Dallas the next morning after the traffic had cleared.

Mom handled the traffic like a pro and we stopped in front of our destination at mid-morning. It was a nice townhouse in one of the new additions on the north side of Dallas.

"Well, here we are," Mom said.

Ringing the doorbell, a black lady greeted us. "What can I do for you?" she asked.

"We're here to see Elizabeth. I'm her daughter and this is her granddaughter," Mom said.

"Yes, ma'am," she said. "Let me tell her you're here."

Returning shortly, she announced, "Ms. Elizabeth doesn't want to see you. I'm sorry. She's very sick."

"Take me to her," I said.

"I-I can't. I'll l-lose my job," she said.

"Wait here, Mom," I said.

I pushed past the lady and found the bedroom where my grandmother was sitting in a recliner in her bathrobe. She looked old and frail.

"Grandmother, we've come a long way to see you. We're not leaving until you talk to us. We love you and are worried about you. The time has come for you to accept us as family."

She glared at me, but didn't respond. I continued, "You're ill and may die. Do you want to die angry and full of hate? I'm a pastor and missionary, having seen more than my share of death in Africa. Families would come together for comfort during these times of sorrow. You need us now and we need you. Please talk to us and maybe we can be a family again."

Nothing. She continued to glare at me. I stood there for at least five minutes before saying, "Okay. We're leaving, but I'm giving my cell number to your nurse. We're going to stay in Dallas tonight and leave for New Mexico at noon tomorrow. Please think about what I said and call me before we leave." I went over to her chair and took her hand. She tried to pull away but was too weak.

"I'm going to say a prayer for you." I bowed my head, saying, "*Wondrous God, we ask for your help to provide comfort and strength to my grandmother during these difficult times. We also ask that her heart be opened up to this family, where she belongs, so we might provide the love that she so desperately needs.*"

I went back to the living room where mom and the nurse were waiting. I gave my number to the nurse and told her what I had said to my grandmother about getting in touch with us.

"Tommie, this is Annie. Annie, this is my daughter. We appreciate anything that you might do to help us."

"She's very ill. Nobody comes to visit her. I'm her only friend, and she depends on me for everything. I'll do what I can to help you," Annie said.

Thanking her, we left. On the drive to find a place to eat lunch, Mom asked me, "What do you think?"

"She's a tough one. I don't know. It's obvious that she's critically ill."

We found a Chili's restaurant, and we had just finished our meal when my phone went off. "Ms. Tommie, she's agreed to visit with you and your mother."

CHAPTER 37

Zack

I HAD STAYED AT THE ranch after getting home from the Texas trip. Lacy had let the air out of my sails with her response to my proposal to be more than friends. This was not a busy time on the ranch, since the hay had been put up for the winter, the calves worked, and grazing was adequate.

I had to babysit Dad while Mom and Sissy had gone to Dallas to visit my grandmother. Dad thought it was a wasted trip since she hadn't spoken to any of our family for the past thirty years. I admit that was a lot of anger, and I kind of agreed with him. She was actually a stranger to me, and she must be some piece of work.

Dad, recovering from surgery, had consented to using crutches for the time being. How long that would last was anybody's guess. Mom was hesitant to leave, but I promised to look after him while they were in Dallas. We made it okay for the four days they were gone. I would cook breakfast and we'd have a sandwich for lunch. Mia would have us over for supper and by then we would be starved. She was an awesome cook, and we looked forward to that meal.

I was in a dilemma as to what my plans would be for the fall. Mom and Dad were doing well, considering it had been less than a year since Jack's death. Lacy had gone back to the tour alone, or without me. One part of me wanted to continue to rodeo, but the other part said I needed to be back in school. I knew one thing for a fact. I had to find out just how good I was. We had made the smaller rodeos but had not been to a major PRCA rodeo with the top cowboys in the world present.

On the way over to Mia's Tuesday evening, I asked my dad what he thought, after explaining my dilemma.

"Zack, you need to do what makes you happy. People constantly encouraged me to go professional, but I was happy right here on this ranch. Don't worry about pleasing anyone else. The other problem can be solved easily. Albuquerque has a major PRCA show in early September. The best cowboys will be there. You can make a couple of the rodeos close to home and then test your skills against the best there. Maybe you can make a decision after that. Of course, the fall semester will have already started; however, maybe you can enroll late if that's the way you decide to go."

That made sense and gave me some short-term direction, at least. We arrived at Mia's, and she had a great meal, consisting of a pot roast with potatoes and carrots. She had homemade rolls and a garden salad to go with the roast. Dessert, of course, was cobbler made with apples from our orchard. Gramps didn't eat with us, saying he wasn't hungry. Mia told us later that it took him so long to eat that he was embarrassed. Mia was unusually quiet, and Dad asked her if she was worried about something.

"Bo, you know me. I'm a worrier. I woke up last night with that dreadful feeling that comes with a terrible event. It's probably nothing, but it worries me. These feelings are the only thing I dislike about my Indian heritage. Changing the subject, but when will Lexie and Tommie be home?"

"Tomorrow afternoon," Dad answered.

"They called last night and were pleased with the trip," I volunteered.

"I'm glad. Tom has always worried about Elizabeth not accepting Lexie or the kids. Maybe she will now," Mia replied.

We visited an hour after supper with Gramps and Mia before leaving. Gramps had difficulty talking because of his breathing. It made me wonder why good people had to suffer.

Mom and Sissy were home late the next afternoon. They were in good spirits, and Mom explained the reason. "The trip was a success, thanks to Tommie. I would've given up on my mom and come home but she persisted and prevailed."

"How much time did you spend with her?" Dad asked.

"We were with her three hours Monday and most of the day Tuesday," Tommie said.

"What did you talk about all that time?" Dad asked.

"Everything. We had a lot to catch up on. Of course, she knew nothing about our family, especially the kids. Strangely, she was interested in Tommie's work in Africa and her ministry. After some encouragement, she talked freely about herself. She hasn't led a happy life. I never would have expected my mom to open up the way she did," Mom said. "That's the first time she's talked to me in thirty years."

"Did she mention Tom?" Dad asked.

"Occasionally, but not in a negative manner. It seemed that the longer she talked, the more her anger diminished," Sissy explained.

"She promised to take our calls and to keep us informed about her condition. Her nurse and caretaker is wonderful and was helpful in getting her to talk with us," Sissy said.

"She didn't even come to Jack's funeral," Dad said angrily.

"Bo, you have to remember, she didn't know Jack, had never even seen him," Mom said. "If I can forgive her for how she treated me, surely you can, also."

Dad didn't respond, and I knew it would be harder for him. That's just the way he was.

I made a rodeo in Alamogordo the next weekend and one in Anthony the following week, winning both of them. Scooter worked great, and I was roping as good as I ever had. Mom and Dad made both rodeos, traveling with me. It was a good time for all of us. We were back at the ranch on Monday, September 2.

I continued to stay in my travel trailer at the barn, and after supper with Mom and Dad, went to bed early. My cell woke me up sometime during the night. I looked and it was 2:25. Seeing it was Lacy, suddenly I was wide awake and frightened. "Hello."

She was having trouble talking but finally got it out. "Jazzy died, Zack. It was colic and the vet couldn't save her." She started sobbing and I waited until she could talk again. "I don't know what to do, Zack. I have another rodeo next weekend. Should I come home or ride Chrome? I'm confused. Why did this have to happen to me now? Isn't losing Jack and my leg enough?"

"Where are you now?" I asked.

"Sitting in my pickup at the vet clinic. I don't know what to do. Help me, please."

"Listen to me, Lacy. Everything will be all right. Go back to your trailer and try to get some sleep. Do you think you can drive home tomorrow? You're in Pueblo, right? It'll be about a seven hour drive. You need to come home and regroup. You're not in any condition to make another show."

"Okay. I can make the drive. I probably can't sleep, but I'll wait until morning to leave," she said.

"Don't leave before daylight," I said.

"Okay. I'll be home tomorrow," she said.

No way could I go back to sleep. I made coffee and took it outside, wondering if anything had changed. After all, she had said, "Help me, please."

I was at Lacy's house when she arrived home the next afternoon. She got out of her pickup and came over and hugged me, saying, "Thank you for telling me what to do. I was devastated at losing Jazzy and couldn't think straight. Coming home was the only thing to do."

"Now what?" I asked, as she backed Chrome out of the trailer.

"I honestly don't know. I was doing great on Jazzy. We had won Pueblo, and even missing the bigger shows the first half of the year, had moved into the top twenty. Chrome can't compete consistently with the best. He's dependable and is a good backup horse, but he's at least a half second off Jazzy."

"I'm going to the fair at Albuquerque this weekend. You can go with me and run Chrome. Maybe we can locate you another horse."

"I didn't even get to bury Jazzy. The vet did cut a piece of her mane off for me. Will you go with me to bury it in the orchard beside Flame and Bear? After we do that, I'd like to go into Ruidoso and see Mark."

Of course I agreed. She cried when we buried Jazzy's mane between Flame and Bear. Later, the reunion with Lacy and Mark was emotional, again. Lacy broke into tears holding Mark for a long time before releasing him.

Carl was not at home, but Diane was understanding when I told her what happened. She offered to let Mark go stay a few days with her, but Lacy declined, saying, "No, he doesn't need to miss school. Maybe he can come out for a weekend soon."

"How's Carl?" I asked.

"Great. His business has taken off with the help of Todd. He has a meeting in New York starting this Saturday, lasting for five days. He's dreading being gone that long. Mark will be lost without him. He doesn't let Carl out of his sight when he's home."

"Tell Carl hello for us and that we're sorry we missed him."

"I'll do that and thanks for coming back to see Mark," she said.

On the drive back to the ranch, Lacy was quiet. To start a conversation, I asked her about going to Albuquerque this weekend.

"I guess so, Zack. I don't want to sit around the house and grieve over the loss of Jazzy. I'll never be able to replace her. I actually think that next year I could have made the Finals. One thing I've learned the last year though… you can't change the past, no matter how you dwell on it. Another is that you need someone in times of joy and sorrow to share it with.

"The rodeo is Friday, Saturday, and Sunday. We'll leave tomorrow and you can enter when we get there. I'm already pre-entered."

"It'll be tough. At least half of the top fifteen will be there," she said. "Are your mom and dad going?"

"Only if we make the short go. Tommie's staying because she's filling in for Pastor Stevens Sunday."

"I thought I could make it on my own. Now I have doubts, after this last week. Thank you again for being there for me."

After saying this, she reached over and touched my arm.

Once in a great while everything seems to come together. We went to Albuquerque Thursday and I roped in the slack Friday morning. I drew a good calf, roped him quick, and tied him in 8.4, which was the fastest time of the morning. Lacy didn't run until Saturday so we had the rest of the day off. The fair was in full swing and we went to the midway, looking at exhibits, eating foot-long hotdogs and riding the tilt-a-whirl. We actually laughed out loud at some of our antics, a first in almost a year. It was one of the best days that I can remember. The midway was crowded and in order to stay together we held hands.

That night she told me I was welcome to sleep in the trailer. I wasn't going there yet and declined. I slept well on my cot in the horse stall, thinking maybe everything was going to work out after all.

My good fortune continued when I roped in the performance Saturday night. Once again, I had a good calf and tied him in 9.1, which was good enough for second in the go-round. I was going into the short go with the best average by almost a second. Lacy had a good run, which barely made the short go. She was pleased with her run, saying that Chrome did his best.

When I called Mom that night and told her the good news, she said they had decided not to come. She was afraid Dad hadn't recovered enough for that long a drive.

Sunday afternoon was a repeat of Saturday. As the old country music lyrics say, "When you're hot, you're hot, when you're not, you're not." I drew good again, tying my calf in 8.7 and winning the short go and the average. I was thrilled with my efforts, discovering that seven out of the top fifteen calf ropers in the world competed.

Lacy had another good run, finishing seventh and just out of the money. Strangely, she wasn't disappointed, saying, "I actually did better than I expected."

The rodeo was over by 5:00 that afternoon, but we decided not to start home until morning. We put up our horses and went back to the carnival to become teenagers, once again.

CHAPTER 38

Lexie

I WOKE UP EARLY, AND rather than lay there without being able to go back to sleep, rose and made coffee. Looking at the clock, it was only 5:15. Today was Sunday and we were going to church. The older I became, the earlier I woke up. Bo was the opposite, sleeping later than he ever had.

We had stayed up late last night after Zack had called, too excited to go to bed. I detected something in Zack's voice that had been missing. I assume it had to do with Lacy. He mentioned her several times in our conversation even though she hadn't done that well.

I sat down with a cup of coffee and thought about the week. I had actually visited with my mother for the first time in three decades. She was 75 years old and ill, ignoring me for a lifetime, yet I was thrilled at being able to sit down and talk to her. After all, she was my mother and I loved her. It would have never happened without Tommie. I was ready to give up and come home.

Bo still went to the family cemetery at least twice each week. Some days, when he returned not speaking for hours, I felt his sorrow and respected his privacy. It wasn't easy, and it would have been better for him to talk about it. That was not Bo and would not happen.

Felicia had actually been better and we had talked several times since she presented her last problem to me. She had agreed to let her daughter, Jolynda, attend school in Texas and pursue a theater arts degree, as I had recommended. She conveyed to me that their relationship had already improved.

My dad's and Bo's race filly didn't do well in the All American trials; however, the outside horse Jimmy trained did qualify and ran third in the big race. He collected a hefty check for the third place finish. I will give Felicia credit; she had been spending more time with Jimmy.

Bo came in at seven, saying, "You got up early."

"Sure did, sleepy head. Ready for coffee?"

"Yeah. Let's go outside and sit on the porch. It looks like a nice day."

It was a beautiful fall morning in New Mexico. The temperature was in the mid-forties, the sky was clear, and the mountains were a deep blue.

"We still haven't started our new house," he said.

"I know. It's my fault. I keep dragging my feet. We raised our family in this house and it's going to be hard to leave."

"Do you want to back out?'

"No. It will be exciting to build our own house. Also, we need to be closer to my dad. Tommie is leaving and Lacy will be gone a great deal of the time. Your mom is going to eventually need help with Dad."

"On another matter, Zack had an awesome rodeo! He has his questions answered now, about how good he is. I knew it all the time. That little horse is amazing and together they're going to be tough."

"Do you think he'll continue to rodeo instead of going back to school?" I asked.

"Definitely. After this weekend, it's hard to imagine him doing anything else."

"In a way, I'm sorry. Not that he did well this weekend, but giving up his dream of being a doctor."

"He may eventually go back to school but not anytime soon," Bo stated.

"How's your leg? I noticed you've already abandoned the crutches," I said.

"Better. I don't need the sticks anymore."

"You better take care of yourself. You're not as young as you used to be," I reminded him.

We left for church at 10:15, giving us plenty of time for the twenty mile trip.

"Bo, I look forward to hearing Tommie preach. I'm proud of her. It's really kind of her to fill in for Pastor Stevens and give him some time off. I'm going to miss her when she goes back to Africa next week."

We arrived at the church, and it was obvious that a large crowd would be present. That was always the case when Tommie preached. She was a favorite, especially with the older people. She had been raised in this church and most of them felt they had been part of her growing into this wonderful young lady.

She was standing outside, greeting people as we arrived. She hugged her dad and me, saying, "Both of you look so nice today."

"Thanks. Are you going to lay it on us today?" Bo asked.

Laughing, she replied, "You probably need it, Dad; however, I have a positive uplifting message today that will make you go away smiling."

Diane and Mark were behind us. They were slow getting to the church entrance. Mark was precious, in his white shirt and bow tie. A good description of him would be huggable and that's what everyone wanted to do. I know he got tired of it, but he was patient. I didn't get an opportunity to speak to them, but I made a note to do so after the service. I was curious as to how Carl was making it on his trip to New York.

The church held about fifty people and it was full, with standing room only. Tommie welcomed everyone and went over a list of concerns of the church, mentioning deaths and illnesses of members. After that she offered a prayer on their behalf. That was followed by a hymn, which was beautiful due to the large crowd and choir.

She came back to the pulpit with her Bible, saying, "I want to welcome each and everyone of you on this beautiful September day in 2001, the year of our Lord. Now, I usually have selected a scripture by this time; however, this morning will be different. I do this occasionally in my Bible study at home. I just open my Bible and point, not looking at the scripture and verse where my finger ends. I have had questions and concerns answered doing this on more than one occasion. It may seem a little strange, but please give it a try some time.

At this point, exaggerating her movements, she opened her Bible and pointed. She looked down and hesitated before saying. "My scripture this morning comes from Proverbs 6: 17-18. *The Lord hates hands that shed innocent blood, and a heart that devises wicked plans.*"

She continued on with her sermon, but the scripture diminished her uplifting and joyous message.

As we exited the church, Bo and I told her she did great. We caught up with Diane and Mark, since they were ahead of us.

"Diane, it's good to see you and Mark," I said.

"Oh, me, Lexie, Mark is getting tired of everyone wanting to hug him. We're trying to escape before more of the congregation ambushes us."

"You can't blame them, Diane. He's darling," I said.

"I know, Lexie, but he doesn't understand."

"I wanted to ask you how Carl was doing at his meeting in New York?"

"Not good and we're doing worse. Mark keeps wanting to know when 'Ibutho' is coming home. He still calls him that after the fight at the restaurant. I feel so sorry for Carl, Lexie. He is miserable. First of all, he hates to fly. He is terrified of heights. Added to this misery is that the meetings are being held on a top floor, and the air conditioning has been off. He said they have been suffering with the heat.

"Where are the meetings being held?" I asked.

"The World Trade Center," she answered.

CHAPTER 39

Bo

I MET ZACK AT THE barn when he came in the next day. He had taken Lacy by her house before coming home. Getting out of the pickup, I gave him a hug.

"What a rodeo! I'm proud of you. Did that performance answer your question about how good you really are?"

"Dad, it was great. I can't believe that many top cowboys were there and I beat them all. A guy followed me to my stall after the short go and wanted to buy Scooter. I told him he wasn't for sale and his response was, 'Just name a price.' I told him again that he wasn't for sale. Then he threw out an astronomical figure that I couldn't believe."

"And you worried about paying too much for Scooter," Dad said. "Now what are your plans?"

"Continue to rodeo, now that I know I can compete," he said.

"Put your horses up and come on to the house. Your mother will want to hear about the trip."

I couldn't help but be excited about his decision to rodeo. That means he would be at the ranch, at least some of the time. When I told Lexie, she was pleased, also.

"Oh, Bo, I hope we're not being selfish, wanting him to be home some of the time. He has always wanted to be a doctor."

"I'm not worried about that, Lexie. I'm just happy to have him around, at least occasionally."

Zack came in before we could continue our conversation, giving his mom a hug.

"I'm so proud of you, Zack. You had an amazing weekend in Albuquerque. I'm sorry we missed it."

"No problem, Mom. Lacy was there to help me celebrate. We had a great time at the fair. I felt like a kid again."

We visited for the better part of an hour, hearing all about the rodeo and a great deal about Lacy. After Zack left, Lexie had an observation that was no surprise.

"Bo, it seems that Lacy has changed her mind about Zack. I haven't seen him this way since we lost Jack. Maybe there's hope after all. It certainly seems that way now."

"It's almost too much to wish for," I replied.

The next morning was Tuesday, September 11. I slept late again, not getting up until after 7:00. After a breakfast of bacon and eggs and three cups of coffee, I was ready to go. I had to service several windmills which needed greasing and repair a gate in one of the pastures that had been knocked off its hinges by an over-ambitious bull.

It was a beautiful day with sunshine and a hint of fall in the air. My favorite time of year was here. I drove to the top of the mountain behind our house and stopped, appreciating the view. This ranch didn't have the trees of the north ranch but it held a stark beauty that I loved. I saw movement to my right at the bottom of the mountain. A large mule deer buck walked out from behind a shrub that didn't look large enough to hide him. This ranch didn't have as many deer as the north ranch, but the trophy bucks sometimes showed up here. Jimmy still loved to hunt, and I would need to tell him about this buck.

I felt for my cell phone and realized that I didn't have it. I wasn't going back to the house. I had a full day ahead of me and it would be nice not to be interrupted. Maybe Lexie wouldn't call. She was the only one I worried about. It always upset her when I didn't have the phone with me. I looked at my watch and it was just past 8:45. I had to start getting up earlier. Sleeping till past 7:00 in the morning didn't allow me a full day's work.

AT 8:46 AMERICAN FLIGHT 11 CRASHED INTO THE NORTH TOWER OF THE WORLD TRADE CENTER IN NEW YORK CITY…KILLING EVERYONE ABOARD AND AN UNKOWN NUMBER OF PEOPLE IN THE TRADE CENTER.

My first chore was to repair the gate that separated two of the pastures. It was an iron gate and going to be heavy. My work consisted of putting it back on the hinges, which was not going to be easy. I brought my large bumper jack, and the first thing I did was stand the gate up against the post with the hinges. Using the jack, I raised the other end, so it was possible to install the gate back on it hinges. It took me several tries, and I was out of breath when I finished. I sat down on the ground and said to myself, *you're not getting any younger,* smiling at Lexie's exact words.

AT 9:03, UNITED AIRLINES FLIGHT 175 STRUCK THE SOUTH TOWER…KILLING ALL ABOARD ALONG WITH AN UNKNOWN NUMBER IN THE TOWER.

Sitting there, with my strength returning, I thought what a great life I had. I never wanted to do anything but ranch, and good fortune allowed me to do that. I could have someone else do this kind of work, but I actually enjoyed it. A day would come when it wouldn't be possible, but I dreaded that time. This land was my life and I wanted to be a working part of it for as long as possible.

Now, on to the windmills. Lexie would raise all kind of hell with me if she knew I was climbing windmills with my leg not completely healed. What she didn't know wouldn't hurt her. She was getting worse about telling me what to do, and especially what not to do. I had brought an extra tube of grease in case I needed it.

I felt good today. I was doing work that had to be done and that I had performed since I was a kid. Thirty minutes after the work on the gate, I was on top of the first windmill. It was going to turn without a squeak when I finished.

AT 9:37, TRAVELING ABOUT 530 MILES AN HOUR, AMERICAN FLIGHT 77 CRASHED INTO THE PENTAGON, KILLING ALL ON BOARD AS WELL AS MANY CIVILIAN AND MILITARY PERSONNEL.

Halfway down the windmill, I heard a honking. Looking back toward the road down the mountain, I saw a car parked at the top. That had to be Lexie, and she was going to be upset if she saw me up here. I finished my descent, hoping she couldn't see this far. She had probably discovered that I left my phone and brought it to me.

It took several minutes for me to reach her, driving faster than I should on the rough roads. She was out of the car when I arrived, and I could see she was upset. She was at my pickup before I could get out.

"Bo, they've attacked the World Trade Center," she cried.

"Who?" I asked.

"I don't know. Planes flew into it! Carl is there! Diane has called and she's frantic! She can't reach him on his phone."

"Let's get back to the house. I'll follow you," I told her.

A few minutes later, we were in the den watching television. We sat there speechless as the South Tower collapsed. Seconds later the phone rang and Lexie answered.

She was silent for a few seconds and then said, "We'll be there as quick as possible, Diane."

"Bo, we need to go into town and stay with Diane. She still hasn't been able to contact Carl, and she needs us."

"Okay. Call Zack and tell him to bring Lacy and met us there. Diane is going to need help with Mark when he gets home from school."

We were at Diane's in twenty-five minutes and found her in tears. She was trying to talk but having a difficult time. "I-I can't reach him. He w-was at a m-meeting in the N-North Tower. I-It collapsed. I-I pray to God he got out."

A few minutes later a news commentator announced that another hijacked plane, United 93, had gone down in a field in Pennsylvania, only twenty minutes flying time from Washington DC.

"Who could've done such a horrible thing?" Lexi asked.

"Bin Laden," I said. "He has labeled us infidels. His goal is to kill us."

Zack, Lacy, and Tommie had joined us, and we sat there for the next two hours being given information about the worst terrorist attack ever suffered on American soil. The longer we watched, the more terrified Diane became.

"What can I do? I have to do something! I can't just sit here and watch and do nothing! Please help me!"

"There's no way a commercial flight will get close to New York. I'll call Stewart and see if he might be able to get you to New York.

"Thank you. If I can just get there, maybe I can find out something," Diane said.

I called Stewart, and after explaining our situation, he told me he would get back with me as soon as possible. They were saying now that the fatalities could number in the thousands. We sat there silently watching the most horrendous event that could be imagined.

Stewart called back in fifteen minutes saying he had found an airport where he could land that was about two hours from New York. He told me that his plane would be ready to leave in half an hour. I relayed the information to Diane, who immediately went to pack a change of clothes.

"I'm going with her, Dad. She can't go by herself," Zack announced.

"No telling what will happen next in that area. More attacks may be coming and I can't lose another son," I said. "Let me go instead."

"No. I'm going and that's final. Maybe I can be of some help with my medical training."

Lacy was crying when we were preparing to leave the house, begging Zack to be careful. Tommie and Lacy promised Diane to take care of Mark. Before leaving, Tommie led us in prayer.

Lexie and I drove Zack and Diane to the airport, arriving at just past two. Lexie had been silent until just before they boarded the plane but couldn't hold her emotions any longer, grabbing Zack and saying. "Zack, please take care of yourself! We love you! Like your dad said, we can't lose another son!"

Lexie hung onto my arm as the plane sped down the runway, lifting off and heading for what was considered at that moment to be the most dangerous place in the world.

CHAPTER 40

Zack

AFTER WE HAD CLIMBED TO our flight altitude, Stewart came back to where we were seated. "Zack, we have clearance to land at the Philadelphia Airport. Hopefully they won't change their minds. With all that has happened, it's not out of the question."

"Once again, you were here to help us, Stewart. We appreciate it," I said.

"That's what friends are for, Zack. I'm glad to be able to help. This is a horrible event for our country. I can't imagine what it looks like at the scene. I know television can't reveal the devastation caused by planes flying into buildings."

Diane, quiet until this time and clinching her cell phone with both hands, said, "He was on a top floor. That had to be the worst place. I-I don't see how he could have made it out. I keep wanting my phone to ring and hear his voice."

"How long a flight will it be?" I asked.

"About four hours, give or take," Stewart answered.

After that short exchange, silence followed for the next hour. Diane sat with a stoic expression, grasping her phone, and seldom moving.

I had a sense, at least, of the agony she was going through, after sitting and hoping for Jack to recover when there was little chance. We still were going to have over 100 miles to go when we landed. The best option was to get a taxi. Renting a car would just create a need for directions and wasted time.

Tommie had wanted to come, but I convinced her she needed to stay with Mom and Dad. Also, she had planned to leave for Africa in four days. I knew that Diane was right about Carl's chance of surviving. She had told us earlier that Jake wasn't with Carl at the meetings. That was good, since it would be a terrible blow to Dad if he lost two friends. Jake was special to him also. He spoke often of how he had befriended him and Jeremiah during their first days at college.

My mind went back to Lacy. Something had changed. I assumed it was losing Jazzy and having that helpless feeling that accompanies tragedy. Just like that, she wasn't independent anymore, but needed someone. I guess being there made me her choice. Had her true feelings for me changed or was I just handy? Since I had decided to continue the pro circuit, we would be together, and time would answer my question. Diane broke her silence.

"I keep asking myself, why did this have to happen now? We were so happy. Carl didn't want to go to New York. He started dreading it weeks before the time to leave. People don't understand Carl. He doesn't make friends easily because he's quiet. If it had not been for Jake, I doubt if anyone would have hired him. When people discover how honest and straightforward he is, they trust him. That is the primary reason he has been successful in the investment business. I am much like him and that is the reason we found one another. Two shy misfits that share a life together. Then we discovered Mark, which made our life complete. Now this horrible event, and I know he didn't make it."

At that point, she couldn't continue. I felt for her and the suffering she was going through. I didn't know what to say, thinking that it was best to only listen and not offer encouragement or advice. Stewart came back and told us that we were about an hour from Philadelphia and everything was looking good for us to be able to land. I looked at my watch and saw it was 5:30, then realized it was 7:30 New York Time.

I didn't have a change of clothes with me, but wasn't going to be concerned with what we were facing. I didn't plan on being here more than a couple of days anyway.

We landed at 9:45. Stewart and his pilot were going to spend the night in Philadelphia before going back to New Mexico. Outside the terminal, I found a taxi, asking him if he could take us to New York.

"That's over a hundred miles. More like 140. Where in New York?" he asked.

"The World Trade Center. Her husband was in the North Tower when it was struck," I said.

"It'll cost you a minimum of $900. More if traffic extends the time past three hours."

"Okay."

We rode in silence for most of the time, arriving as close to our destination as possible a few minutes past 12:30. Streets were blocked and we still had a long walk to get to the site.

We walked for half an hour before reaching the devastation. It was dark but light plants had been set up at the site and there was a lot of activity. The smell was terrible, consisting of fumes which reeked of gas that burned your eyes. Gray ash covered everything. We inquired as to where we should go to find information about victims and found the area more quickly than I thought possible.

There was a line moving slowly toward a desk with two men behind it. Diane took her place in line while I stood off to one side and waited. It was difficult to see with the poor lighting and the dust in the air.

Diane returned in an hour, saying, "I have no information on Carl. Only half a dozen survivors have been found. At this time, the only way they have of knowing who is missing is relatives asking about them. I have brought several pictures of Carl. I'm going to show them around and see if anyone has seen him."

Rather than just stand around, I joined a bucket line that was removing debris from the site. A man who was coordinating the effort explained that heavy equipment couldn't be used for fear of causing some of the pockets where there might be survivors to cave in on them. The man in front would pass me a bucket and I, in turn, would pass it on to the man behind. The last man would dump it in a pile, to be removed later.

It was about 1:30 A.M when I started and seven hours later I was still in the line. I was amazed that nothing like shoes, purses, or personal items were ever in the buckets. Most of the debris was ash, with occasional rocks or small pieces of metal.

Visibility was poor, but as daylight came, I was terrified at the scene that slowly unfolded before me. I could make out fires burning in what was left of the main structure and pieces of steel sticking up. The air was thick with dust and the stench of gas. I had been given a filter mask when I started which I hope kept out some of the pollution. When I could fully make out what was before me, I said to myself, *this is what hell will be like.*

I, along with everyone in the area, was covered with ash. At good daylight, several men relieved some of us and gave us direction to a place where coffee and rolls were being furnished. On the way there, I saw several bulldozers and graders being brought in. One of the men with me commented, "It looks like they've decided to use heavy equipment and not worry about the pockets. I thought that would happen. We'd never move enough to get to survivors, if there are any left."

I saw several people with frantic looks showing pictures to everyone coming by. I didn't see Diane but knew she was doing the same thing. Suddenly, I realized how tired I was. My legs didn't want to work and my arms ached. There were firefighters, policeman, and search dogs everywhere I looked, and I knew that more volunteers would come later.

I heard a woman scream, and looking in that direction, saw her staring at a body that had been recovered. We found the place that was serving food and drink. Coffee had never tasted that good, and I forced down a roll before searching for Diane. I went back to where I left her, thinking she might be in that area. I found her, still stopping people and showing them Carl's picture.

"Zack, no one has seen him. Every minute it looks more hopeless. I don't know what I-I am g-going to do," she said breaking into tears.

"Come with me. You need coffee and something to eat." We went back to the rest place, and with me a refill, and her a large paper cup of coffee, sat down at a table. I didn't know how long she was going to be able to hold up. In fact, I didn't know how much more I could take.

"Do you want to go back the way we came and see if we can find a place to rest?" I asked.

"No. I have to keep looking," she answered. "I've rested enough."

I was back in the bucket line shortly after that and stayed there the remainder of the day. There were a steady stream of ambulances coming and going, with body bags being loaded. I commented to a fellow worker that they were finding a lot of bodies. His explanation will stay with me for as long as I live.

"Those are the easy ones to recover. They were trapped on the top floors above where the planes struck. The North Tower was struck between floors 93 and 99. The South Tower between 77 and 85. There was no escape from the fire and many of them jumped. Their bodies were not covered with as much debris."

When he told me this, I tried to imagine what it would be like to make that decision... be burned alive or jump to your death. My next thought was; I wish whoever was responsible for this, would meet a worse fate, if that was possible.

I was relieved for a break to eat a sandwich around noon. By five that afternoon, I could barely stand. I realized that was it! I couldn't go on any longer. I hadn't slept in 36 hours and had received very little rest. My entire body ached. My hands were bloody where the bucket handles had cut them and my throat burned from breathing the fumes. I had a coat of ash covering me from head to foot, similar to everyone else.

It was not hard to find Diane. She was in the same location, continuing to show her pictures to everyone that passed. It was obvious that she could barely stand. I told her we had to rest and would come back afterward to resume our search. She didn't agree or disagree, just dropped her head.

I knew neither of us were capable of walking far enough out of the area to find a hotel. I flagged an ambulance coming by and asked them if we could ride. Thankfully, they consented. It was over two miles before they let us out at the first hotel that was still open.

I asked the desk clerk if she had any rooms. I could see the pity in her eyes when she said, "Sort of, if you're desperate. We have told our single guests upon check-in that they might have a roommate since people are so desperate. All of them have been understanding. I can get you a room but it is already occupied. Of course, your roommate will be a man. The same goes for the lady with you, only hers will be a woman."

I turned and looked at Diane. She was staring at the floor, not looking up. "That will be fine," I said.

I registered for both of us, paid, and the clerk gave me the keys to the rooms. Mine was room 571 and Diane's was 283. I took her to her room, knocked on the door, and a young woman answered.

"Would it be all right if this lady stayed with you? Her husband is missing." I said.

"Of course. Come in. I'm so sorry. I'll be glad to have her and help anyway I can," she said.

Going to my room, I thought, tragedy brings out the best in most people. I had witnessed it firsthand many times the last day and a half.

I found room 571 and knocked. I knocked again and waited but no one answered. I assumed my roommate was out. I inserted my card, entered the room and heard the shower running. He didn't come to the door, because he couldn't hear me. There were two beds and two chairs in the room. I collapsed in one of the chairs, lay my head back, and was asleep in seconds.

A scream startled me awake and standing just out of the bathroom was a woman with only a towel in front of her. She turned and ran back into the bathroom.

"What're you doing here?" she screamed.

"The clerk said I could share this room," I said.

"You pervert! Get out of here now! This is my room."

"I'm sorry. The clerk said there would be a man in this room."

"Well, I'm not a man,"

"I would have to agree with you on that," I said, smiling for the first time in 36 hours."

"Get out now! I saw you looking at me, you pervert!"

"I'll go back down to the lobby and see what's going on," I said.

"Good. Don't come back, either," she said.

The clerk was apologetic, saying, "I made a mistake. The person's name in your room is Jerri. I thought that name would belong to a man. I never dreamed it was a woman. What is worse, I have nothing else available. I'm sorry."

"Are you sure you can't find me something. I need a shower, as you can see, and rest."

"I have nothing. I am so sorry for the mix-up. You're welcome to try and get some sleep in one of the chairs here in the lobby."

"Thank you, anyway," I said. Well, the only thing to do was go back to Jerri's room and try to reason with her. That was a long shot, but the only way I could get a shower and rest. I arrived, knocked on the door, and waited.

"Who is it?"

"Me."

"The pervert?"

"No. Just a tired guy that needs a shower and some rest," I said, as meekly and humbly as possible.

"Go away," came the answer.

"Please?" I begged.

"No way," she said.

"Okay, let's compromise. I need a shower in the worst way. You can leave while I shower and then when I'm finished, you can come back. I'll be gone before you get back. That way, at least I'm able to clean up a little."

Silence followed and I thought she was going to ignore me. I waited several minutes and turned to leave before she answered "Okay. You go to the lobby and come back in ten minutes. You have fifteen minutes to shower. I'll be back in twenty-five minutes and you better not be here. If you are, I'm going to call my daddy and tell him you saw me naked. My daddy is big and mean."

"I'm not in a position to argue, ma'am. I'll do whatever you ask."

I did as she instructed and the shower was great. My clothes were filthy but at least I was clean. I shook them out the best I could prior to dressing. I left then, not wanting to exceed my fifteen minutes. I met her coming down the hall. I smiled and thanked her, but she kept walking, not making eye contact. She looked smaller with her clothes on. She couldn't be over five foot with black hair that was cut as short as mine. Her skin was dark, and I assumed she was Hispanic. She was a fiery little thing.

I found something to eat in a vending machine and then went to bed in one of the lounge chairs. It was actually quite comfortable, and I was asleep in minutes. I woke several times due to bad dreams but went back to sleep. Diane woke me up before daylight, saying we had to resume our search. The hotel had coffee in the lounge, and after filling our cups, we started off for Ground Zero, as it had been named. This time we walked the entire distance in silence and arrived just as it was becoming light enough to see.

More people were in the area and heavy equipment was moving debris into dump trucks. Diane spoke for the first time since leaving the hotel. "Zack, I'm going to check at the victim's booth and see if they have any new information."

I decided to go with her. The line was much shorter today and she was talking to the men within minutes. She looked back and motioned me to come over to the table.

"They found three more survivors early this morning. Two are women but the third is a man. He was unconscious and had no identification on him. They have taken him to the hospital. I know it's a long shot, Zack, but I have to go see."

"Do you still have the two women here?" I asked.

"One of them has left but the other is in that building, pointing down the street," the man answered.

"Diane, let's go talk to her first. Maybe she can tell us something before we make the trip to the hospital."

We found the woman immediately, surrounded by her family. Diane explained that her husband was missing and could she describe the man who was rescued with her.

"He was covered in ash so I couldn't tell you what he looked like. He saved my life and my friend's. We would never have gotten out without him. He's an angel. That's all I know. I'm sorry I can't tell you more."

"Was he a large or small man?" I asked.

"Huge," she said. He carried me down several flights of stairs. I couldn't breathe."

I looked at Diane and saw the tears. "What do you think?" I asked.

"I don't care. I have to be sure. You can stay here and I'll get to the hospital some way."

One of the men sitting beside the survivor said, "We feel so blessed. I'll be glad to take her. My car is parked about two miles from here, but we can walk out or maybe catch a ride on one of the trucks."

That settled it. I didn't try to persuade Diane to change her mind. She was only going to be disappointed again.

I went back to the area where I had been working. A policeman with a dog approached me and asked if I was a volunteer. I told him I was and he asked me to help him. I agreed and for the remainder of the morning we followed Max, his dog through the rubble looking for victims, either dead or alive. The policeman's name was Chad and we quickly bonded.

I wasn't ready for what we discovered. We only found one body, but throughout the morning, Max would hit on an area and we would uncover debris and find a body part. Sometimes it was an arm or a leg and once a torso. The first time this happened, I threw up. Embarrassed, I apologized to Chad.

"Don't worry about that. Just think that this body part can be identified by DNA and some family will have closure. It's a terrible job, but we're doing something good."

I accepted that and did better after his response to my apology. The dog was amazing. He worked so hard that eventually Chad had to stop and take him away from the Pile for water and rest. The Pile was the name given to the jumble of rocks, steel, and debris that we were searching.

At noon, Chad stopped and said, "Zack, we have to rest. If we're going to do good work, we can't exhaust ourselves. We can get something to eat and rest for an hour before we return."

We found the area that was serving lunch, and I had just taken a bite out of my sandwich when I saw Diane. She was walking fast and obviously looking for me. I stood and waved at her. When she saw me, she screamed and started running. She grabbed me around the neck, saying, "It was Carl! Thank God, it was Carl! He's going to be all right!"

When she calmed down, I asked her, "Why did the woman say he was huge?"

"I talked with the other survivor. She was in the same hospital as Carl. She said that no way could a little man perform such a feat.

Zack, I'm so thankful. I haven't gotten in touch with Mark yet. Thank you for coming with me. Your family continues to be there for us. Carl will be able to travel in a couple of days, and we're going home."

"That's wonderful, Diane. I assume you'll stay at the hospital with Carl."

"Yes. Most definitely. I haven't been able to get you on my phone. I'll let you know when we're going home. You may want to leave now and that would be fine."

"No. I'll wait until you and Carl leave," I said.

She hugged and thanked me again before leaving to return to the hospital and be with her hero. We discovered later that the meeting that Carl was attending was moved to a lower floor due to the air conditioning not working where they were scheduled to meet.

I went back to work with a renewed vigor. Max continued searching, and by dark that evening we had uncovered several more victims. Chad got me a ride back to the hotel in a police car.

When I knocked on room 571, there was no answer. I opened the door and the room was vacant. I assumed Miss Fireball had left for a while which was fine with me. I still had my grungy clothes on, but the shower was wonderful. I felt better immediately after getting out and toweling off. I needed to see if I could get a razor from the hotel. My three-day stubble was beginning to bother me. I heard the door open and thought, oh, no!

"You're back, pervert. What nerve you have! This is my room! Can't you understand that?"

"Sorry, I borrowed your shower. I'll be gone in a few minutes. Back to my suite in the lobby."

"Five minutes. That's it! You better be gone by then!"

"Thank you," I meekly replied.

I was gone in three minutes. Once again, I used the vending machine for my supper and went to sleep in the lobby.

CHAPTER 41

Tommie Rose

I POSTPONED MY PLANS TO return to Africa. With Zack gone and my gramps doing poorly, I decided to wait for at least another month before leaving. Diane had made an appointment in Dallas with a specialist to determine if anything could be done to help him. The appointment was scheduled for next week, and I was going with Mia and Gramps.

We had received the wonderful news about Carl yesterday, after all but giving up hope that he survived. We were keeping Mark at the ranch, and he had been asking about Ibutho. Diane had called this morning and Mark talked with him. The improvement in his English was amazing. Lacy had been taking him to school and picking him up in the afternoon. She had considered staying in town but decided against it.

I had been talking to Ted daily since the attack in New York. He had not mentioned me returning to Africa, which was a disappointment. I had thought he would at least attempt to persuade me to stay longer here in the States.

Lacy continued to be a mystery. Now she seemed to be interested in Zack. She talked about him constantly and kept repeating that she wished he would come home. Overnight, she had gone from apathy to caring about him. I had offered to help her look for another horse to replace Jazzy. Her response had been, "I want to wait and let Zack help me find another horse."

Diane and Carl arrived home on Monday, September 17. They were able to get a commercial flight and were in Lubbock by noon. Mom and Dad picked them up, arriving home by late afternoon. Zack wasn't with them, which didn't surprise me, and for some reason, I can't explain why.

He called me at seven that evening and asked if I could take Lacy and go to Mom and Dad's. He wanted to have a conference call to talk with all of us at once. Immediately, my curiosity kicked in, wondering what was so important that he wanted all of us included.

I did as he asked, and we were all sitting in the den when Mom's phone rang. Answering, she put it on intercom and his voice came in loud and clear, saying. "I hope everyone is good there. I wanted to convey my change in plans to all of you at one time. Can you hear me?"

"Yes," replied Mom. "We can understand everything you say."

"Good. I'm going to stay in New York. I don't know for how long. I have teamed up with Chad, a policeman, and his wonderful dog, Max. We search the Pile, as it is called, at least 10 hours a day for victims. Everyone has conceded that we'll not find any more survivors. You know I've always heard that one death is a tragedy but thousands are only a statistic. That's not true. I think of all those people who rose last Tuesday morning, had coffee and breakfast with their spouse and maybe their kids and went to work in the Twin Towers, Pentagon, or boarded one of those flights. I'm sure most had plans for the evening, maybe dinner out, or a special TV show that came on Tuesday night. Instead, their life ended in a horrible manner that day. All of this makes me fill insignificant and somehow very small."

He paused and then continued, "Whenever we find a body or even a finger that allows a victim to be identified through DNA, I know that some family is going to have closure and hopefully begin healing. I'm telling you this, not to shock you or tell you what a terrible place Ground Zero is, but hoping you will understand why I'm making this decision."

"What about your rodeo?" Lacy asked.

"Oh, me. I dreaded telling you this, especially Dad. This has been a life-changing event for me. I see everything much more clearly now than before. I'm going back to school the second semester. I've always wanted to be a physician, like Dr. Sadler, and help people live a better life. I became sidetracked when we lost Jack. I'm not sorry for the last year. It helped me to heal from our loss, and I believe it was good for our family."

"Zack, I'm not the least bit disappointed in your decision. We're proud of you. Your dad and I have talked recently about your desire to be a doctor," Mom said.

"Your mother's right, Zack. Please don't worry about what pleases us. Remember, I chose not to go professional because I didn't want to do anything but ranch. I've never regretted that decision. I don't believe that thirty years from now you will either."

"Now, Lacy, please listen carefully. I want you to take Scooter and start working him on the barrels. He's only eight, and I know it usually takes years to make a competitive barrel horse. Scooter is special, and in six months he'll be running the barrels as good or better than Jazzy. Being a roping horse is an advantage, since he won't get silly like many horses that only have one job."

"But aren't you ever going to rope again?" Lacy asked.

"Sure, and when I do, it will be on Scooter or Cotton. I won't have time to rope much. School will take up most of the year. When I get out of medical school and start a practice, I should be able to rope more; however, that will be several years. I never intend to go professional."

Zack paused and when no one commented, he continued. "Lacy, Tommie will help you with Scooter. Horses listen and respond to her. Also, ask Jimmy to help. He knows more about horses than anyone I know. You're going to be surprised at how quickly Scooter picks up the barrels. He's an extremely talented and intelligent horse. Dad, it would be good for you or Tommie to run some calves on him occasionally. After all, he enjoys that and can handle more than one job.

"Little Brother, it appears that you have everything under control. I'll pray for you each day and be thankful for the work you are doing. Remember, we all love you," I said.

Mom and Dad made similar statements to Zack, but Lacy remained silent. Her expression seemed to reflect a stark reality that she hadn't expected.

After the call ended, the room was silent for several minutes before I said, "Lacy, I'm going to Dallas tomorrow with Mia and Gramps. When I return on Thursday, we'll go right to work with Scooter. I agree with Zack about him. He's an amazing horse."

"Okay. I just don't see how he can compete anyway soon. Even for a full year," she responded.

Mia, Gramps, and I drove to Lubbock the next morning and flew to Dallas. We arrived, rented a car, and were at the Adolphus Hotel by mid-afternoon. Gramps had insisted that we stay at his favorite place. We had an early evening meal and retired to our rooms early.

Ted called before I went to bed and asked me if it would be okay for him to come to New Mexico next weekend, which would be September 29 and 30. I don't know if he would have even been upset if I said no, which I didn't. We visited about his work and Gramps' doctor appointment. I also told him about Zack's decision to stay in New York and return to school in the spring.

"Your brother is a good man, Tommie. There is something about him that exemplifies integrity and honesty. He will be an outstanding physician."

After ending the call and lying in bed, I reflected on Ted and my relationship, if you could call it that. Suddenly it dawned on me; Dr. Adders was "in like" with me. I had coined a new term. One that meant someone really enjoyed your company and needed you in their life but desired nothing else from the relationship. No warm cuddly moments, unspoken glances of affection, and romance at special getaways. I better stop there before I went any further into my psychological evaluation. My last thought, before going to sleep, was that maybe Dr. Adders considered me the equivalent of a nun rather than a Methodist pastor.

Gramps started his tests early the next morning, while Mia and I watched television in the waiting room or thumbed through magazines. We moved from one room to another as he completed each series of tests. It gave us a lot of time to visit. I always enjoyed listening to Mia tell of our family.

"Tommie do you have any recollection of the trial here in Dallas when you were only three years old?"

"Maybe. I can't say for sure. I've heard Mom and Dad talk about it and that could be what causes me to think I recall some of it. I do remember Reno and playing with him."

"That was a long time ago, but I remember it like yesterday," Mia said.

"B-Boy was something else, wasn't he?" I asked.

"Yes, you could say that about my dad," Mia answered.

She commenced to tell me several stories of B-Boy and Gramps, including their partnership in the racing business. I had never heard the story of when they bought a new car for her.

The reminiscing ended when a doctor came in and told us the tests were completed, and he would take us to an office to wait on the report.

We waited two hours for the doctor to come in. I had about given up, but finally two doctors arrived. They introduced themselves, and I could tell by their expression that it was not good.

"We have completed and evaluated the tests. We are going to change some of the medication and hopefully that will improve Mr. Warren's heart function. I'm sorry to inform you that we can do nothing more than that. He is not a candidate for surgery and with his age and condition would not be eligible to be placed on the heart transplant list. He will need to be careful about what he does and get plenty of rest. We are concerned about the altitude of your home. He would do better living several thousand feet lower. An altitude of 6,000 feet does make his breathing more difficult.

Gramps spoke, almost angrily, "I live in the mountains of Southwest New Mexico, and I will die there a happy man."

Smiling, the other doctor, said, "Good for you. I hope when I'm your age I feel the same way."

That ended the meeting and we went back to the hotel. Actually, Gramps was in good spirits. We had supper in the hotel restaurant and watched a movie in their room before retiring for the night.

CHAPTER 42

Lacy

I HAD BEGUN TO THINK that my life was going to be one disappointment after another. Zack wasn't coming home and furthermore wasn't going to rodeo. I only had one horse and he couldn't win at the top level. Scooter was a roping horse and knew nothing about the barrels. He would never be able to compete on the professional level. It was kind of Zack to let me use him but it would accomplish nothing. My only chance was to find and buy another horse.

I had changed my mind about Zack. I realized after Jazzy died that I needed someone. Zack was a wonderful person and I should not have brushed him off when he confessed his feelings toward me. That was a stupid move. I don't know what I was thinking. Now he had decided to return to school, and with Tommie leaving, I would be alone.

Tuesday night was long and lonely with Tommie gone to Dallas. On these occasions, I would dwell on my handicap, becoming depressed and feeling self-pity. I knew that I had much to be thankful for. Many widows were left penniless and had to scrounge for a living. With the trust that Jack had received and I had inherited, I would never have to worry about money; however, that was a poor substitute for losing the love of your life.

Wednesday morning, I decided to go to the cemetery. It was cloudy with a cold north wind, and I had to go back inside and get a jacket before leaving. I saddled Chrome and rode the mile to my destination. Had it only been six years since we took that wild ride from the house to the cemetery for our wedding? Before I knew it, tears were rolling down my face as we climbed the hill, much slower than we did six years ago.

I rode directly to Jack's grave. I dismounted, and standing, looking at the headstone, wondered how life could be so cruel. I spoke in a whisper, *I miss you so much, Jack. At this moment, I am miserable, with no desire to move forward with my life. What can I do? How can I ever be happy without you? I can do without a leg, that's nothing, but I'm lost without you.*

I stood silently for another few minutes before turning to get back on Chrome. Suddenly, I had the strangest feeling, similar to after your second cup of coffee in the morning, except a hundred times greater. I had not mounted my horse so easily since losing my leg. Feeling lighter, even with the cold wind, a warm feeling spread through me. I eased down the hill and ran Chrome at full speed back to the house. Both of us were exhausted when we stopped in front of the barn. I screamed as loud as possible…*I am alive*! Quickly, I looked around, to make sure no one was present.

I allowed Chrome time to cool down and then fed him. I went inside, looked in the refrigerator, and took out a carrot. I then drove to Bo and Lexie's where Scooter was stalled. I went inside to his pen, and he came over to me. I spoke aloud to him. *Well, it's you and me, Scooter. We might as well get to know one another. We have a lot of work to do. You sure don't look like much. Chrome will put you to shame in that category.* He came over to me and started munching the carrot I held out to him. Looking into those big eyes,

I saw something. Maybe it was only my imagination, but I believe he understood what I said.

After Scooter finished his carrot, I drove up to Bo and Lexie's. It was almost noon and Bo's pickup was home. Lexie answered the door, saying, "Lacy, come in! You're just in time for lunch."

"Thank you. I'm sorry to interrupt you."

"You're not. We're glad you came by. We need company."

Going into the kitchen, Bo hugged me, saying, "You probably came over to see your new barrel horse."

"Yes. I brought him a carrot," I replied.

Laughing, Bo said, "You made a friend for life. We spoil him, especially Zack. He takes him a treat every time he goes to the barn."

"Would it be all right if I kept him at my place?" I asked.

"Sure. I expected you to. It'll be more convenient," he answered.

"I didn't bring my trailer, but I'll come back this afternoon and get him. Tommie will be home tomorrow and will want to start working him on the barrels."

I stayed and ate lunch with them. We had a nice visit but stayed away from the subject of Zack and his decision to return to school.

I left, went home and hooked on my trailer, and returned to pick up Scooter. Bo sent several bags of his feed with me until I could buy some. When I got him out of the stall to load, he moved liked he was thirty years old. My horses usually pranced around, especially Jazzy. It was like he was thinking, *ho hum, wonder what we're going to do.*

Tommie was home by mid-afternoon the next day. After explaining the results of their trip, she asked me how I was doing.

"Better. I'm ready to start on Scooter," I said.

"You don't think much of Scooter for a barrel horse, do you?" she asked.

"No, not really. He has never been around a barrel, and he's so laid back. I've never seen a good barrel horse with his disposition."

"Lacy, when you start training a horse on the barrels, what is your first objective?"

"A young horse has to learn to change leads at the barrel," I answered.

"Well, you can forget that with Scooter. You probably haven't noticed, but when he's tracking a calf and it doesn't run straight, he will change leads each time the calf turns. Name something else that is important in a good barrel horse," Tommie said.

"He has to rate in order to be under control to turn," I said.

"Scooter will rate a fast calf or a slow calf and give you a good shot. Something else, you need in a top barrel horse."

"Speed, and the ability to accelerate away from a barrel," I said.

"Have you ever watched Scooter leave the box? I've run several calves on him, and he throws me back in the saddle every time. I anticipate his quickness but am never ready for it. And speed, I'll quote what Uncle Jimmy said. 'Scooter could outrun over half the horses at the track for a hundred yards.' Uncle Jimmy had a saying about a race horse he trained for B-Boy and Gramps. This was a great horse, and Jimmy said, 'He's got lightening in his feet and thunder in his heart.' That's Scooter, Lacy. His heart is probably twice as big as most horses. Now tell me another requirement of a barrel horse."

"They need to not become crazy about the alley."

Tommie laughed loudly. "Do I need to even comment on that?"

"I give up, Tommie. Maybe you're right and he'll work for me. I brought him over here, and if you're not tired from the trip, I'll ride him."

"Good. I'm anxious to get started. You saddle and I'll set the barrels up for you."

Within a few minutes I was warming Scooter up, trotting him, and then doing some figure eights. I rode over to Tommie and said, "He doesn't want to go. I didn't wear my spurs. Do you think I need them?"

"No, just move your reins forward when you want more speed. He'll respond to that. Also, Zack clucks at him. Try that and see if it helps."

It worked. Whenever I moved the reins forward he would respond. The ride was smooth, even in a long trot, and his lope was like riding in a rocking chair. He put my horses to shame in this respect.

Tommie had me walk him around the barrels several times. She made the pattern tight to save time. She then had me trot him half a dozen times. I had to rein him around the barrels but that was no problem. He neck-reined so much better than any horse I had ridden.

I rode over to Tommie and she asked, "What do you think?"

"I'm surprised. What's strange is that he's so quiet and well behaved. Will he stay that way?'

"Welcome to the world of the roping horse. Most are that way. Not all, of course. Cowboys sit around on them, waiting their turn, and that usually causes them to be sensible and well-mannered. Contrast that to a barrel racer who runs her horse on a pattern, and then goes and ties him to the trailer or puts him in a stall. My horse, Flame, was different, because we roped on him, also."

"How long do you think it will take him to learn the pattern?" I asked.

"Not nearly as long as it would a young horse. He'll begin to recognize the barrels and his job within a few months. It'll take longer to run him full speed. I truly believe that by early summer he'll be ready to enter."

"Do you think I need to look for another horse to make the early 2002 rodeos?" I asked.

"That's up to you, Lacy. You certainly could afford to buy another horse. I do believe that we could improve Chrome with some work if you're willing to make some changes in the way you run him."

"Sure, I'd be willing to do anything to improve Chrome.," I said.

"Okay. That's good. We'll start on him tomorrow," Tommie said. "We've done enough today. It's a good start. Let's feed the horses and find something for us to eat."

After our evening meal, we sat on the porch and visited. Tommie expressed her disappointment that nothing else could be done for Tom to make his life better. It also gave me an opportunity to tell her about my experience.

"Tommie, I need to ask you something. It's kind of personnel, and hopefully you can help me." I commenced to tell her of my experience at the cemetery the previous day and the change that occurred in me. She listened, without interrupting.

"Lacy, I never try to preach to individuals. If I did, people would run when they saw me coming. I preach on Sunday and attempt to live in a way that others will see that I live by what I say. I have never preached to you. I know that it would make you uncomfortable. However, I do emphasize in most of my sermons that God is everywhere. What I don't say is that His presence is felt more in some places. For me it's at the family cemetery. If I'm struggling with preparation for a sermon, I'll go there.

Predictably, I'll find the words needed to fulfill my message before leaving. If I'm worried or confused, I can find the answers there. I know it's hard to believe, but what I tell you is true. I haven't shared this with anyone else."

"Are you saying that what I experienced was spiritual?" I asked.

"That would be up to you to decide. I will tell you this, Lacy. To win a World Championship will require a fast horse and a strong faith. At this time, I know that you have one of the requirements."

CHAPTER 43

Zack

I WOKE UP THURSDAY MORNING, after sleeping in the lobby chair for eight days. She was sitting there, looking at me with those big black eyes, holding two cups of coffee. I squirmed around, doing my best to look uncomfortable. I rubbed my lower back and grimaced, trying to look like I was in pain.

"I felt guilty," she said.

"Oh, I'm fine. Just a little stiff. Thank you for the coffee," I said, taking one of the cups. I studied her and admittedly had never seen anything quite like her. I identified her as Hispanic so in order to impress her, I said, "¿cómo estás esta mañana?" (How are you this morning?)

Is that Spanish?" she asked.

Feeling like a fool, I apologized, saying, " I'm sorry. I thought you were Hispanic."

"No. Are you?"

"No. I just speak a little Spanish."

"You identified me by the color of my skin, right?" she asked.

"I'm sorry," I said, apologizing again. This was not going well at all. Maybe I could move on to something else. "Are you here because of the attack on the World Trade Center?"

"Yes. My college roommate was in the South Tower. They haven't found her yet," she said, a single tear rolling down her cheek. "I'm staying until they find her. She was my best friend."

"I'm sorry."

"You?" she asked.

I explained my reason for coming, telling her that Carl and Diane had gone home. Maybe the less I said the better. I should have known she wasn't Hispanic. Her skin was more of a copper color. Her face was oval with full lips and she was not wearing make-up. I kept trying to think of a way to describe her. Suddenly it was there. She was just plain cute!"

"I'm glad your friend was found alive. Are you going to be here much longer?" she asked.

"I don't know. I'm going back to school after the first of the year. Right now, that's all I know for sure."

"Just because I brought you coffee doesn't mean you can stay in my room," she said.

"That's okay. I can sleep in this chair until a room comes open. Could I buy your breakfast? We could eat here at the hotel restaurant."

"No. I need to get to the Site. I work in one of the booths that provide food and drink to the workers. I need to be there shortly."

"Well, at least, could I walk with you?" I asked.

"Suit yourself. I have to go back to the room for a few minutes before I leave," she said, getting up and walking away. I don't know whether she walked like that all the time or if it was for my benefit. It definitely got my attention and gave me something to think about until she returned.

It was a half hour walk to the Site and she did most of the talking. After my communication breakdown earlier, I was glad to be a good listener. She worked in Dallas as a Physical Therapist and had gone to school at North Texas

State. Her roommate had been a business major, and her dream had always been to live in New York. She had been hired by a large firm in the World Trade Center, living here for the past five years.

I kept trying to think of some way to ask her if she was married, engaged, or in a relationship, but couldn't come up with anything. I had better not press it since this was the first real conversation since meeting her eight days ago. It was the shortest half hour I remember. We came to my destination before she reached hers.

"Are you going to let me use your shower again tonight?" I asked.

"Sure. Same as the last eight nights. You get twenty minutes and then you're out."

"Thanks," I said, as she was walking away. I guess she did move that way all the time, with that wiggle. Suddenly, I was encouraged. She had only given me fifteen minutes the last eight nights.

Chad and Max arrived a few minutes later and we went to work. Spray paint was used to mark areas that had already been searched. It was no problem finding areas that had no markings. We followed the same procedure of working for two hours and then taking a break to allow Max time to rest. If we hadn't stopped, Max would have worked himself to death. He never slowed down while he was working. We would rest for about fifteen minutes, give him water, and then go back to work.

Chad had invited me to stay with him a number of times, saying he had an extra bedroom and bath.

"I appreciate it, Chad, but I'm fine at the hotel." I didn't dare tell him I was sleeping in a chair.

"Anyway, you're going to have to meet my family. I've told my wife and two boys about you. They boys are excited about meeting someone from New Mexico. They'll probably expect you to ride up on your horse."

I promised him that I would meet his family before leaving. If it wasn't for Jerri, I would've taken him up on the bed and bathroom. It was tempting to imagine sleeping in a real bed.

We would stop at 6:00 each day and Chad would give me a ride back to the hotel. I didn't see any other way than to explain my situation to him. I told him about Jerri and that I wanted to wait and walk with her.

Smiling, he said, "So now the truth comes out. You don't want to stay with my family because she's at the same hotel as you. That's fine. Hopefully something good will come of this horrible tragedy."

I thanked him for understanding before he left and sat down against a wall and waited. Twenty minutes later, I saw her coming. Thank goodness, she was by herself. She was close, before seeing me.

"What are you doing?" she asked.

"Waiting on you. Would it be all right if I walked with you?"

"Suit yourself. It's a free country," she said.

This "suit yourself" response was becoming old. On the way back to the hotel, I asked how her day went.

"Sad. I keep thinking they'll find her. I don't know how much longer I can afford to stay."

"Does she have any other relatives here?" I asked.

"No. She wasn't married, her parents were divorced and have new families of their own. I talked with her on the phone almost every day."

I guess now was as good a time as any to ask her. "Are you married?"

"No. I was in a relationship, but he's angry now because I've been gone so long. He doesn't understand."

I then asked about her family and she ignored my inquiry, changing the subject to me. I gave her a brief description of my family and where I lived. I didn't tell her about Jack, not wanting to relive any more grief. I did tell her about my desire to be a physician.

By this time, we were back at the hotel. "What time can I use your shower?" I asked.

"It'll take me an hour to clean the ash off me and out of my hair. I'll come down when I'm finished."

After she had left, I punched in Sissy's number on my phone.

"How are you doing?" she asked.

"Better. I didn't throw up today. I'm still working with Chad and Max. Both are amazing." I then told her about meeting Jerri.

"Sounds like she made an impression," she said.

I tried to explain but found myself rambling around without making a point. Frustrated, I said, "She's cute."

"Well, Little Brother, that's not much of a description of someone you sound enamored with. Tell me more about her appearance."

"She's, uh, tiny. Short hair, really short black hair. Dark, maybe more of a copper with smooth skin. Black eyes. When she walks, she takes these short steps. She has a big attitude and is aggressive."

"Does she like you?"

"No. She's still angry with me." I explained what happened the first day, when I thought a man would come out of the shower.

"No wonder she's mad at you. Did you apologize?"

"Sure. More than once," I answered.

She then told me about Gramps' report he received in Dallas. "It's amazing how positive he can be, Zack, the way he's suffering. It hurts me to watch him breathe."

We visited another few minutes before hanging up, with her last words being, "Hang in there with this girl. She may be the one."

After an hour, Jerri came back down to the lobby, saying, "Okay, you can go up now. I'll wait here until you come back."

It was amazing how dirty I was at the end of each day. Maybe ash-covered was the correct term. Chad had brought me some clothes on several occasions, and she had reluctantly allowed me to keep them in her room. I always felt better after a shower. He had also brought me a razor, toothbrush and deodorant, which I kept in the bathroom.

When I returned to the lobby, she was sitting in my chair, looking at a magazine.

"Okay, Jerri. We're both cleaned up, now we need to go somewhere. Let's get a taxi and find a department store or shopping center, even if we have to drive for two hours."

"I can't afford a taxi," she said.

"Don't worry, I'll take care of that."

She didn't respond for several minutes and finally I said, "Please."

"Okay. I don't like the idea of you paying my way. You'll probably want something in return," she stated.

"You're right. I would like for you to be nicer to me and stop thinking of me as a pervert."

Then she smiled… for the first time.

Fortune was kind, and a taxi was available when we walked out the door. I told the driver we wanted to go to Macy's. He was talkative, asking us if we were visitors to the city. I explained the reason we were here and that we were working at Ground Zero. Then for the next part of the trip we heard all about his family, including his grandkids, which he dwelt on more than anything else. We arrived, and exited, presenting my credit card for the fee.

"Don't worry about it, he said. You've paid your fee to this city in it's time of need."

I thanked him and we entered the store… ordinary shoppers. It was crowded even though it was only an hour until closing time. I took a chance and reached for her hand. Relief, she didn't pull away.

We found the men's department, where I bought two pairs of jeans, two shirts, socks, and underwear. I also found a light-weight jacket that would feel good on cool mornings. Feeling guilty, I asked her if she would allow me to buy her something.

"No, but thank you," she replied in a civil tone.

I checked out, paying with a credit card, and worked our way to the front door. "I'm hungry. Will you have supper, I mean dinner, with me?"

Smiling again, she said, "Yes."

Things were looking up. We didn't have to go far down the street until we found a neat little café.

"Can we get pizza?" she asked.

"Sounds good to me," I replied.

While we waited for our order, I asked her again about her family. She brushed me off, saying there was nothing interesting to tell. She did share more information about herself, describing her work as a physical therapist and talking about some of her patients.

Out of the blue, she asked, "Why aren't you married? You're much too good looking to be single. Plus, you must have money."

Caught off guard, I thought a few seconds before attempting to answer. "I haven't found anyone yet that is willing to spend their life with me, who I care about."

"But there is someone, but she's not willing to marry you?" she stated as a question.

"Yes. You're perceptive. My turn. Why aren't you married? You're much to attractive to be single."

"I'm too particular. I look at a man and compare him to my daddy. My relationships don't last," she explained.

"Is your dad really big and mean?" I asked.

"No. He's a kind and gentle person who wouldn't harm anyone."

"Tell me about your college experience," I said.

"Not a great deal to tell. I needed a field that would allow me to be employable that I would enjoy. Physical therapy fits those requirements perfectly. My parents helped me, but I still had a loan to repay when I graduated. I finished in four years, accepting a job in Dallas, actually Plano. I wanted to stay in the area. Oh, I was also a cheerleader for three years."

Surprised, I asked, "You were a college cheerleader?"

"Yes, don't sound so shocked."

"But, you're tiny. How did you hold those others on your shoulders?"

"Most of the time, I was the one on top," she replied.

Our pizza arrived and while eating, I told her about my high school football and rodeo. She didn't seem to be impressed until I began explaining my decision to become a physician because of Dr. Sadler.

We stayed until just before midnight. Outside, we walked back toward Macy's, thinking that we would be more likely to find a cab there. The sidewalk was mostly clear now, and suddenly, she ran a few steps and did three flip flops, landing lightly on her feet. It scared the daylights out of me.

"What do you think?" she asked.

"Goodness, I'm impressed! You must have taken gymnastics."

"No. Not one lesson. It just came natural."

The next taxi driver was not as generous, as he took my credit card and charged more than I had expected. Well, it was worth it, I thought.

"Do you want me to see you to your room?" I asked, wistfully.

"No, I can find it. I had a nice evening and thank you," she said, turning and leaving.

That seemed to be a cue for the hotel desk clerk to come over and tell me that a room had opened up. I thanked her and with new energy, registered and went to room 446. The last thing I remembered, before waking up the next morning, was lying down on the bed fully clothed.

The next four days followed a similar pattern. Even though I now had a room and didn't have a need to use Jerri's shower, we still met each morning for the trip to the Site. Chad had started picking us up at the hotel on his way. In the afternoon, he dropped us off on his way home.

For the past four nights we had eaten at a small café about five blocks from the hotel. It was a neat place with great food. During these times, she told me about her roommate. She also went into detail about her work.

Monday night she finally opened up more than usual and told me about her mother who had been a refugee from Viet Nam. She described the hardship she went through in her country, barely escaping with her life.

I responded by telling her about losing Jack and how it had affected my family. I also described Sissy and her work in Africa. She had questions about Jack as well as

Sissy that I attempted to answer. She also asked me to describe life on a ranch, which seemed to fascinate her.

I summoned up the nerve to ask her about the relationship in which she was involved. Her response was both encouraging and discouraging.

"It's not easy to describe. Clarence and I have talked little about the future. My parents don't care for him, especially my dad. He was very direct with me, saying, 'he's not good enough for you.' My dad is stubborn, and the chances are slim that he'll change his opinion. Clarence didn't go to college and currently works as a bartender, at Papasitos. We don't live together, as many unmarried couples do today. I have my own apartment."

"How long have you been involved?" I asked.

"Almost two years," she answered. "He's still upset because I've been gone so long."

"Are you ever going back to school to work on your master's?" I asked.

"Probably not. I'm happy with my job and not interested in an administrative job."

"I would imagine you're a Dallas Cowboy fan," I stated.

"No. I like the Oilers," she replied.

"But you live in Dallas, not far from the stadium," I reminded her.

"My hometown is Houston," she replied.

"Would it be all right if I came to Dallas to visit you after we leave New York?"

"Suit yourself," she said.

"I would have preferred a more positive response," I remarked.

"It's better than no, isn't it?"

We finished eating, and it was midnight when we started our walk back to the hotel. She held my hand, probably making her feel more secure with all the strangers passing by. In the lobby, I asked her once again if she wanted me to walk her to her room. I received the same reply but had a surprise.

"No. I can find my room, but come with me," she said, taking my hand and leading me to a door that opened to the stairway. She positioned me at the bottom and standing on the second step, ordered me to close my eyes. She kissed me and then said, "You're nice," and ran up the stairs, leaving me standing there dumbfounded and numb.

The next morning was Tuesday, September, 25, two weeks from the date of the attack. We rode with Chad to the Site and followed the same routine as previous days. His wife had packed us a lunch, as she had been doing. We worked until 6:00 and when Jerri didn't show up, I told Chad to go on and I would wait on her. He objected, but I convinced him to do as I asked.

I sat down against a wall and waited until 8:00, finally giving up and returning to the hotel. I went directly to her room and knocked several times, receiving no response. I went back to the lobby and asked the clerk if she had seen her.

"Yes. She checked out after lunch today and asked me to call her a cab to take her to the airport. She was upset and having a hard time. I felt sorry for her. They had discovered her friend last night and she was going home."

I was confused. Why would she leave without at least telling me bye, especially after last night? Then I panicked, realizing we had not exchanged phone numbers. There wasn't a reason since we stayed in the same hotel and had our schedule set. My confusion turned to anger as I thought she could have at least told me she was leaving or even left a note. It was just plain rude to leave without a word.

I spent a restless night, tossing and turning, and looking at the clock, until I dozed off around 5:00. I only had too much to drink one time at a college party, but I remember the next morning, and that's how I felt when I awoke.

When Chad picked me up, he knew immediately something was wrong. I explained what had happened, sitting quietly the rest of the way to the Site. I was hoping that going to work would get my mind off the disappointment but I was wrong. The day seemed to last forever, with the work even more depressing, if possible.

When we stopped in front of the hotel that evening, Chad said, "I'll wait while you get a change of clothes. You promised me you would met my family, and this is a good time to do that."

I didn't argue, coming back shortly, with my clothes. It was an hour's drive to his house, and I kept the subject away from Jerri. I told him more about my family and the ranch, while he, in turn, talked of his wife and two boys.

He had called his wife and told her we were coming. The boys were waiting outside when we arrived, running to meet their dad. He introduced me to Spencer, who was 7, and Jeffery, who was 5. They extended their little hands, and we were friends immediately.

Chad's wife, Darla, welcomed me with a hug, saying she had heard so much about me the last two weeks. I thanked her, apologizing for the inconvenience that came with an unexpected dinner guest.

"I consider you family. All we've heard the past two weeks is Zack this or Zack that. It's a pleasure to have you in our home."

We had a great meal, and I spent a wonderful evening with Chad's family. The boys were interested in the ranch and the fact that I was a cowboy. I had to tell them about the horses and cattle we raised. I really got their attention when I told the story of when my dad killed the huge mountain lion.

I stayed the night, but before the boys went to bed, I invited them to come visit me in New Mexico. We would ride horses and go fishing. Both hugged me before leaving.

That night before going to sleep, I thought, this is the kind of family I want.

I worked another two weeks at the Site before deciding to go home. I spent several of those evenings with Chad's family and that helped get my mind off Jerri. My decision to leave was influenced by several things. First and most important, Gramps was doing poorly; each time I talked with Sissy, she asked me when I was coming home, saying, "He's not going to be with us much longer."

Another reason was that I had spent a month in New York, and it was obvious that it would take years to clean up the devastation. Chad, being very honest with me, said, "You have done more than your part, Zack. I know you miss your family, and they need you." He promised me that he and his family would plan a trip to New Mexico during a time that I would be at the ranch.

I boarded my plane to return to the ranch on Tuesday, October 7. As the plane circled over New York, headed for my destination, I understood what a dramatic effect this experience would have on my life. I had witnessed horror first hand and saw how fragile and unpredictable life can be; however, the compassion, strength, and heroism of the people of New York would remain with me always. I would never allow anyone to make a negative comment about this city and its people.

Eventually, the number dead would be placed at 2,973. Only eighteen survivors were rescued. Only 291 bodies

were discovered intact. Over 21,000 body parts were discovered. No remains were found for 1,115 victims.

Condolences and donations came from all over the world. An outpouring of sympathy came from people who we knew loved us and those we thought hated us. One of the prominent newspapers in France had the following headlines on September 12, 2001: WE ARE ALL AMERICANS.

Maybe the most generous and loving tribute of all came from the Massai tribe of Africa who inhabited one of the poorest regions of the world. They donated fourteen of their best cows.

CHAPTER 44

Tommie Rose

Ted came in on Friday, September 28. He was good to accompany me to visit Gramps that afternoon without complaining. In fact, I wish he would complain or disagree with me occasionally. He was staying with Mom and Dad at night, and they actually looked forward to seeing him. Mom kept hinting that maybe he would propose on one of these visits. I didn't want to disappoint her, but that was about as likely as snow on the Fourth of July.

On Saturday, she insisted on preparing a picnic lunch for us to take to that beautiful little waterfall on the north ranch where we used to swim in the summer. I know what she was thinking; create a romantic setting and anything might happen. She called me early Saturday morning saying, "You know, Tommie, you might want to go swimming, as warm as it's been. Ted could wear a pair of Bo's swim trunks, and I kept that swimsuit you had in high school. I imagine it would still fit."

"Mom! That thing is indecent. I was eighteen years old then."

"Well, Tommie, he might enjoy seeing what you looked like when you were eighteen. What do you think?"

"I think Ted would be embarrassed, seeing me in that thing."

"The waterfall was the first place your dad really kissed me. We had a picnic with fried chicken that your Mia fixed for us. I'm going to fry a chicken this morning to send with you."

"Mom, I'm thirty years old and Ted is thirty-four. We can't conduct ourselves like high school kids."

"Why not?" she asked.

"Because... well, because." I couldn't think of anything to say.

"For once, Tommie, trust your mother and don't act your age. Now, when Ted comes in for breakfast this morning, I'm going to tell him about your plans to go swimming today. When you come to get him, you can put your swimsuit on under your jeans and disrobe at the waterfall."

I was lost for words. After a moment of silence, I said, "Okay, but I feel like a fool and he will too." After we ended the call, I tried not to think about what I had agreed to do. It was still early and an hour before I needed to leave, so I took a cup of coffee out on the back porch to watch the sunrise.

I was at Mom and Dad's by 9:30. Dad had already left, but Mom and Ted were sitting on the porch waiting for me. The first thing Mom said was, "I told Ted you were going swimming."

He had this frightened look on his face. A world renowned neurosurgeon afraid to go swimming with a minister. Maybe this wasn't such a bad idea after all. I went into the house and to my old bedroom, finding the swimsuit lying on the bed. Stripping down, I put it on. Looking in the full length mirror, I blushed, saying *"This is ridiculous."* Standing there, my next comment, was *"Not bad."* It was amazing how well the two piece still fit. If the congregation saw me in this, I would never be allowed to preach again.

With my clothes on over the suit, I went back into the kitchen. The fried chicken smelled delicious. My mother and Ted came back inside with Mom asking, "Did it fit?"

"Yes," I answered.

"Told you so," she said, with a smile.

Ted still had that look of a child that was dreading to get a shot at the doctor's office. I asked him if he was ready to go.

"I guess so. I borrowed swim trucks from your dad. They're a little too big," he said.

We took our picnic lunch and were at the waterfall 45 minutes later. Ted had been silent on the drive but when we stopped, he said, "I don't like cold water. I imagine this water will be freezing cold."

"We swam here all the time when I was growing up. You'll get used to the water after awhile," I said.

"It is a beautiful place," he said as we stood looking at the pool. The waterfall was only a trickle at this time of year.

"Okay, here's the deal. We always just dove in. You adjust to the water better that way. It's easier than wading in the shallow part. Right here the pool is deep enough to dive." I started taking off my clothes, noticing that he was looking in the other direction. Down to my swimsuit, I dived head first into the water, which was so cold, it took my breath away. When I came up, he was still standing on the bank, fully clothed.

"Well, hurry up! The water's fine," I said. He slowly started taking off his shirt. He hesitated before removing his pants.

"I do not look good in a swimsuit. Not anything like you do."

"Dr. Adders, I hope you don't look anything like I do. Besides, how do you know? You didn't even look at me. Come on in before I'm forced to come get you."

Reluctantly, he started pulling off his pants. I should've known my dad's swimsuit would swallow him. I dared not laugh, but it was about three sizes too big. Standing there with his skinny legs, my heart went out to this famous brain surgeon. He was out of his element and was doing his best to please me.

"Come on in. I think you look great," I said.

Maybe that was all he needed to get the confidence to dive in. He hit the water and came up gasping for air. I noticed something floating on top of the water behind him."

"I lost my trunks!" he exclaimed.

I couldn't contain myself and started laughing. Finally, able to talk, I said, "Don't worry, I'll get them for you." I paddled over, got his trunks, and gave them to him. His lips were blue from the cold and his teeth were chattering as he tried to talk.

"I-I have to stand u-up to put t-them on. I n-need to go t-to the shallow w-water. C-could we g-get out then? I-I a-am f-freezing."

I didn't respond, so I assumed he took that for a yes. I felt guilty for putting him in this situation. He was uncomfortable and embarrassed. He was in a totally foreign environment from the operating room, only consenting because he wanted to please me.

He was in chest deep water, trying to put on his trunks. He kept losing his footing trying to stand on one leg and going under water. He went under several times before I went to help him.

"Here, let me hold you up while you get one leg in and then the other." He didn't object, and with my help, was fully covered when he walked out of the pool. He was having to hold the swimsuit up with both hands to keep it in place. I followed him out and retrieved a blanket from the pickup. He sat down, and I wrapped the blanket around him; however, he continued to shiver.

"Thank you. I told you I did not like cold water," he said.

"You did fine. We'll keep you wrapped up still you thaw out and then the sun will finish the job." He continued to shake, and I put my arm around him and held him as close as possible.

Without warning, he began to laugh. He laughed so hard that he laid back on the grass and tears came to his eyes.

"What is it?" I asked.

"The Medical Journal is doing a feature on me that will appear in the December edition. My picture, in scrubs, will be on the cover. If they could only see me now."

He continued to laugh and I couldn't resist the temptation of leaning over and kissing him. It lasted longer than I expected but it was nice.

"That was worth the freezing water. I'll go back in for another kiss," he said.

"That won't be necessary," I said, leaning down and kissing him again.

"How can you be so beautiful and be attracted to me?" he asked.

"I find you extremely handsome," I said.

"I am skinny. I look like the 'before' picture in one of those muscle building ads. On the other hand, you look like the 'after' picture in an aerobic video ad."

"Let's not worry about that. I believe we're good for one another. We enjoy one another's company and that's special," I explained. "Now are you hungry?"

"Yes. Very much so."

I went to get the picnic basket and was surprised when I opened it, seeing a bottle of wine with two glasses. Mother thought of everything. The fried chicken was unreal and Ted ate like a 300 pound linemen in the NFL. We each had a glass of wine with the meal. Afterwards, we lay in the warm sun and dozed, off and on, for several hours. I was surprised when he told me he was ready to go back into the water.

"This time I am going to jump in feet first," he announced.

"Are you sure? The water is still cold."

"Absolutely. I am going to show you how tough I can be," he said.

For the next hour we played in the water until we were exhausted. The sun was going down when we collapsed on the bank. He was shivering again, and I wrapped the blanket around him.

"Are you ready to go?" I asked.

"Do we have to leave? What about building a fire? Can you do that?"

"Are you kidding? Of course I can. You gather up some small pieces of wood while I get rocks to build a fire ring," I instructed.

We had a nice fire going before the sun went down. The warmth after the cold water and the cooling night was fantastic. I broke the silence by asking him if he could dance.

"It's been a long time."

I rose, went to the pickup, and found a county music station in Roswell. Leaving the door open, it came in loud and clear. We both dressed and then for the next several hours danced to the radio music. He actually picked up the two-step and was very good. The longer we danced the closer we held one another.

At midnight, we put out our fire, and ended a day that resembled two teenagers on a picnic rather than a

34-year-old surgeon and 30-year-old minister. *Mothers are always right,* was proven once again.

The next day, which was Sunday, Mom, Dad, and Ted picked me up on their way to church. Mother was all smiles as I got into the car.

"How are you this morning, Tommie?" she asked.

"Fine, Mother. How're you?"

"To tell you the truth, I didn't get much sleep. I kept waiting for Ted to get home. You shouldn't worry your mother like that," she said, smiling and loving every second of it.

Ted had sunburned badly and resembled a lobster. I'd need to put some aloe lotion on him after church. I asked him if he was hurting.

"A little. Mainly, the front of my legs and feet," he replied.

We arrived at church and attracted a crowd, as usual. Everyone wanted to greet Ted, knowing he was here to visit me. Thank goodness, I wasn't preaching today. One of the older widow ladies came up, hugged me, and said, "I don't see a ring yet, Tommie. This young man had better not let you get away." Of course, Ted heard her, but looked almost as frightened as he did before he dived in the pool yesterday.

We sat in our customary seats and Pastor Stevens delivered his usual good sermon. As we exited the door and greeted Pastor Stevens, he said, "My, my, Dr. Adders, it looks like you visited the swimming hole yesterday." If possible, Ted turned more red than he already was.

On the drive to Mia's, where we were going to have lunch, Mother talked constantly. She was on a roll, exalting in her successful matchmaking, or so she believed. We had tried to talk Mia out of doing lunch, but she would have none of it.

After lunch and visiting for an hour, we left. Mom and Dad let us out at my house. Lacy was visiting her mother, which she had been doing once a week. We spent the afternoon in Ruidoso, going up and down main street, looking in the shops but buying very little. Ted wanted to buy me something and we ended up in the jewelry shop. I picked out a turquoise cross that was beautiful. I insisted on returning the favor and asked him what he would like.

"Promise you will not laugh. It's going to cost more than your gift."

"Sure. No problem. Let's hear it."

"Cowboy boots," he announced. I bought boots when your mother took me shopping, but they weren't like your dad and brother wear."

"I know just the place. It's on our way out of Ruidoso. I'm impressed. You'll be riding in no time."

"Whoa! I did not say anything about a horse," he replied.

We stopped at the western store and found a perfect pair of boots. They were black with six to eight inch tops, much like the ones B-Boy wore. We left the store with him wearing the boots and acting much less like his age or profession.

"I'm going to cook your supper tonight. What would you like?" I asked.

"What is the specialty of New Mexico?" he asked.

"That's easy. A green chili cheeseburger using Hatch chilies."

"That's what I want."

"You got it, Dr. Adders," I said, pleased that it was going to be easy.

I have to admit the burgers were delicious. Ted confessed it was the best burger he had ever eaten. Actually, he ate two. After finishing our meal, we sat on the porch and watched the sun go down over the mountains. It was a beautiful early fall evening. Whatever the reason, the conversation became serious.

"Have you decided when you are going back to Africa?"

"I need to be there now, but I can't leave because of Gramps," I said.

"Eventually, you'll go back though," he stated.

"Yes, of course. That's where my work is."

"I am completely out of my element with romance."

"I would never have guessed that; however, you are a quick learner. Every kiss gets better."

"You are making fun of me."

"I'm sorry. Go ahead with what you were saying."

"I would like for you to stay in the States so we could be together more. If you return to Africa, we will not see one another but once or twice a year."

"That's not possible," I replied. We were interrupted by my phone.

"Hello, Mom."

"Tommie, it's getting late, and your dad goes to bed early. I was just thinking that since Ted is leaving early in the morning it might work out better if he stayed over there tonight."

Before I could respond, Dad's voice came through in the background, telling Mom to let him have the phone. I then heard giggling and scuffling, and evidently he took the phone away from her.

"Tommie, honey, don't pay any attention to your mom. She's a desperate woman who is on a mission." More giggling and then I was disconnected. I hoped and prayed that when fifty years old I would have a marriage like they did.

"What did your mom want?" Ted asked.

"Meddling where she doesn't belong," I answered.

"Why isn't it possible for you to stay in the States and be a pastor in a church close to my work?"

"Because, Dr. Adders, my work is not your work. Mine takes me 9,000 miles from you."

His next response surprised me. "Do you want to have a family with children?"

"Yes. That's my plan."

"I would not know anything about raising children," he said.

"That's not correct, Ted. Many times the best knowledge we receive comes from the worst experiences we have. You'll know everything not to do because that was the kind of childhood you had. You were denied love, and you'll shower love on your children. You were made to feel like nothing, and you will make certain that your children vision themselves to be everything. You will be a wonderful parent."

"I would have no idea about how to make a woman happy," he said.

"This woman you speak of just might be happy sharing her life with you and being your friend."

Then, out of the blue, he changed the subject, saying, "I need to leave early in the morning. My flight leaves Lubbock at 10:00. Since I have the rental car at your mom and dad's, it will not be necessary for you to rise early."

That could be the closest I've come to repeating one of B-Boy's favorite observations.

CHAPTER 45

Lacy

IT WAS TUESDAY, OCTOBER 9, and Zack was coming home today. Bo and Lexie were picking him up in Lubbock. I was relieved, afraid he would stay right up until the time to return to school. I had given a lot of thought to what I was going to say. I believed it best to be honest with him and tell him exactly how I felt. I didn't love him, but maybe in time that would change. I was willing to give it a chance if he was. I knew he cared deeply for me and always had, even when I was going to marry Jack.

My problem was that only a short time ago I had disappointed him with my response when he expressed his feelings toward me. Being the kind of person he was, I believed he would understand.

I'd been riding my horses each day for the past two weeks. Scooter was doing good, and I had begun loping him around the barrels. He had already started to look for the barrel as he approached. The most amazing progress was with Chrome. Tommie had given me some advice about how to run him to the first barrel. We had gone back and looked at some videos of past rodeos, with her explaining that I needed to adjust my approach to the first barrel. He needed more room than I was giving him; hence, he was slowing down to turn the barrel.

She had explained it the following way. "Lacy, horses have much different ability levels and Chrome has less than Jazzy. Jazzy could make the first barrel without much room but Chrome needs his rear to be parallel to the second barrel when he starts his turn. That way you won't choke him off. Run him toward the middle until you reach a point and then go to the barrel. You will have him set up for a half turn, which will make it an easy barrel."

After following her instructions, I could see an immediate improvement, even though it was awkward for him at first. By the time a week had passed, he was doing much better. I couldn't wait to take him to a barrel race.

My movement continued to improve with my prosthetic. It would be difficult to recognize my handicap by watching me walk. One of my regrets was that I always had to wear pants. Dresses and shorts were out. I wasn't comfortable enough, and might never be, to expose my leg. I had always enjoyed dressing up on certain occasions and still had some of my wardrobe.

I'd been going to visit my mother once a week. Our relationship was better than it had ever been. She was finally rid of that man who I detested. She had received the payment for the hunting lease on her property, and with the cash, could start stocking the ranch again. The big surprise was the person I discovered at the ranch on my last visit. I thought he looked familiar before the introduction.

"Lacy, this is Cody Lowe, who you probably don't remember. We go back a long way."

Of course I remembered him. He was the man Bo had defeated in the match roping when I was just a little girl. In later years, Lexie had told me that he was crazy about my mother. He had blamed Bo for not being able to win her affection.

When I left that day, she followed me to the car and explained. "Lacy, Cody's probably the only man who ever truly loved me besides my daddy. He's changed after he's grown older, and after being with him a number of times, I believe we might have a future. I'm not getting any younger and my choice of men has been poor, to put it mildly. At this time, I want someone who cares about me and treats me good."

"Mother, I want you to be happy. That's all that matters. I'm glad Roy is no longer a part of your life. As far as I'm concerned, he's the scum of the earth. How did you get him to leave?"

"As you know, this is a large ranch. I had five sections surveyed on the far southwestern part of our property and offered it to him if he would get out of my life. He signed the papers, agreeing to the divorce and settlement."

"Good for you! Now you can move on with your life." I said, hugging her.

"Lacy, I'm going to be a better mother. I hope it's not too late."

"Of course not. I'm going to be a better daughter, also," I stated.

On the drive back through Cloudcroft and to the ranch I thought, how strange; I lose Jack and a leg but gain a mother.

Mia had everyone over for supper the day Zack came home. Tommie and I were already there when Bo, Lexie, and Zack arrived. He hugged us both saying he was glad to be home.

During the meal, he avoided conversation about his experience in New York at the attack site. However, Tommie brought up a subject which caught me off guard.

"Okay, Little Brother, tell me about this girl you met. The family needs to hear about her."

I panicked, anticipating his reaction.

"Not a lot to tell. She had a room at the hotel and allowed me to use her shower each day. We started spending time together and getting to know one another. Her roommate was in the South Tower when it was hit. She had told me if they found her remains she was going home. That's what she did, without saying goodbye. I don't have her phone number or address."

"What are you going to do?" Lexie asked.

"I know she's a physical therapist and works in Plano. I'm going to Dallas and try to find her," he stated.

"Is she involved with someone else?" Bo asked.

"Yes. But I have to find out how serious it is. Maybe it was just that horrible place with the grief and death that brought us together. Each day I went through that hell, I would concentrate on getting to see her that evening.

"What's her name?" Mia asked.

"Jerri Johnson," he answered.

"How old is she?" asked Lexie.

"At least a couple of years younger than me," Zack said.

Thank goodness, Mia changed the subject, saying, "Tom has been doing better the last couple of days. We're hoping and praying that the new medicine is beginning to work."

"Nancy's right. I have been breathing easier and even felt like going for a ride around the ranch this morning," Tom said.

"Gramps, that's wonderful!" Tommie said.

"I know you've been staying at the ranch because of me, Tommie. That is not necessary and please don't let me keep you here any longer. You have important work awaiting you."

We stayed an hour longer visiting, but Zack didn't mention the girl again. I rode with Tommie back to my house and asked her, "Are you leaving now that your gramps is doing better?"

"Probably. I'll wait a few days and see if he continues to do well."

"It's going to be lonely without you," I said.

"I know you were surprised and disappointed with Zack's announcement about the girl. He told me about her several days ago and it surprised me, also; however, I'm happy for him. This is the first girl that he has really cared about besides you. I know that's not easy for you to accept, especially now. Please try to be happy for him. He's a special man, and if anyone deserves to find love, it's Zack."

"I know that. It just seems that every time my life clears up and I see what direction to go, a cloud covers me up."

"Lacy, of all people, you have every right to experience ups and downs and indecision after what you've been through. Losing Jack and your leg would have devastating consequences for anyone. You have done remarkably well in your recovery."

"I could never have gotten through this without you, Tommie."

At home, I went directly to my room, cried while showering, went to bed, and cried some more.

The next morning, I made up my mind to find a barrel race to attend this weekend. Andrews, Texas was having a three day 4D competition beginning Friday. It wasn't that far and would give me a chance to try Chrome.

Tommie suggested that we work the horses since she wouldn't be here but a few more days. I ran Chrome first and was amazed at how much better he was doing. Riding back to the alley, I said to Tommie, "He's a different horse. I think he's going to be more competitive."

"Let's hope so," Tommie replied. "Now let's work with Scooter."

I trotted Scooter around the barrels twice and then loped him. He did well. I decided to take him one more time, and I have no idea why I did it, but when we turned the first barrel I moved the reins forward. He lunged forward and the next thing I knew, I was sitting on the ground, flat on my rear. Thank goodness we had loads of sand put in the arena. I wasn't hurt, except for my pride, and I started laughing. I guess that answered my question as to Scooter's quickness. After dumping me, he went around the second barrel and then came back and stood beside me.

Tommie came running down to me, asking, "Are you hurt?"

"No. You're right, Scooter can move when asked," I said, continuing to laugh.

"He's amazing. Look at him standing there, as if asking, 'What next'? I predict that he will win many rodeos for you," Tommie said.

I left for Andrews Friday after lunch with Chrome and Scooter. Tommie had suggested that I take Scooter and do several exhibitions on him. She had promised not to leave before I returned Sunday. Roany was riding in the front seat with me, and I was feeling better.

I was at the arena by four, and locating the office, paid for stalls and a hook-up. There was a jackpot that night and I entered Chrome and purchased exhibitions for Scooter, which would begin at 5:00.

Returning to my trailer, I saw that a neighbor was unloading her horses from a very expensive rig. I went over, introduced myself, and offered to help. She was a short, somewhat overweight woman, in her mid to late thirties. She introduced herself as Twiggy.

"Are you running tonight?" she asked in a deep gruff voice.

"Yes. I also have some exhibitions," I replied.

"Have you seen any men around?" she asked.

"No. Are you looking for someone in particular?"

"Just one that breathes and will do what I tell him to," she answered in that same tone. "That's the problem with these 4D barrel races. Very few men."

She thanked me for my help and I saddled Scooter for my exhibitions. He did great and I continued to be amazed at how calm he was. I was careful not to ask for any speed.

In the jackpot, Chrome made one of his best runs ever. No doubt, the change Tommie suggested was going to be successful. I was one of the first to run, so I put Chrome up and went back to watch the rest of the competition.

My time was a 15.21 seconds and the closest to it was a 15.5 that Twiggy had. Her name was really Katy Stockholm and I remembered seeing her run last December at the Finals in Vegas. She was an excellent rider and had good horses.

I ended up winning and when I went to get my check, she was there also. "You made a good run," I said.

"Not good enough. You have a nice horse."

"My best horse died this year, and I've started another one to take with Chrome."

"Have you eaten?" she asked.

"No. I never do before a race."

"Good, I know this place in town that serves great food and stays open till midnight," she said, in the form of an invitation.

I couldn't have asked for a more enjoyable evening. A win, good meal, and being entertained by Twiggy. She was funny, with story after story of her life, mostly pertaining to her three marriages. Her first husband, who was thirty years older, had died and left her a fortune. She described what happened to the next two.

"Lacy, they just couldn't keep up with me. I wore them out and they finally dropped out of my life. I have a lot of energy and it was too much for them. I'm sorry, but that's the truth of the matter."

I didn't ask what she meant by, "They just couldn't keep up with me." We sat out in front of her trailer and talked until 1:00, and I hadn't laughed so much since losing Jack. Roany, who was a good judge of people, took up with her immediately.

The barrel race started the next morning at 11:00, with exhibitions at 8:00. I did several exhibitions on Scooter again, letting him out a little the last time. Amazing is an understatement of how he did. Each time I rode him my respect increased.

There were over two hundred entries and I didn't run until after 3:00 that afternoon. The tractor would drag the arena after every five riders and I was the first after the drag. I had one of the most awesome runs of my career. I didn't hear my time announced, coming out the alley.

I heard the announcer say, "I'm sorry, Lacy. Our electric eye didn't get your time. There are ten runners left. You can make another run after that."

No way was I going to run Chrome again. I went to the press box and told them my decision. "You can give me my money back. I won't run him again today."

"Sorry, we can't do that," the lady in charge said. "You can run again and we'll be sure and get your time."

Before I could answer, I recognized the voice behind me saying, "What do you mean, you can't give her money back? Of course you can and you will. Lacy had a winning run and you cost her several hundred dollars with your mistake. You didn't even check the eye after the drag. You give her money back and don't you even think about giving me any lip."

The in-charge lady blinked and started to reply but was interrupted before a word came out. "Don't go there, lady. I told you what was right. Now, get on with it."

She reached in her money box and took out cash, giving it to me, not saying anything.

"You make sure and check the eye after every drag," Twiggy instructed.

I won the next day and completed an interesting and successful weekend. I made a new friend and companion, as did Roany. We agreed that we would begin hauling together immediately. We looked at the fall schedule of PRCA shows and selected the ones we would attend. I left Andrews feeling more confident, looking forward to my next rodeo.

CHAPTER 46

Zack

I WAS GLAD TO BE home and for several days did very little except accompany Dad around the ranch. I tried to avoid talking about my experience in New York. Maybe, in time, that would be possible, but not now. I asked Dad about Lacy, who had been acting strangely since I arrived home. He shrugged, and said, "Who knows? She's a woman. I quit trying to figure them out a long time ago."

I couldn't get my mind off Jerri, regardless of how hard I tried. On Saturday night, after supper with Mom and Dad, I announced, "I'm going to Dallas in the morning and try to locate Jerri. With the information I have, maybe I can find her."

"I hope you're not disappointed," Mom said.

"Either way, I have to try. I need to understand why she left without a word."

Addressing Mom, Dad asked, "Zack is puzzled about Lacy's strange behavior. I don't know what's going on. Do you?"

"Yes, I'm afraid so. Tommie and I were hoping Zack wouldn't notice."

Turning to me, she continued, "Lacy has had a change of heart about you, Zack. We believe it comes from the realization that she will be alone when Tommie leaves. We're only guessing but it makes sense. Tommie thinks she was ready to express her feelings about you when you surprised everyone with Jerri. Now she's disappointed and can't hide it."

"That doesn't change anything for me. Lacy made it clear that she wasn't interested in our relationship being any more than what it is at the current time. If she has changed her mind, more than likely she would do it again."

"I agree with you," Dad stated.

"Let us know if you find Jerri," Mom requested.

I left early the next morning. I didn't want to fly since it would have required renting a car. I immediately began thinking about what had happened with Jerri. Surely there was some kind of logical explanation for her behavior.

It was a beautiful day and I didn't mind the drive. The traffic was not bad, it being a Sunday. I only stopped twice, for gasoline and bathroom breaks. I was in Dallas by 6:00 in the evening, and after looking at a map, stayed on I-30 until reaching Highway 75. I turned North on 75 and it took me straight to Plano. I found a hotel, checked in, and used their internet service to search for home health care units in the area. Knowing that she worked for a home health care group narrowed my search somewhat. Still, I was amazed at the number of such groups.

I then spent a long restless night, dozing and waking up every so often, looking at the clock. I finally rose and dressed at 5:00. I had a list of nineteen home health care agencies in the area. I had acquired a map of Plano from the lobby and would begin by locating the closest and working out from there.

I left the hotel at 7:00, and the traffic was unbelievable. I thought Houston traffic was bad but this was worse. It was 10:00 before I found the first clinic. I asked the person at the desk if there was a Jerri Johnson working for them.

"Why are you looking for her?" she asked.

"She's a friend and I'm trying to locate her."

"We have no one who works here by that name," she answered.

I left and two hours later found the second name on my list. I had no success there either, and by the third inquiry, I realized my tactics needed to change. I was viewed with suspicion by each of the people who responded to my inquiry.

At the fourth clinic, my approach was different as I spoke to the woman behind the counter, "Good morning, how are you today?"

I received a smile and, "Fine."

"Could I talk with the boss? I'm not a salesman but just need a few minutes of his time."

"Let me check and see if she's available," was her response.

Within a few seconds, an older woman appeared and asked me to come into her office. I introduced myself and told her the entire story of how Jerri and I met. She didn't respond until I hesitated, describing the carnage at the Site.

"That's okay, young man. I can see it's difficult for you to speak about. You say the young lady's name is Jerri Johnson. You must have been impressed with her to come all this way to find her."

"Yes. I guess so," I replied.

"She doesn't work here. I'm sorry," she stated.

"Well, thank you anyway," I said, getting up to leave.

"Wait just a minute, young man. I didn't say I wouldn't try and help you. Wait in the lobby and give me a few minutes to see what I can do. With what you've been through, you deserve consideration, and who am I to interfere with love?"

She came out of her office twenty minutes later with a smile, sayings, "Jackpot. Here's the address. I hope she's glad to see you." She also gave me directions to the location of the clinic.

I thanked her profusely and left, thankful that I had changed my approach at just the right time. Within an hour I was at the health agency. When I asked about Jerri, the receptionist said she was making her rounds and would probably be in around 5:00. I looked at my watch and it was 3:45. Rather than wait in the office, I went back to my pickup. It was a long hour and fifteen minutes. From where I sat, I could see the walk leading to the front. Expecting to see her at any time, I waited.... not patiently.

At a few minutes after 6:00, Jerri came out the front door, wearing sweats and a cap turned backward. Evidently they had a back entrance she'd used. I got out of my pickup and started in her direction; however, before she saw me, a man met her. They were far enough away that I couldn't tell much about him, except he was African American. He hugged her and they continued to the parking area. I wasn't surprised that a man met her, but I didn't expect him to be a Person of Color. The last thing I wanted was to cause a scene. Returning to my pickup, I sat there, not knowing what to do.

By now, I had lost sight of them. I decided that the best option was to come back tomorrow and, hopefully, she would be alone.

Disappointed, I returned to the hotel.

Sitting in my room, I thought how ridiculous this whole experience was turning out to be. Evidently, she didn't want anything to do with me, or she would have told me goodbye before leaving and left me her address and phone number. My excuse for finding her was to understand why she left without telling me. That wasn't much of an excuse.

Mother's explanation of why Lacy was acting strangely was a surprise. I should have been pleased to learn this information; however, now, I was not anxious to enter into a relationship with Lacy. That was strange, since a month ago I had a totally different attitude. I spoke softly to myself, *but that was before I met Jerri.*

The next afternoon at 4:30 I was back at my spot, watching the front door of the home health clinic. This time, she came out the door at a few minutes after 5:00. I met her at the end of the sidewalk. She had a look of surprise but recovered quickly.

"Jerri. Could we talk?"

"Why?" she asked.

"I want to know why you left New York without a word," I stated.

"I didn't owe you an explanation. You shouldn't have assumed that I did."

"No, you're right. It would have been the right thing to do, though. You have to admit that. Will you talk to me about why you're acting this way?" I asked.

"You came all the way from New Mexico to find out why I didn't tell you goodbye?" she asked.

"Yes, and also because I wanted to see you again. Is something wrong with that?"

"Probably. My dad is an African American so that makes me one-half black. Would your family and friends be shocked when they saw you with a little colored girl. Your rich New Mexico family would disown you. You might have to work for a living like other people."

I had to wait a few seconds to control my anger. "You're wrong. You have no idea what my rich New Mexico family is like! You have no right to judge them. You can't imagine how your comments anger me! Maybe you're not who I thought you were after all, and I'm not speaking of your color." I turned around and started toward my pickup.

"Wait. Wait a minute," she said, just loud enough for me to hear.

I stopped and turned around.

"I thought you wouldn't want anything to do with me when you discovered I was black. It was easier to disappear and not have to tell you."

"You were wrong. I don't care about your race. Now, can we go somewhere and talk?" I asked.

"I can't now. My mom and dad are in town visiting. I have to get back to my apartment. We're going out for dinner later. You can join us if you like. Where are you staying?"

"Was that your dad who met you yesterday when you were leaving?"

"Yes. Why?"

"Never mind." I told her the name of the hotel and her apartment wasn't that far from it.

"There's a Chili's down the street from your hotel. My dad likes to eat there. We can meet you there at 8:00."

"That's great. I look forward to meeting your parents. Could I have some time with you alone after dinner? I could take you home."

"Let's just wait and see how things go," she replied.

Not wanting to press it, I told her 8:00 would be fine. Driving back to the hotel, I thought, it could have been a lot worse. At least I was going to be able to spend time with her, even if it was in the presence of her parents. It made sense now why she had left without telling me. I felt sure she had experienced humiliation because of her race, and it had definitely made her defensive. I could care less that her daddy was black. Convincing her of that might not be so easy.

I had brought enough clothes to last several days. I chose a white shirt and jeans with boots and my good black hat to wear. She hadn't seen me wear anything but jeans and work shirts that Chad had furnished.

I tried to guess what we would talk about during supper, hoping it wouldn't be about New York. Not knowing her parents, I had no idea what their interests would be.

I left early to make sure I could find the restaurant. It was no problem and by 7:40 I was in the waiting area. They came in at 8:00, right on the dot. Her parents were small, in fact, not much taller than Jerri. Her dad was stocky and her mom was dainty, both appearing too young to have a daughter her age.

Jerri brought them over to me. Standing and looking down on them, she began the introductions. Before she even mentioned my name, I saw tears roll down her dad's face. I panicked, thinking, *this is going to be terrible.*

Then after the introductions, he reached out and hugged me. Her mom was beginning to cry also.

"What's the matter?" asked Jerri. "What's going on here? I introduce you to this man from New Mexico and both of you start crying."

"Let's get a table and I'll explain," Jeremiah said.

For the next two hours, there were more tears, this time from everyone at the table. We talked about Jeremiah's and my dad's special relationship, my mom, Jerri's mom, and football.

"I knew who you were the second I saw you. You look so much like your dad. That white shirt and black hat with that dark complexion. Your dad and I could never have made it without each other. He was something special, and we couldn't have won a national championship without him. We would have followed him off a cliff and never hesitated."

"Bo is the reason Jeremiah and I were able to get together," her mother said.

Jerri said very little during the entire time we visited. Of course, with Jeremiah and LyAnn doing the reminiscing, I didn't say much either. We decided to break up our meeting before the manager asked us for our table.

"Dad, Zack is going to take me to my apartment. Don't wait up for me. We have a lot to talk about."

CHAPTER 47

Bo

IT WAS A RELIEF TO get Zack home and out of danger. Now he was gone again on a wild goose chase after some girl he hardly knew. She must be some looker. I'd been surprised at his decision to leave the ranch and resume his education after the first of the year. I had put on quite an act to convince him that I wasn't disappointed in his decision. With him and Tommie both leaving it was going to be hard on us.

The most discouraging aspect of them leaving was the future of this ranch. It had been in the family for four generations and the future for that continuing was not promising. I had always known Jack would be the fifth generation to continue the tradition that I loved. Mother had scolded me on more than one occasion about putting too much emphasis on the land, saying, "Land does not give one immortality, only God can do that." It still depressed me greatly to think of someone other than my family owning this ranch.

Jimmy had taken the horses to Sunland Park. He continued to believe the filly that didn't run well in the All-American trials would be successful as a three-year-old. Jimmy was seldom wrong about horses, and I had learned to never doubt his judgment.

Lexie's talk with Felicia must have done some good. She'd been staying in El Paso much of the time with Jimmy. Also, her decision to allow Jolynda to attend school in Texas and major in theater arts had proven to be a good move. Lexie said their relationship had made a 180 degree turnaround.

It was October and my favorite time of the year. The cattle had been worked and feed put up for the winter. The days were becoming cooler and the nights colder, with a frost likely this week. The trees were turning along the creek, further evidence that a change was coming. I had seen several bucks together this past week. Soon they would split off into singles to find a group of doe for the rutting season. Jimmy still loved to hunt and had been after me to go with him this year. He would have liked for us to camp out the way we did when we were in high school.

It was only three weeks until the anniversary of Jack's death. I thought about him every day. I couldn't help but wonder what life would be like if it had never happened. I would still go to his room occasionally and sit on his bed, remembering when he was a little boy. Sometimes I would question whether others missed him as much as I did.

My leg was doing better, with the pain diminished to the point that I seldom noticed it. I wanted to start roping again but wanted to give it plenty of time to heal. Turning 50 did give me an opportunity to compete in senior ropings, better known as old-timers. Chuckling, I said to myself, *helluva note to be called an old-timer. I'm not ready for that.* That settled it; when I felt 100 percent I was taking Cotton and going to some jackpots that wouldn't be seniors.

Lexie still reminded me of how much like Grands I had become, mainly when she told me how stubborn I was. I hadn't developed a taste for Jack Daniels, even though I did have a drink with Tom occasionally. He always mentioned Grands during this time and how much he missed him. He'd been gone twenty years; however, I was reminded of him almost every day by something he had taught me or had said. It never failed that when I visited the family cemetery I could always smell smoke when I returned to my pickup.

I had been going back home for lunch every day since this was not a busy time of year. Today, Lexie met me at the door, kissing me, and saying, "Hello, Cowboy."

"What's the deal?" I asked.

"Just glad to see you. Dinner's about ready. It's one of your favorites. Just sit down and relax while I put it on the table."

I knew a surprise was coming. We had been eating sandwiches and chips for lunch. When she put the meatloaf, potatoes, and fried okra on the table, all doubt was removed. When she took the apple pie out of the oven, I was prepared for the worst.

"How's that look, Cowboy?"

"Wonderful. What's going on?" I asked.

"I'm just trying to be a good wife. Let's eat before it gets cold."

While we were eating, I asked if she had heard from Zack today.

"No. It's Tuesday, and he left Sunday morning. I suspect he hasn't been successful in his search or we'd have heard." she replied.

Whatever the reason for the meal, I enjoyed it immensely. Then, when I was stuffed and ready for my afternoon nap, she hit me with it.

"Cowboy, what would you think about a cruise?"

"In a boat?"

"Yes, I believe most cruises occur there."

"I don't like cruises," I stated.

"How do you know?" she asked.

"I just do. Besides, I don't need to be gone that long."

"I haven't told you how long we'd be away," she said.

"More than three days?" I asked.

"Three weeks. It would be so romantic! I still have that bikini that I wore when we went to Florida after we married. Do you want me to try it on for you?"

"You're pulling out all the stops, aren't you? Tempting me with indecency."

"Please, Bo. We haven't been on a trip of any kind for years. Just the two of us. You'll enjoy getting away. You like to fish. We could get a guide on one of the islands and go deep sea fishing."

Maybe the fishing did it. Probably it was because she deserved a trip and I wanted to please her. At times like this she reminded me of the Little Girl I married. Anyway, I consented, and my afternoon nap was an hour later than usual.

At 6:00 that afternoon, while I was watching the local news and weather, the phone rang. Lexie was outside and I answered.

"Dad, I found her. A lady helped me and I'm going to eat supper with her and her family tonight. I'm nervous about meeting her mom and dad."

"She must be something else, Zack, for you to be this excited."

"I don't know what it is about her. She's just different from anyone I've ever known. She's not beautiful like Mom, but so cute it's impossible to look at her without smiling. She's aggressive to the point it's kind of scary. She can do flip flops on the sidewalk."

"Well, Zack, I'm glad you found her. I hope you like her as much after you get to know her."

When Lexie came in, I told her about Zack's call, asking, "What's being able to do flip flops on the sidewalk have to do with anything?"

"I don't have the slightest idea. From what I understand, Zack may not know either. He's just fascinated with this girl, whoever she is. I hope he doesn't get his heart broken."

"What about this cruise?" I asked, moving to another subject.

"I scheduled it for after the first of the year, when the kids will be gone. It'll be a sad time, and we need to get away."

"You've already made reservations and paid for it, without asking me?"

"Yes."

"How did you know that I'd go with you?"

"Oh, I just had a feeling," she said, smiling.

The phone rang that night, and looking at the clock before answering, it was 1:05. Frightened, I answered, hoping it wasn't bad news.

"Hello, Cowboy. What's going on?"

"I was sleeping. Who is this?" I asked.

"Your old college roommate, Scoot-Scoot."

"Jeremiah! What're you doing calling in the middle of the night? Is something wrong?"

"I don't know. That's why I called. Maybe you could help me out. My daughter's not home and it's getting late."

"Have you notified the police?".

"No, not yet. I wanted to talk with you first. Well, it's like this, Cowboy. She's out with a young man wearing a white shirt, black hat, and wranglers, that looks a whole lot like you."

CHAPTER 48

Tommie Rose

TED HAD CALLED ME EVERY day since he'd been gone. He asked me on more than one occasion to postpone going back to Africa. Of course, I refused. He gave an indication of wanting us to have a future, all on his terms. That was not going to happen. Maybe it was meant for me to remain single and die a shriveled up old maid.

It was Wednesday morning, October 17, and I had slept late. Dad had called this morning at one o'clock telling me the news about Zack. He had found the girl and it was Jeremiah's daughter. Dad was so excited it was difficult to understand him. Mom had finally taken the phone and given me the details of how it happened. It had to be labeled as a miracle, being brought together by one of the greatest tragedies ever experienced by this country.

Lacy had been ecstatic with her runs last weekend at Andrews. She was also excited about making a friend that she was going to haul with. I believed that she had turned the corner and was now headed in the right direction. I think the ups and downs she had been experiencing were in the past.

I had booked a flight to Johannesburg this Sunday. I dreaded leaving but was looking forward to getting back to my work at the mission. I had been home for over a year and was going to miss the ranch. I loved this country and planned to eventually live here. I had no idea when that would happen.

I was on the back porch and had just begun reading my Scriptures for the day when my phone went off. Noticing it was Mia, I answered immediately.

"Tommie, your gramps wants to talk with you."

"Good morning, Tommie. How are you today?" he asked.

"Good. Just enjoying this beautiful morning," I responded.

"Tommie, the reason I'm calling is to invite everyone over Saturday evening for a family gathering and meal. I would like to ask you to make sure everyone is here, including Lacy. I know you're leaving Sunday, and would like to have the family together."

"Sure, Gramps. I'll get right to work on it. Are you still doing okay?"

"I feel better than I have in months. The medicine is working," he replied.

Before ending the call, I told him I loved him. Each time could be the last that I talked to him. I was afraid he was exaggerating his well-being to prevent us from worrying. My heart ached every time I thought of leaving him, knowing it would probably be the last time I saw him.

It was early, but I called Zack anyway. His phone rang several times, and just when I was expecting his voice mail, he answered. "Hello, Little Brother. You must not have gotten much sleep last night."

"No. We stayed up talking till three this morning. I guess you heard about my good fortune."

"Of course. Dad woke me up at one. You probably got more sleep than he did last night. Is she still everything you expected?"

"More. I can't wait for you to meet her."

"The reason I'm calling is that Gramps wants everyone at his place Saturday evening. I'm leaving Sunday, and he's given me the job of seeing that everyone is at the family gathering."

"It shouldn't be a problem. I'm going to try and convince Jerri to take off work Friday and come home with me for the weekend. That'll be the only chance you have to meet her."

"Just make sure that you're here by Saturday," I said.

"Of course. I'll be home by then."

After the call ended, I said to myself, *how in the world could two people whose families were so connected find one another? It had to be more than a coincidence.*

I was successful in the responsibility that Gramps had given me. The last to arrive was Zack and Jerri. Due to the fact that she had taken off work during her stay in New York, she wasn't able to take off on Friday. They left early Saturday morning, with Zack calling me several times assuring me they would make it. The last time I talked with him, it was agreed he would come to my place.

I greeted them in the yard when they arrived at 5:00. From Jack's description of Jerri, she looked much like I expected. The short black hair with oval face, full lips, and dimples when she smiled was enough to melt anyone's heart. I didn't realize how short she was until we hugged and her head was below my neck. It could have been my imagination, but it seemed I could feel the energy coming from that little body when I touched her.

I invited them into the house and showed Jerri the bathroom. When she left, Zack asked, "What do you think, Sissy?"

"She's darling. Is she as nice as she looks?"

"Well, she's aggressive, but nice. She's unpredictable and has plenty of confidence. She's sensitive about her race. She told me that she didn't know what to call herself, since she's half black and half Vietnamese."

"Were you in the least disappointed when you got to know her better?" I asked.

"Not at all. In fact, I was more impressed. She was involved with someone else, but he broke it off because she was in New York so long."

"You going to have to take her back to Dallas tomorrow?" I asked.

"Yeah. Nothing else would work. I brought her so the family could meet her, especially you, since this is your last day at the ranch."

"Boy, this looks like a whirlwind courtship," I said.

"I don't know, Sissy. Maybe it was the circumstances in which we met. We were in a war zone together for two weeks. It seems I've known her much longer than I have."

Jerri was back before Sissy could comment further, saying, "This is a really a nice place."

"Are you tired from the long ride?" I asked.

"Not at all. It was exciting seeing new country. My dad told me that your parents had invited us to visit many times. It fact, my dad had promised to bring us for a visit, but he never got around to it."

"Are you nervous about meeting our family?" I asked.

"A little. I have heard so much about Mr. Skinner from my dad. He also told me how beautiful your mom is."

"We better be going. We're going to eat at 6:00," I said.

I have to admit I was impressed with Jerri. She met the family, appearing at ease with the situation. She was courteous, respectful, and answered all the questions from the family with poise. Zack was beaming the entire time.

I had worried about Lacy but that went fine. Her most impressive response came from a question from my Uncle Todd. He asked her what it was like at Ground Zero.

She hesitated so long I thought she wasn't going to respond. Finally, she said, "I'm angry and don't trust myself to express my thoughts. I lost my best friend, who I talked with most days. Maybe in the future I'll write my feelings down and be able to express them. I'm sorry, but it's too early to speak of now. To make my point, Zack and I just finished a ten-hour drive, and our experience in New York was not mentioned one time."

Of course, Dad had to ask about Jeremiah and tell some of the stories about their college days. I'm sure that Jerri had heard most of them. His favorite was how Jeremiah and LyAnn met during a television interview.

We had a wonderful meal as always, amid a comfortable setting. After finishing, Gramps asked us to move to the den. With everyone seated, he began, "It is ironic, but I feel good enough to talk about my demise. I never felt like a wealthy man until I moved to New Mexico and met my good friend, Bob Matthews. Lexie believed she had made a mistake that ruined her life. Now, because of that mistake, here we sit, a wonderful loving family. The lesson is obvious; there are times when a mistake can lead to many blessings.

Now, on to business. I will not mention amounts of money involved in my wishes. Please trust me when I say they will be sufficient. First, I am appointing Tommie as the executor of my will. That should not surprise anyone. I want my wishes implemented immediately and not prolonged until I am gone. There should not be a problem since my attorneys have spent considerable time formulating a document that would be difficult to challenge.

It is customary for the executor to receive compensation for her work. Tommie, there will be a deposit made to an investment firm in Johannesburg that will be at your disposal. I would suggest that you only take the profits from the investments each year and leave the principal intact. The funds are to be used at your discretion and no one else's.

Todd, of course, the bank in Ruidoso will go to you. Also, I am in the process of purchasing a bank in Alamogordo that is in dire trouble. I know you will relish the challenge of fixing it and make a profit in doing so. Now, I am meddling where I don't belong, but humor me. You have never remarried after a bad experience...find yourself a good woman, who will be your friend and companion, so you will have someone to grow old with.

Lexie, I gave you a generous trust that I understand is mostly intact. I know the reason for that is you have a stubborn husband, whom I respect and adore. I am leaving you some stocks that have done well. Maybe Bo will change, but I doubt it.

Zack, you will have sufficient funds to set up a practice when you finish your medical degree, including a building fund.

Lacy, I know you have inherited Jack's trust and you will have enough to live on; however, in time you will own your mother's ranch, which is one of the largest in the state. You will inherit one-third of this ranch also. If you agree, I would like to buy your part of this ranch now. I will have this ranch appraised and pay you whatever the price comes out to be. I would suggest that you invest the money until you retire from rodeo and take over Alejandra's ranch. At that time, you will have the funds to operate the ranch as it should be. I know your mother's ranch is in need of help at the present time. If you wish, you can help her now, but I would be careful in doing so.

My wonderful wife, Nancy, I could never repay you for the past twenty-six years. It seems an insult to say I'm leaving you money. I know you will not spend it, but I am making sure you will never have to worry about anything you want or need.

Tommie, Jesse and his boys will be left enough so they can retire and live comfortably here on this ranch.

Also, the Methodist Church will be left an endowment that will relieve much of their financial worries. A retirement fund will be set aside for Pastor Stevens, who has been with this family for the past thirty years.

I am leaving Jimmy my half of the horse operation, Bo. I know you will ensure that he has an adequate retirement.

Does anyone have a question about my wishes?"

You could have heard a pin drop in the room. I know everyone was thinking what a strong and generous man it took to give away his fortune while living.

"Good. It's settled then. Now, in honor of Bob Matthews, I would like to propose a toast to this wonderful family. Nancy, would you get the glasses?"

Mia returned from the kitchen with eight glasses and produced a bottle of Jack Daniels from a cabinet.

"Thank you, Nancy. Please feel free to put water in your glass or a soft drink if you prefer."

As my gramps raised his glass and said, "To my wonderful loving family," seven other glasses were raised, some with a generous amount, others with a few drops, but all containing contents from the same bottle.

I slept very little that night, with so much to think about. I was leaving early and had told my gramps bye. I cried and he cried. My mind was filled with doubt; if I was doing the right thing in leaving the ranch at this time. I had prayed about it but couldn't say that I received guidance.

Compounding my confusion and doubt was the relationship with Ted. I was leaving the States and wouldn't see him for months. When he called yesterday, he had told me a Methodist Church in Colorado Springs was looking for a pastor. It was difficult to control my anger since I had told him over and over that my commitment was the mission in Africa. As hard as I tried, he kept coming into my thoughts. I had to admit that he meant more to me than I had realized. Then, I heard a tiny voice inside my head say, *don't be so naive and stubborn, you love him.*

I was at Mom and Dad's by 7:00 the next morning. They were taking me to Lubbock to catch my flight. Zack and Jerri were there, and we all had breakfast together.

"Are you ready to leave?" Dad asked.

"No. I feel guilty leaving Gramps. I know last night will be the final time I see him. I considered changing my plans several times during the night."

"But you didn't," Mom said.

"No. I have missionary work 9,000 miles away. My commitment to those people are greater than my guilt about leaving."

"Gramps understands that, Sissy."

"I know, Zack, but that doesn't make it any easier to leave him."

We left for Lubbock at the same time that Zack and Jerri headed back to Dallas. My flight was at noon, with a three-hour layover in Denver and then my next layover was in (IAD) Washington. From there, I would change planes in Dakar (DKR) for Johannesburg.

My depression grew, the further we traveled from the ranch. The conversation was sparse, with most of it centering around Gramps' announcements last evening. I should be thrilled at the prospect of having funds available for the mission, but my sadness at leaving had dampened everything. Adding to my mood was the fact that Ted had called early this morning, saying he was coming to the airport at Denver to tell me goodbye. If I could make it to the mission and resume my busy schedule, hopefully I could put this sadness behind me.

In Lubbock at the airport, saying bye to Mom and Dad was even more difficult than leaving the ranch. I cried, Mom cried, and Dad couldn't stop the tears either. After boarding, I cried some more, until the stewardess came by and asked me if I was okay. I assured her I would be fine but wondered if that was true.

The flight to Denver took less than two hours. I immediately started looking for Ted in the terminal, hoping to get the goodbye over and done with. I kept telling myself, *you're not going to cry this time.*

I had reading material to help pass the three-hour wait. I would stop frequently and look for Ted. With only an hour before boarding he hadn't shown up, and my spirits reached a new low. How ridiculous, I thought angrily! I was a mature woman, acting like a school-girl, not being able to control my emotions.

When the announcement came for flight 623 for Washington to load, I grabbed my travel bag and stalked with new resolution to the gate. The line was not long and moved quickly. As I was entering the ramp, someone pinched me on the rear. I turned around, prepared to slap someone, and Dr. Adders was standing there, blushing, with his travel bag.

"Surely I can find someone to cure in Africa," he said with a smile.

CHAPTER 49

Lacy

TWIGGY AND I LEFT FOR Fort Worth on Wednesday, January 9, to compete in the first major professional rodeo of the new season. We were going to stay in Denton Wednesday night with a friend of Twiggy's who had an arena. It would give me a chance to work Scooter, which I did at every opportunity. We were traveling in my rig. We would switch out about every other month, so I'd picked her and her horses up in Amarillo. I enjoyed hauling with her throughout the fall and couldn't imagine going by myself now.

Twiggy was rough talking and gave the impression of being tough as nails but was actually kind and sweet. Her passions were men, Marlboros, and Budweiser, in that order. If I didn't want her to smoke in the cab, I'd have to stop every few hours for a break. I could always tell because she would become fidgety.

We hadn't done that great in the fall but both of us placed in several shows. She had two horses; the difference being that both were seasoned. I had only competed on Chrome, since Scooter wasn't ready; however, like Zack had predicated, he showed all the signs of being a great barrel horse. Twiggy seemed to know everybody and frequently we would stop and spend a day or two with one of her friends.

By noon, we were about ten miles out of Denton when I noticed a car behind us. Looking in the mirror more closely, I could see it was a policeman. When he turned on his blinking lights, I exclaimed, "I wasn't speeding!"

Looking back, Twiggy, said, "Well, Honey, it looks like you were doing something wrong. You better pull over."

I slowed down and finally stopped on the shoulder, as far from the traffic as I could get, without being in the ditch. The car stopped behind but no one got out. "What's going on?" I asked. That seemed to be the cue for a person to exit the car.

"Oh me. Oh my! Look at that cop, Lacy. Smart off to him! Maybe he'll handcuff us and take us to jail."

"Be quiet. You want him to hear you?" I said.

I rolled the window down and when he bent over to look inside, I recognized him, even though he had on sunglasses.

"Ma'am, you're excessive. Do you realize that?" he asked, with a stern look.

"What do you mean? I've done nothing wrong."

"Well, I'll tell you ma'am, it should be against the law to be as beautiful as you are," he said, taking off his sunglasses and smiling.

"You're not so smart. I recognized you immediately, Cop John." I said, returning the smile. "This is my friend, Twiggy."

"Hello, Twiggy. Nice to meet you."

"How did you know it was me?" I asked.

"Your rig. Also, a quick license plate check. You heading to Cowtown for the rodeo?"

"That's right, but we're staying in Denton until lunch tomorrow," I said. "Aren't you afraid you'll get in trouble for stopping people for no reason?"

"No. Besides, I had a reason. I wanted to see you again. I'm sorry for not showing up at the rodeo last year. I was in the hospital with a knife wound that sidelined me for several weeks. Now, what about dinner tonight? I'll let you pay since I helped you out last time you were through here."

"No way. I'm not falling for that again. Do you pull that trick on all the ladies?"

"Just the ones I'm trying to impress. What do you say about tonight?"

"I don't even know where we're staying tonight." I stated.

"6506 Pecan Drive, one mile west of town, turn right at the Shell Station, follow the road to the second house on the right. It has a big red barn behind it. You can't miss it," Twiggy blurted in rapid succession.

"I know that place. I'll be out around 7:00," he said, putting his shades back on.

"I haven't said I'd go."

"She'll be ready," Twiggy announced.

"Great," he said, turning and walking back to his car.

"Girl, I'm having trouble breathing," Twiggy said, fanning herself with an entry form that was on the dash. "That could be the best looking specimen I've ever seen. I'm glad you accepted his invitation."

The place we were staying had a hookup and nice stalls for the horses. We had lunch with Melba and Twiggy talked nonstop about my date tonight.

"I'll tell you, Melba, who he resembles. Did you see Baby Boomers? He looks like Sam Shepard, only more rugged and handsome, if that's possible. I've always adored Sam Shepard. He has this crooked little smile."

She went on and on until I finally left, saying, "I need to ride Scooter." I shouldn't have accepted in the first place. Wait a minute; I didn't accept. Twiggy spoke for me, before I had a chance to decline. I said to myself, *get real, you wouldn't have declined.*

Melba had the barrels already set up in a pattern, and after warming Scooter up, I trotted, lopped, and then made a run. I couldn't believe he was this far along, after only four months. He might outrun Chrome now. With his ability, he didn't need the room to turn the barrels that Chrome did. Plus, he had more speed, to go with the flex. I kept waiting for him to get excited in the alley or refuse to enter. He was the same every time. I knew one thing for sure; I was going to enter him somewhere in the near future.

After I finished with Scooter, I put him and Chrome on the walker that was beside the barn. I sat down and watched them make the circle for the next half hour, trying to decide what to wear for the evening. When you were forced to wear pants, it limited your wardrobe.

I was dressed half an hour early that evening. I had decided on a pair of Rocky Mountain jeans that were too tight to ride in and a white long sleeve Mexican embroidered blouse. I was wearing my leopard print Lucchese boots, which I never rode in. I had washed my hair, leaving it loose to fall below my shoulders. When I modeled for Twiggy, her response was, "Oh, if I had your figure and looks, men would be swarming me."

I was alerted by Twiggy, who was watching from the front window, that he was here. Coming up the sidewalk toward the house, I wondered, how many ladies in Denton County would like to be in my shoes tonight. Answering my own question, *probably at least half of them.*

We left, with Twiggy shouting as we were getting in the car, "I won't wait up for you!"

"That lady's something else," he said.

"Yes. You could say that. However, I've not met a nicer person and she's loads of fun."

"What's your favorite food?" he asked.

"I'm not particular. What about you?"

"I'm partial to this little barbecue place on the east side of town. The atmosphere suits me, but I don't know about you.

"Atmosphere comes behind the food," I responded.

"Great, it's settled," he said.

We wove our way through a part of town where the streets were not paved and the houses would be considered shacks by any standard. We stopped at a place with a flashing neon sign that read Leroy's Barbecue. Most of the cars parked around the building were older models. Loud music was coming from the building, with laughter. This was going to be interesting, I thought.

We entered, and it became deathly quiet. Suddenly, loud applause erupted and shouts of "Sheriff John". A smiling man approached us, shook hands with John, and led us to a table in a dark corner of the room. A candle burned in the middle of the table. John politely pulled a chair out for me and sat down himself.

"What do you think?" he asked.

"Are there any white people here?"

"Certainly. There's two," came his answer.

The waitress came over with a bottle of red wine and menus, saying, "Sheriff John, good to see you, and thanks for helping me with Lyondell. He's doing better. Do you need a few minutes to decide what you want?"

"No. The ribs will be fine, with potato salad, beans, and cornbread."

After she left, he opened the bottle of wine, pouring, first me, and then himself a glass. I took a sip and it was delicious, asking, "Do you come here often?"

"Mostly in the evening, when I get the chance. I live on the other side of town, so it's not convenient."

"They call you Sheriff and you're only a deputy."

"It's kind of an honorary title. The sheriff has never been here," he stated.

There was a piano, and when the man began playing, the room became quieter. He would alternate between Blues and Spiritual. He was amazing and continued to play throughout the evening. On several occasions, a lady joined him and sang the lyrics.

While waiting for our meal to arrive, the man who met us at the door came to our table, saying, "John, I'm sorry for interrupting, but Everest insists that he needs to talk with you. He promised it wouldn't take but a few minutes. He's in my office. I've already told them to hold your food until you return."

John left, and the man sat down, introducing himself as Leroy, and apologizing again. "Ma'am, I'm sorry. A man can't even eat a meal in peace with his beautiful lady."

"Have you known John for long?" I asked.

"Yes, ma'am, since he became a deputy."

"People seem to really like him," I said.

"No, ma'am. People love him. Did he tell you how he was hurt?"

"No. He hasn't mentioned it except to say he had to stay in the hospital for some time."

"Domestic fight. A couple out toward Decatur. In fact, they were a few hundred yards across the county line, not even in John's jurisdiction. He stepped between them to break it up, facing the man, and the woman cut him across his back. It was a bad wound, requiring over 100 stiches. They were both high and she swore to John it was an accident. They did call an ambulance."

"Were they arrested?"

"When the ambulance got there, the couple was gone. They haven't been found. Arrest would have been the least of their worries after they almost killed John. I've begged him to carry a gun, but he won't do it. He told me that he had sworn an oath not to ever take another life. He was in the military, Special Forces. Something terrible happened that has caused him to feel this way."

"Does he bring many women out here?" I asked.

Smiling, he said, "I can't go there. You'll have to ask him."

John came back to the table and thanked Leroy for staying with me. Immediately, a plate piled high with ribs was set down in front of me. I looked down at my white blouse and thought, this could be ugly. Before I could begin eating, the waitress came back with a large cloth napkin, when tied around my neck, covered my blouse. It was the best barbecue I'd ever eaten. I had another glass of wine and we talked for an hour after finishing. The subjects were mostly about my barrel racing and his work as a deputy.

When leaving, we went by the register and Leroy appeared out of nowhere, saying, "John, you know your money's not good and never will be here. Get on your way now and enjoy the rest of the evening with this beautiful lady."

I was a little tipsy after two glasses of wine. John must have noticed because he took my arm on the way to the car.

Melba had breakfast the next morning, with the interrogation beginning before I even sat down.

"Where did you eat? I bet it was an expensive restaurant with gourmet food. Did he order for you? What about champagne?"

"Which do you want me to answer first?" I asked.

"I want to know if he kissed you?"

"Yes," I answered.

"Okay. That was the most important question. Now, let's eat and you can tell me more later."

After breakfast, I rode Scooter again. He did even better this morning. Twiggy was watching and when I came back from my run, she said, "That's some horse to look so common. Doesn't he ever get excited?"

"No. He perks up when you take him in the alley because he knows he's going to get to run."

I rode Chrome around just to loosen him up, and Twiggy rode both of her horses. We left after lunch for Fort Worth and The Will Rogers' Coliseum.

Both of us had several good runs, but we were now competing on another level and didn't advance to the final round. We did have an opportunity to compete at a 4D barrel race in Stephenville, which was only about 60 miles from Fort Worth. It was a three-day event with over 400 entries, lasting the 18th, 19th, and 20th. I entered Scooter all three days, but Twiggy decided to rest her horses for the next rodeo.

In the Friday night competition, with 250 entries, I had drawn number 239. When they called my name and I rode Scooter into the alley it was after midnight. He exploded toward the first barrel and I thought, he can never turn it at this speed. He made it and also the second barrel, and it was going to be one of my fastest trips ever. When he reached the third and started the turn, he slipped and fell. Thank goodness, I was thrown clear, escaping injury. People came running up, asking me if I was hurt. I looked for Scooter and he was standing off to one side holding up a foot. Panicked, I made it over to him as quickly as possible. Picking up the injured foot, I saw that the shoe was hanging by one nail. I flexed his leg back and forth and it looked like he was not injured but holding up the foot because of the loose shoe.

Back at the stall, Twiggy pulled the shoe off, and walking him up and down the alley between the stalls, he didn't show any signs of being lame. Breathing a sigh of relief, I said a prayer, giving thanks that neither of us were injured.

"Are you going to run him again tomorrow?" Twiggy asked.

"I doubt it. I think he's okay, but falling at the third barrel, I doubt if he'd make a run. I know Chrome wouldn't and Jazzy wouldn't have either."

"I try not to give you advice, Lacy, but this is not an ordinary horse. I don't know if I've ever seen one like him. I suggest that you give him a chance."

"We'll see how he walks out in the morning. If he's sound, I'll take your advice."

The Saturday morning race started at 9:00 with 415 entries. This time I had drawn number 224. I kept hearing the other contestants talk about how terrible the ground was. They were also obsessed with their draws. The arena was drug after every five riders and they talked about how important it was to be the first to run in the next five. They called it the "top of the ground" and it was hard not to remind them that at the National Finals fifteen ladies made their run without a drag of the arena. Several had come up to me today telling me my horse fell because of the horrible ground. I didn't respond to them, but I would've liked to say, "You ran on the same ground and your horse didn't fall, in fact, I didn't see another horse fall."

When I rode into the alley for my run, Scooter showed no signs of being nervous or agitated. I was surprised when he shot out of the alley going full speed toward the first. This time he made all three barrels with a run that would be the fastest of all 415 other riders. Coming out of the alley, the first thing I did was get off and hug him, saying, "You are so brave!"

Before I gave him his bath, I produced a carrot from my feed bin. He was munching on it when Twiggy walked up announcing, "You have a visitor."

"Who?"

"Who would you like it to be?" she asked.

"Where is he?"

"He's supposed to be off duty this weekend, but he was on his phone when I left him, talking business."

"Let me give Scooter a bath, and then you can take me to him."

"The little horse with the big heart," she said.

I withdrew from Sunday's race, not wanting to run Scooter again until the next rodeo. I never placed lower than third in the next ten professional rodeos, winning five of them. I rode Scooter in each of the shows, and by the middle of July, I was going back and forth between number 1 and 2 in the World.

Tommie Rose had presented me with a Bible before she left. It was a New King James Translation with study guides. I had been rising early each morning and doing a lesson. I practiced this on the road or when I was back at the ranch. Also, I would find a church to attend wherever we were.

On Tuesday, July 9, we were in Casper, Wyoming for the Central Wyoming Fair and Rodeo. When we went to the office to enter and get our stalls, I noticed they were having a church service Wednesday morning at 8:00, inviting all the participants to attend. The first of five rodeo performances was that night.

The next morning, I was one of about two dozen who made it to the service. A young pastor from the Presbyterian Church in Casper brought the message. The devotional was short, simple, and sincere. When he finished, I made my way down and introduced myself, telling him I enjoyed his talk and was glad I came.

"Thank you. I appreciate it. My wife and I have a small study group of young people at our house each Wednesday evening. We have a few refreshments and generally it doesn't last much over an hour. Please join us and we can show you some Wyoming hospitality."

I didn't commit one way or the other, but he did give me directions to his house, which was only a few blocks from the fairgrounds. I had made a decision that the next good sized town we stayed in I was going to buy a dress. I realized at some point that I couldn't hide my handicap and it wasn't right to do so. I found a mall later that morning and bought my first dress in nearly two years. It was not short but my prosthetic was visible.

Tonight might be the perfect time to wear the dress. I would not know anyone except the pastor and wouldn't be nearly as self-conscious in this setting.

That evening, when Twiggy saw me dressed, she said, "Well, it's about time, girl. You look gorgeous."

"Thank you. I just hope people don't stare at me."

"Sure they will, since there won't be anything in the room as beautiful."

I found the pastor's house without a problem and was a few minutes early. He introduced me to his wife, whose name was Sarah, and invited me into the room where the meeting was being held. There were already several others present. Most were about my age or younger.

"Let me introduce you to Lacy," he said to the group.

With each new arrival he would introduce me and tell them I was a participant in the rodeo this week. When the group had grown to eleven, including myself, he began.

"Our study tonight is on the Book of Job in the Old Testament, believed to be the oldest Book of the Bible. Job refutes the idea that we suffer because of our wrongdoings and are rewarded for our good behavior. Throughout the book we wonder why many times the innocent suffer while the guilty live in comfort and peace."

The longer he spoke, the more I saw myself struggling with this same scenario in my life. Occasionally he would take questions and encourage discussion. I sat there almost in a trance for twenty minutes. He concluded by asking if anyone had further comments. When he received no response, he looked at me and said, "Lacy would you like to tell us something about yourself? Feel free not to, but something tells me you're a remarkable young lady."

"I guess so." I was uncomfortable at first, but as I told about growing up on a ranch and rodeoing it became easier. When I came to the accident it became difficult, having to pause before continuing. The only time I cried was when telling of Jack's death. I tried to explain the feeling that came over me at the cemetery that morning. I described my life as a yo-yo, with ups and downs being the norm and not the exception. I finished by saying that my faith was becoming stronger and I believed that was one of the reasons for my success. When I finished, the group applauded, and each one came over and hugged me.

"When do you ride?" asked one of them.

"I'm up tomorrow night in the show," I replied.

When I left, Jacob and Sarah followed me to the door and told me how much they appreciated me coming and sharing my story.

That next night, before the grand entry, every member of the group came to the trailer to wish me well. Maybe that had something to do with the reason that by the end of the week I had won both go rounds and the average.

By the time Twiggy and I arrived in Las Vegas in December for the finals, I was sitting number 2 in the standings, trailing the leader by $1,265. With ten go rounds and ten runs, the little horse with the big heart was about to face his greatest challenge.

CHAPTER 50

Announcer at the National Finals In Las Vegas

"LADIES AND GENTLEMAN, WHAT AN exciting week we have had in the barrel racing. Now, it all comes down to the last two contestants in the final round. Charlotte Largos and Lacy Skinner have fought it out all year, and coming into this final round, Charlotte leads by a mere $2,154. However, here's the catch. Lacy has left all the barrels standing in her previous 9 runs. She is the only one of the 15 ladies who has made clean runs in every go round. All she has to do to become the World Champion for 2002 is leave the barrels standing. The average money will put her over the top.

Lacy, in an interview today, said that this run was going to be dedicated to her late husband, Jack Skinner. He died as a result of an auto accident in 2000 in which Lacy lost her left leg. She will be riding Scooter, voted the World Champion Barrel Horse for 2002.

I imagine we are going to see a very careful run by Lacy. Her time is not important, only the fact that she leaves them standing. She's coming down the alley, riding a horse that looks as if he is on a trail ride. The crowd is on their feet. She has become a favorite at this year's Finals.

She's off, and not being the least bit careful! This is amazing. She tips the first barrel but it comes back up! The little horse is flying! What is going on? Doesn't she understand the importance of a clean run? Scooter is flying to the third and with only slight hesitation, turns it and heads for home. The noise is deafening with the crowd screaming! The clock stopped at 13.51. Ladies and gentleman, that is a new arena record.

She's coming back in the arena for her victory lap. The new World Champion. The crowd is going wild! I've never seen anything like this, even for a bull ride. The sell-out crowd of 17,000 in the Thomas Mac Center is on their feet, continuing the applause as she circles the arena."

A half hour later, during a break, Lacy's interview was seen by millions watching the Finals on television.

"Everybody was surprised, Lacy, that you were anything but careful on your final run. What made you go throw caution to the wind when a world championship was at stake?" asked the interviewer.

"The run was for my late husband, Jack, and not for the World Championship. Jack was not a careful man, and he would have been disappointed to see me play it safe. I was going to make the best run possible, and I believe that Scooter understood that. I know that Jack would be proud of me."

"You have your family here tonight with you. Would you like to introduce them?"

"Yes, definitely. They have been supportive throughout the year. From left to right, Alejandra is my mother,

Bo and Lexie are my father-in-law and mother-in-law. Tommie Rose is my sister-in-law and Nancy is my grandmother. The man on the far right with the badge is a special friend."

Epilog
2011

"LEXIE, WE NEED TO BE moving. I know how long it takes you to get ready," Bo said.

"Bo, it's only 8:30 and the rodeo doesn't start until 1:00. It's only a little over an hour's drive. What's the hurry? Just calm down."

"I don't want to be late. We've got to hook on and load the horse," he reminded her.

"That will take about ten minutes, Bo. You need to just settle down."

"You need to get Potato up so he can eat breakfast," he said.

"Bo, stop calling him Potato. The kids at school are calling him Tater already. He's seven years old and has a name. He has enough problems with his identity, being a fourth African American, a fourth Vietnamese, a sixteenth Indian, and I guess, what's left, Anglo. Go to the barn and feed Cotton while I start breakfast. I can't believe we're even taking him to a roping. He hasn't caught a calf all week."

"He deserves a chance. It'll be exciting for him and he's roping better on the ground."

"You're a stubborn man, Robert Skinner."

"Stop! Don't say it. You and my mother have reminded me at least a thousand times that I'm just like my grands.

When he came back from feeding, Lexie had breakfast on the table. He hugged the little boy sitting next to him who was short and stocky with black hair. "Are you ready to go this morning, Potato?"

"Yes, sir. I hope I do good. Mother and Daddy won't be there, will they?" he asked.

"No. They're in New York for the ten-year anniversary of 9/11. They let you stay with us."

"Bo, did you even tell Zack and Jerri we were taking him to a rodeo?" Lexie asked.

"No. I didn't see any reason to," he answered. "I've been the one working with him. Zack doesn't have time, with his practice in Ruidoso. He works too hard. People come from all over the country for him to treat them. Can you believe he's even made some house calls? He needs to limit his patients."

"You know how much he respected Dr. Sadler and wanted to be like him. Dr. Sadler made house calls. I'm glad we can help out. It's convenient that they live on the ranch. I keep thinking they'll move to town, but Jerri tells me that will never happen. Since we built our house here on the North Ranch it has worked out for them to live at our old home in the Hondo Valley.

They were loaded and on their way to Tularosa by 10:00, with Lexie still complaining about leaving too early.

"What are we going to do for two hours?" she asked.

"We can practice on the ground. We also need to warm up Cotton."

"I wouldn't warm him up much, after all he's twenty-one. He might not have the energy to catch a calf."

"Have you talked to Tommie Rose lately?" he asked, trying to change the subject.

"Yesterday. She's pleased with her move to Johannesburg, so the family will be together. She's sure that the mission can do without her now. She believes there is a greater need at some of the camps outside Johannesburg. Dr. Adders has been traveling back and forth to the mission on weekends for years. I know it's a relief for him. It's hard to call him Ted. They're saying now that he's the most respected neurosurgeon in the world. Of course, Tommy still leads him around by his nose."

"Did you talk to the girls?" he asked.

"I talked to Nancy. Of course, she's six now. I can't get much out of Mary, but she's only four. I can't wait to see them Christmas. Every time I talk with Tommie she tells me what a wonderful daddy that Ted is."

"We wanted grandkids and we have them now. I wish the girls were closer, but at least we have Zack and his family here on the ranch," he stated.

"Don't forget Lacy. Her little boy is five now and she has already told me she wants you to teach him to rope. It's hard to believe she found such a wonderful man. John is everything that she needed after what she has gone through. Only thing about it I don't want Alejandra hanging around over here."

"Lexie, we're over sixty. Surely you can let that go."

They arrived at Tularosa and waited two hours until finally the rodeo began.

"Bo, he's only seven and he's entered in the eight-to-ten-year-old group."

"I know that. As long as he's younger, it's legal."

The announcer was calling for the breakaway roping for the eight-to-ten-year-olds to begin. There were seven entries in the group. He called each boy's name and finally got to number six.

"Bo, I still think you should've gone to the box with him. He looks tiny on that big horse. He'll be the only child without an adult to help him with his horse."

"You know the family rules, Lexie. We don't put our kids on a horse that needs help in the box."

The announcer's voice was loud and clear. "Our next contestant hails from Hondo, New Mexico. We're ready for you, Bobby Jack Skinner."

The little boy rode his horse into the box, built his loop, gave a nod of his head and was out behind the calf. The calf was not fast, as they had been chosen for the youth. He swung his rope four times and let go a beautiful loop that settled gently over the calf's head. Cotton stopped, the breakaway came off, and Bobby Jack threw both of his little hands high into the air, and another generation of cowboys from the Skinner Ranch was born.

Made in the USA
Middletown, DE
10 July 2023

34795520R00235